# The NHS

Facing the future

# The NHS

Facing the future

Anthony Harrison and Jennifer Dixon

Published by
King's Fund Publishing
11–13 Cavendish Square
London W1M 0AN

© King's Fund 2000

First published 2000. Reprinted 2000

ISBN 1 85717 219 1

A CIP catalogue record for this book is available from the British Library

Available from:

King's Fund Bookshop
11–13 Cavendish Square
London
W1M 0AN

Tel: 020 7307 2591
Fax: 020 7307 2801

Printed and bound in Great Britain

Typeset by Peter Powell Origination & Print Limited

# Contents

## Section 3
## Overview

# Preface

This book takes a 'helicopter' view of the NHS at the end of the 20th century. Our starting point is the widespread perception that the NHS is under pressure and may not be able to survive in its present form as a universal publicly financed service. Given the NHS's objectives, we argue that the current form of finance is the most appropriate, but as long as it is financed in this way, the NHS will actually be, and will be perceived as being, under pressure. The central question, therefore, is whether that pressure can be managed better.

We begin by arguing that the reforms carried out during the past 20 years have been inadequate in this respect: indeed they may have made matters worse by encouraging rather than reducing demands on the Service. The sources of those demands are familiar – new technology, an ageing population, rising expectations – but perhaps the key change in the last few years is that the external environment within which the NHS operates has become more critical. If the NHS is to respond to this new environment, it will have to change. That leads us to consider just what changes are consistent with what might be known as a 'national health service'. The precise role of the NHS has never been systematically defined. Over the years the Service has adapted to changing circumstances, but the most significant reforms of its structure and the scope of services provided have largely taken place without public debate. Furthermore, the balance between what should be nationally determined and what is a proper matter for local discretion has never been systematically addressed. In the new environment, we argue, such implicit policy-making cannot continue.

Whatever form the NHS takes in future, it must, as deliverer and purchaser of health care, be better able to discharge certain technical tasks. In the second part of this book, we consider the core technical tasks of maintaining control over costs, delivering services effectively, ensuring the availability of human resources to deliver them, managing the demand on services and distributing resources fairly. In looking at these tasks our prime focus is on whether or not the NHS has what we have referred to as the 'technical capacity' required to discharge them effectively. Our overall conclusion is that it does not.

However, most of the weaknesses we identify have been already apparent for decades. That leads us to conclude that the NHS suffers from a systematic weakness – a failure to find and implement adequate solutions to some key long-standing problems, such as linking workforce and service planning. This stems from a failure to acknowledge the requirements of managing the service delivery system effectively, which in turn is reflected by the relative paucity of resources devoted to the search for new knowledge and development in the area of service delivery and management rather than clinical matters.

Another reason for this systematic weakness also stems from the fact that the NHS is a 'central' and 'national' service delivered locally. The Service is too complex to be project-managed from the Centre, at the same time a 'national' health service cannot be run entirely locally.

At the centre of our discussion of these technical tasks is the question of whether or not the NHS has succeeded in finding the right balance between central and local responsibilities. While successive governments have supported the principle of giving more responsibility to localities, they have at the same time made more aspects of running the NHS a central responsibility. We argue that the increasing ambition of successive governments has not been matched by a corresponding increase in their capacity to manage the Service centrally. But within the current political system, which focuses responsibility for NHS performance on the Secretary of State, it is hard to see a realistic alternative. Only major political change will open up new options. Without it, the prospect is that the Government will try to do more and fail, while not allowing localities to take initiatives of their own.

Nevertheless, we do believe that in many respects the NHS is better able to 'face the future' than it was once: it is more flexible and responsive than it was only a few years ago and it is beginning to make many of the changes we believe are necessary. Further improvements in its technical capacity can be made within the existing framework, and in this book we suggest how this could be done.

Many of the key challenges the NHS faces, however, require more than merely technical solutions. At a deeper level, they also require a re-balancing of the fundamental relationships between the State, the professions and the public. The responsibility of the medical profession for the Service (as opposed to patients) has been largely implicit for most of the life of the NHS. Now the professions are faced with both a more critical and demanding Government and public. In our view the professions as a whole must urgently develop their roles to comprise a wider responsibility for the overall delivery of health care – in other words, managing the *system* as well as the *specific clinical intervention*.

Without this fundamental shift, we argue, the power of the professions will be significantly reduced and, more importantly for the NHS, a vital source of expertise in service delivery will be lost.

At 'helicopter flying' level, the view is wide and the horizon a long way off. The surface to be described is of dismaying dimension. Although we aimed to 'see the whole', in practice we have had to be selective, focusing on only some of the key tasks that any publicly funded health service has to perform well. Because we have adopted a broad approach we have not attempted to evaluate in detail any of the vast range of policies that have been introduced over the last 20 years. Rather we have aimed to set individual initiatives within the long-term context of the enduring issues that the NHS must continually face and try to resolve. For that reason we have, however briefly, set much of our analysis in a historical context, to emphasise one of the NHS's central features: that the enduring issues have long been recognised by official reports and academic enquiry and most remain to be systematically tackled. We have tried to show at least in part why this should be so.

Naturally, our debts are large. We are particularly grateful to Ken Judge for the original idea of writing a book, to Bill New for his help with Chapters 10 and 13, to John Appleby for his comments throughout the text, to Barbara Barrett and Shirley Harrison for their help in preparing the text for publication, to Kim Stirling and Urannie Small for secretarial support, and also to a number of King's Fund colleagues who directly or indirectly contributed to our thinking. We have borrowed frequently from the large volume of shared understanding of how the NHS works and where its weaknesses lie, without at every point citing those who have set down this or that point to be found here. In the Bibliography we have listed the works we have cited, but also many other books and articles that have influenced our thinking or which set out, at greater length than we can here, the evidence and argument for particular points.

Finally, both of us believe in the objectives the NHS was designed to promote. We also believe that a *national* health service is the right vehicle for promoting them. But what form it should take is another question, indeed it is *the* question that is addressed in what follows. No change is not an option if the NHS is to survive and thrive.

AJH
JD
King's Fund
August 1999

# Summary

The NHS was founded on the principle of fairness, to provide equal access to all on the basis of equal need rather than on the ability to pay. It thus eliminates price as a method of bringing demand for services into line with available supply. Without price as a mechanism to allow users, or other payers, to decide how much health care they are prepared to fund, it is left to the Government to make such decisions. Whatever level of funding the Government decides, there will be a 'gap' between supply and demand. The resulting tension is managed at national level by the Treasury and NHS Executive; at local level by health authority purchasers and the new primary care groups; and at the individual level by clinicians, in their dealings with patients. Managing scarcity is the most important task facing the NHS; the ability to manage it will determine the future of the NHS.

## Section 1: Setting the Scene

### Chapter 1: Crisis and response

Government is constantly vulnerable to criticism because of its role in setting the overall level of funding. It has been in the interests of all major stakeholders in the NHS, including its staff, to attack the Service on the basis that it is inadequately funded, and to represent it as being in crisis.

Coping strategies introduced by successive governments have largely failed, in that the tension between supply and demand in the NHS has patently not been eliminated – 'crisis' remains. There are three main reasons why. First, the gap will never, and we argue should never, be filled. It is not possible to quantify what is the 'right' level of funding for the NHS, and therefore to know with certainty that the NHS is 'underfunded' – such a judgement is subjective rather than objective. A gap, therefore, does not necessarily mean a 'crisis'.

Second, some major policies introduced to the NHS, particularly in the last 20 years, have not borne effectively on the fundamental issue of managing the tension between supply and demand – and indeed may have made it worse. For example, the requirement to increase productivity in the NHS may have increased demands on hospital care inappropriately.

Third, too little attention has been paid to the external environment within which the NHS must operate to enable solutions to be sought, designed, implemented and explained successfully.

## Chapter 2: A changing environment

Demography apart, the 'market' the NHS services is not growing, but the environment in which it operates is becoming more critical and more demanding. Traditional methods of managing scarcity by controlling access to, and utilisation of, health services are weakening because they are less tolerated by the public. New methods of managing scarcity will have to be adopted that are more in tune with the times, for example methods that rely less on the vagaries of the judgement of individual professionals, methods that are less secretive and more open, which involve the public more, and which strike up a different relationship with the mass media.

Although we argue that there has always been a gap between supply and demand in the NHS, and that it is neither possible nor desirable to fill this gap with extra resources, the important point is that any gap will be less tolerated in the future because of changes in the external environment. Policies, we argue, will need to be devised to take account of this.

## Chapter 3: A changing service

The precise nature of the National Health Service has never been formally defined. What services are available on a 'national' basis varies considerably, but without any clear rationale. Significant change, for example in the availability of dental care on the NHS and long-term care, has been made without public debate. How far the NHS should be a public provider of 'service' rather than a just a purchaser of care has also never been seriously debated. The role of the NHS towards the voluntary and private sector has been largely ignored in official policy-making.

We argue that there are a number of ways to structure a national health service so that it can be legitimately called such, and so that it can achieve the stated objectives of the NHS. There is no one blueprint as to what a national health service should be. But the scope for reform is limited by attachment to specific structures, such as hospitals and general practices. To achieve major reform Government will have to convince conservative stakeholders – public and professional – that it is serious about the basic objectives to be achieved.

This means that changes to the scope of the NHS should not be made silently or by default, that variations in access should be tackled where appropriate, and that positive reasons for diversity in what is available should be explicitly stated.

## Section 2: Key Tasks

The chapters in this section are concerned with how the NHS might technically manage better the supply-demand mismatch. Four main areas are examined: how more 'supply' or finance could be raised; how existing resources could be used more effectively and efficiently; how demand for care might be managed better; and how a better relationship with the public might be forged to allow a greater understanding of scarcity and how it can be managed. The aim of each chapter is to examine how well the NHS is equipped to discharge the technical tasks required in each area, and how its capacity to do so could be improved.

### Chapter 4: Raising finance

This chapter examines four main ways of raising finance for the NHS, through general taxation, hypothecated taxation, social insurance and private insurance.

Since the NHS was established, successive governments have tried to find additional, or alternative, sources of funding. Each has largely failed because all the alternatives examined ran counter to the equity objective that underpins the NHS. Furthermore, alternatives do not offer any advantages over existing arrangements: taxation remains the cheapest and most equitable method of raising funds. As a result, alternative funding streams to general taxation and National Insurance contribute only marginal extra resources, a situation that is largely unchanged since 1948.

It may be that, if pressures on the NHS increase, additional funds will be sought by means that are neither equitable nor efficient to collect, but they might be more tolerable to the public than explicit rationing. The real question, which cannot be ducked, is not 'are there suitable alternative sources of finance for the NHS?' but 'how much public money are governments prepared to commit to the NHS?'. If the answer is 'not enough to modernise the NHS adequately for the needs and aspirations of the public in the 21st century' then that paradoxically implies that the Government itself can no longer be trusted to run the NHS.

## Chapter 5: Controlling costs

One means of managing scarcity is to increase the efficiency with which the available finance is used: controlling the costs of the resources the NHS requires is part of this aim. The conclusion is that in none of the five areas examined (pay, pharmaceutical drugs, supplies, capital projects (such as hospital buildings) and clinical services as a whole) can there be confidence that the NHS gets the best possible deal through existing policies.

The NHS requires a renewed and clear focus for taking seriously the issues discussed in this chapter. This might be provided initially by a 'Costs Inquiry' or a Commission mirroring the Guillebaud Committee of the 1950s. This might, as that Committee did, identify systematically gaps in information and understanding in each of the areas reviewed. As a result, programmes of research could be defined and commissioned, and adequate policies designed.

One recurring theme in the NHS has been the absence of the most basic information bearing on the five main areas of costs defined above. The recently published National Schedule of Reference Costs is a step in the right direction, but it will only work properly if the data used are regarded as reliable and, more importantly, if the capacity exists to interpret the data and help is made available to NHS organisations to make necessary changes – a tall order in a climate in which the cutting back of 'management' costs is seen as a good thing. How these broad requirements should be met – whether by strengthening analytic expertise or skills in organisational change inside the Service, centrally, regionally, locally, or outside it – is an issue we return to below.

## Chapter 6: Designing systems of care

Since 1948, remarkably little attention has been paid to the design of the health care 'system' in the NHS as a whole: most of the emphasis of research has been placed on discrete parts of the NHS such as the GP consultation or admission to hospital.

New developments, such as Government proposals for national service frameworks (NSFs) – initially for coronary heart disease, mental health, diabetes and care of elderly people – are a step in the right direction since they relate to the design of a whole system of care for patients in each group. But while they are a good start, they relate to only specific groups of patients and not the health care delivery system as a whole.

Even using such an incremental approach, as represented by the NSFs, progress will be slow because much of the required information will be missing. The range of factors to be considered is formidable, and the way they interrelate is highly complex. Because of past neglect, there are large gaps in information and knowledge about the design of a 'whole system' that will produce effective care efficiently.

We make a series of proposals to strengthen the NHS's ability to deal with these issues.

## Chapter 7: Organising systems of care

Until the late 1980s, debate about the organisational structure of the NHS was largely focused on its administrative and supervisory structure, for example how many administrative tiers there should be and how large each should be. The NHS and Community Care Act 1990 changed that by introducing new forms of organisation, such as providers and purchasers, with new lines of accountability, for instance those applied to NHS trusts. There is little hard evidence as to whether these new organisations proved valuable.

Nevertheless they created more scope for diversity, innovation and experiment than previously, particularly as a result of local initiative rather than national directive. But three main issues arise.

First, local innovation and experiment reveal a series of tensions. However, they are entirely appropriate in the rapidly changing environment within which the NHS operates and opportunities for both should be increased.

Second, for effective ways of organising care to be developed, clinicians must be far more involved and must take more responsibility for the Service in future. We believe that this requires no less than a radical change in the definition of the role for clinicians, in particular doctors, and thus a change in the knowledge base required for training, at undergraduate and postgraduate level.

Third, many recent and radical changes to the way NHS services are organised have taken place with the complete absence of information as to whether or not they might work. There is similar ignorance about how organisational change affects the relationships between different parts of the Service.

We believe that local innovation and experiment is entirely appropriate in a rapidly changing environment. New ways of organising care should be developed by clinicians themselves. A greatly expanded R&D programme for service design and delivery should support them in this. Changes in their knowledge base, and hence the content of their training, will also be required.

## Chapter 8: Ensuring the supply of human resources

The key resource for the NHS is its staff. The NHS employs almost 1 million people – the largest number of, and best educated and trained, staff of any organisation in Europe. Improving the effectiveness and efficiency of staff is crucial. This chapter largely concerns how the numbers of staff, and how the roles of clinical staff, are determined in the NHS. We conclude that the NHS has still to find a satisfactory way of determining both.

A realistic assessment must be made of the scope of long-term workforce planning. The less confidence that can be placed in forecasts of future requirements for staff with particular skills, the greater the emphasis should be on retraining and promoting flexibility between specialties and professions, or even redefining the professions themselves. Facilities to retrain staff in different specialties are, however, hard to find. Professional boundaries, and boundaries between specialties of medical staff, remain largely inflexible.

In planning the numbers of staff and skills needed for the NHS in future, more emphasis should be put on the need for staff to take on the emerging roles of designing, planning and commissioning, as well as delivering, effective integrated systems of care. These roles require skills that may be found or developed in people from different professional backgrounds, for example areas poorly represented in the NHS at present such as statistical analysis, simulation, analysis of futures and forecasting, as well as more prosaic needed skills such as commissioning.

## Chapter 9: Managing demand

Since 1948, very little attention has been paid in the NHS to monitoring changes in the demand for NHS care, analysing reasons for this (including existing policies) and designing policies that do not stimulate demand inappropriately. The medical profession has had little or no reason to scrutinise, or manage, demand. That this approach has been inadequate to respond to the powerful forces driving up pressure on the NHS budget is not surprising. While most of these forces result from changes in wider society, which are impossible, and undesirable, for the NHS to hold back, the Service need not be entirely passive. It can determine how to respond positively to these pressures.

Demand for NHS care is initiated in three domains: from the public (so called 'patient-led' demand), from professional providers ('professional-led' demand)

and from policies introduced into the NHS (so called 'Service-led' demand). The NHS should increase efforts to manage demand better by focusing on all three areas.

Regarding patient-led demand, we reject blunt measures to curb demand such as increasing user charges or removing whole services from the NHS menu, because this would deter both inappropriate and appropriate demand. Instead it is argued that it would be better to pursue policies that increased access to NHS care, but which also routed patients to more cost-effective and appropriate sources of care inside or outside the NHS (for example self-care).

If patient-led demands are inflated by measures of this type, then it will be all the more important for the Government to create an environment within the NHS so that only appropriate demands are met. This will require much closer scrutiny of professional-led and Service-led demands, and the creation of a conducive environment for routing demand appropriately. This means that professional behaviour bearing on service utilisation must be systematically scrutinised.

On Service-led demand, we argue that a mandatory 'demand audit' be performed on all new and existing policies, starting with the introduction of primary care groups, NHS *Direct*, policies to reduce waiting for elective care and, especially, policies to increase productivity. 'Demand audit' of major policies should be a key strand of the NHS R&D programme – it currently is not.

Finally we conclude that of the three types of demand – patient-led, professional-led, and Service-led – the Government has most capacity to influence Service-led and then professional-led demands. This is where effort should be focused in the short term. But in the medium term, the nettle of managing patient-led demand will need to be grasped.

## Chapter 10: Sharing the cake

Since the foundation of the NHS, there has been substantial progress in making the allocation of resources to different parts of the country more equitable for hospital and community health services; there has been less progress for family health services and for capital projects.

There is no way of guaranteeing that similar needs in different parts of the country will be met with an identical response by the NHS. Media scrutiny of variations has grown more intense: disparities in access to service, for example the availability of drugs or infertility treatment, have contributed to public concerns about the sustainability of the Service.

Successive governments have been understandably reluctant to admit that beneficial health care should ever be withheld. Decisions of this kind have been largely delegated locally, to purchasers and clinicians. The danger of continuing in this way could be that it will only breed mistrust amongst the public at large about the NHS as a whole, creating unease that they will be denied care, apparently arbitrarily, when they need it. We argue that the fact that resources are finite needs to be explained more fully, and positively, by the Centre – no significant progress can be made in establishing a fairer or more democratic means of choosing between claimants if the Centre refuses to acknowledge scarcity in a fuller way than it has done so far.

A broad framework to guide the allocation of resources at different levels of the NHS should be made explicit and available, making clear what are national and local responsibilities. At national level, the reasons for including or excluding services from the NHS menu should be explained and justified.

## Chapter 11: Ensuring the knowledge base

The central finding of this chapter is based on the conclusions of previous ones: there is a lack of basic information and a paucity of research in some of the key areas in which knowledge is required for cost control and effective service delivery. Starting with the formation of the NHS R&D programme at the beginning of the 1990s, efforts have been made to redirect the research effort in the NHS towards service priorities. Although this is a move in the right direction, it does not go far enough. The resources devoted to understanding the NHS as a 'system', for example in the areas of service delivery and organisation, and human resources, remain tiny. Other important issues have also been neglected, for instance the role of the NHS in relation to the public and the informed user.

The conclusions we draw are the following. First, the priorities of the NHS R&D programme need to be pushed further towards operational, organisational and policy issues.

Second, the significance of the developing role of the user in health care, combined with developments in information and communication technology, requires a fundamental assessment. The 'People's Panel' and the NHS National User Survey are welcome, but are only a start. A more systematic approach to understanding what the public thinks of the Service is required, taking in evidence from other existing surveys, such as the General Household Survey and the British Social Attitudes Survey.

Third, given the conclusions above, the field of responsibility of the Director of NHS R&D is too narrowly defined. Either this role needs to be expanded significantly, or better still a new locus – inside or outside of the NHS – should be created to span the full range of knowledge and intelligence bearing on the NHS, for example taking in the information and communications industry and relevant social and economic trends as well as clinical developments.

Fourth, and this is perhaps a vain hope, the design and implementation of all major new policies should be based on a proper understanding of the impact of previous policies.

Fifth, the implications of our analysis for the education and training of all health professionals need to be assessed. As argued in Chapter 8, analytic and other management skills need to be strengthened across the board, before and after professional qualifications are acquired.

## Chapter 12: Managing the Service

More than 20 years ago, the Royal Commission on the NHS criticised the role of the central departments, arguing that they interfered too much in detail and failed to play a genuinely strategic role. Since then, the role of the Centre has grown massively, first under the Conservatives as they attempted to raise productivity and efficiency, and now under Labour. But the capacity of the Centre to manage the Service has, if anything, been reduced.

The role of the Centre has become incoherent and inconsistent. The incoherence lies in the growing central role combined with slimmed-down and overloaded central institutions; the inconsistency in the fact that initiatives have often been in conflict with each other, for example by laying claims on the same resources, or by pushing the Service in different directions. The requisite knowledge base typically does not exist, locally or nationally, to allow for interactions between policies to be taken into account or to implement individual policies successfully.

Whatever the division between central and local roles, as long as the NHS is a centrally financed service, the central role will continue to be demanding. Our first proposal, though, echoes those made in earlier chapters, that the capacity of the Centre, especially policy-makers, to 'understand the whole' needs to be strengthened.

Our second recommendation is that any proposed change to the balance between the Centre and the local NHS, for example through a new central policy initiative, and any addition to the management responsibilities of the Centre, Regional Offices of the NHS Executive, NHS trusts, health authorities and primary care groups should be accompanied by an explicit estimate of the management implications of implementing it, the human or other resources required, and its expected impact. To be effective, the Centre must either boost central capacity or reduce the scope of its ambitions. The current commitment to reduce management costs should be assessed in the light of the new responsibilities the NHS is being asked to take on.

Our third recommendation is that the range and scale of centrally inspired initiatives put forward in any given period should be limited, thereby reducing the number of priorities defined at any one time. Ideally this would involve bringing together, at the very least, senior health service managers and policy-makers to determine jointly what the Service might realistically be taking on.

## Chapter 13: Making the Service accountable

As things stand now, political, administrative, and now clinical, accountability in the NHS runs 'upwards' to the Secretary of State. Lines of accountability 'downwards' to the public are much weaker. Short of major constitutional change, which, within England at least, is still some way off, this situation is likely to persist. Accordingly, we make a number of recommendations to improve accountability that can be taken up within the existing framework.

First, the current system of external monitoring of the NHS, including the proposals made in *The New NHS*, could be rationalised and developed into a coherent system of external scrutiny.

Second, the Centre (either the Department of Health or NHS Executive) should take upon itself a genuine mission to explain, in non-partisan terms, the forces making for change in the way that health care is delivered, the changes actually taking place and the reasons why policies have been adopted. Ideally this would be backed up by evidence from routine indicators and commissioned research through the NHS R&D programme or the Department's policy research programme. It would mean using non-political spokespersons in the national and regional media to explain the case for change.

Third, freedom of information must be realised in ways which do not, as such measures have in the past, embody new barriers such as cost or physical access. Recent experience with patients' records has shown this.

Fourth, a fundamental review is required of the way in which the Service interacts with the public and patients. New ways of engaging the public in key decisions need to be developed: there is no set recipe for ensuring this is done effectively, so the only practical approach is to experiment.

## Section 3: Overview

The two chapters in this section summarise the arguments from earlier chapters, and focus on how the Government could forge a new relationship with the major stakeholders in the NHS, to smooth the path to more radical reform that will be needed in future.

## Chapter 14: Where the NHS is now

On the basis of evidence and arguments set out in previous chapters, we conclude that although the NHS faces enormous challenges, it is in better shape than ever before to meet them. At a minimum it can be concluded that the Service is:

- encouraging innovation and flexibility in service delivery and organisation
- making a start in tackling areas that for most of its history the NHS has neglected – the evidence underpinning clinical practice and its relationship with the public and users
- developing the role of clinicians as managers of resources
- better informed than ever about its performance through the development of external audit, the greater availability of information, and developments in information and communication technology.

Nevertheless, some significant weaknesses remain in the areas of:

- monitoring change in the environment external to the NHS, and assessing its impact on the NHS
- designing effective patterns of service across the 'whole system' of the NHS
- controlling costs in key areas
- understanding the nature of demand and managing this appropriately
- developing staff and breaking down barriers between professional groups towards a more flexible workforce

- managing the balance between central command and control and local discretion and innovation, which in turn acknowledges the power of clinical professionals locally
- the knowledge base concerning service delivery and organisational issues
- 'explaining' the need for change, and the inevitability of scarcity, to the public.

## Chapter 15: Facing the future

The starting point of this book is the initial settlement made between the State and the medical profession when the NHS was established. The central thread running through the subsequent chapters is that this settlement is changing and must change further. Any fundamental change within the NHS requires an adjustment to the NHS's implicit constitution, that is the balance of power between professionals, the State, and the public.

Underlying the whole of our analysis is the view that, as far as the management of the NHS is concerned, the distinction between medical and clinical issues on the one hand and other issues on the other, is unhelpful. Virtually all the critical issues that NHS management must face require a broad view, not that of a specific discipline or profession.

We have not attempted in this book to put forward solutions or particular proposals except in broad terms. But our analysis suggests some key requirements for the future:

- the NHS will have to continue to change and adapt in the light of new circumstances and new knowledge
- its basic orientation should be shifted from a preoccupation with the requirements of Government, and of the professions, to those of its ultimate financiers, the public
- within the NHS, the role of clinicians should be extended to comprise responsibility for the management of resources and of services: clinical training should be overhauled to reflect this
- communication between the Service and the public should not primarily run through the political process. The NHS itself needs a clearer non-partisan voice
- in policy-making, there should be less emphasis on process, and more emphasis on overall direction and an honest assessment of longer-term impact of policies.

Progress in each of the areas discussed above can be made in isolation, and indeed there are signs of change in what our argument suggests is the right direction. But the most important changes needed essentially involve mutual adjustment of roles between the three main stakeholders – the State, the professions and the public. This must start with the political role. Time will tell if there is the understanding, or more importantly the will, to begin.

Section 1

# Setting the Scene

# Chapter 1

# Crisis and response

The wartime White Paper[1] that committed the then Government to a national health service described its aims as follows:

> the Government … want to ensure that in the future every man, woman and child can rely on getting … the best medical and other facilities available; that their getting them shall not depend upon whether they can pay for them or on any other factor irrelevant to real need (p.5).

Despite widespread public support for these objectives, there was significant resistance from the medical profession – represented by the Royal Colleges and the British Medical Association – which was deeply antagonistic to the possibility of State control of medical practice through a nationalised health service and restrictions on private practice. To persuade enough doctors to sign up to work in the new NHS, Aneurin Bevan, Minister of Health in the first post-war Government, granted concessions that effectively guaranteed clinical freedom and independence from the State. These allowed general practitioners to continue to be self-employed rather than salaried employees of the NHS, and hospital consultants to practise privately. The result was an implicit bargain between the State and the medical profession, that the former would set the overall level of funding for the NHS, while the latter were free to spend it largely as it wished. The general public were not, except through their elected representatives, a party to the negotiations that produced this bargain.

The bargain has been a constant source of tension. Without any obvious reason to hold back, the medical profession has pushed against the ceiling of the global budget for the NHS since it was imposed in the 1950s. Since the Government was responsible for setting the overall level of funding, it has been constantly vulnerable to the attack that the level has not been enough.

While the initial hope was that improved access to health services would lead to reduced spending because more people would receive care before they required expensive treatment, it very soon became apparent that it would not. The cost of 'the best medical facilities' rose as the growth of clinical knowledge and the introduction of new technology vastly extended the range of conditions the NHS could treat. Demographic changes have increased the number of older people with greater need for health care and social change has inflated expectations of the kind of service the NHS should be providing.

The evident failure of the NHS to meet all the demands placed upon it throughout its history has meant that financial crisis and the NHS have been familiar partners. It was a financial crisis in the autumn of 1988 that led more or less directly to the NHS and Community Care Act 1990. In that year, a short-term squeeze on funding prompted letters of protest to *The Times* from Presidents of the Royal Colleges. In the same year the case of a child in Birmingham, whose heart operation was cancelled five times for want of intensive care nurses, caused uproar in the media and encouraged Margaret Thatcher to announce the fundamental review of the NHS. This led to what were seen at the time as the most far-reaching reforms the NHS had ever been subject to, the so-called '1991 reforms', resulting from the NHS and Community Care Act 1990.

Nevertheless, in the years that followed, and despite substantial increases in funding, financial 'crises' appeared almost every year – NHS trusts and health authorities appeared to be struggling not only during the winter months when demands on the NHS were at their highest, but also early in each financial year. Pressure on resources resulted in some services, such as free dental checks and eye tests, being redefined out of the NHS at a national level and others, such as treatment for infertility and cosmetic surgery, at local level by health authority purchasers.

It was against this background that Healthcare 2000 – an independent group financed by the pharmaceutical industry – offered the prognosis in 1995[2] that without even more radical action than that taken by the Conservative Government, the 'gap' between supply and demand would widen and hence additional sources of finance for the NHS should be sought. The same conclusion was drawn by many other individuals and groups.

But perhaps the most vociferous attacks have come from within the NHS itself: Enoch Powell had noted in the 1960s that those working within the NHS were the first to criticise it. Thirty years later in 1995, Sandy Macara, General Secretary of the British Medical Association, likened the NHS to the *Titanic* saying that it would sink unless substantial extra funding was forthcoming. In 1997, a new Labour Government came to power pledged to spending plans that appeared to make the NHS unsustainable, allowing as they did for virtually no growth in resources. In the event, it made extra funding available for the NHS both later in that year and in the March 1998 budget. Later in 1998, substantial increases were announced following the Comprehensive Spending Review. But with waiting lists rising and the constant threat of another winter of overflowing casualty departments in the offing, the sense of 'crisis' remained and indeed was realised in the period over Christmas 1998 and New Year 1999. The plea for new sources of finance was widely reiterated in the press in early 1999, as once again the NHS appeared not to be coping.

Representatives of the professions have been robust in their criticisms of perceived governmental parsimony, not least because the task of reconciling the demands upon the service with the resources available to meet them has been largely discharged by individual professionals, choosing to meet this need rather than that, deciding one need to be more urgent than another.

But this role has become increasingly difficult to discharge. Media scrutiny of the NHS has intensified, and the use of the media by interest groups has grown more sophisticated; all such groups have an incentive to portray the Service as underfunded, whether in order to lever more funds from the Treasury or to promote other – for example commercial – objectives. The performance of the NHS has become more transparent, through, for example reports from the Audit Commission and the Health Service Commissioner, while media scrutiny of the NHS, be it during the annual winter crises that afflict the hospital service or particular events such as those at the Bristol Royal Infirmary, has become more searching. At the same time, a relatively quiescent public has been transformed into increasingly powerful and interested consumers who are less blindly trustful of NHS professionals. Travel and greater information from abroad, often via the Internet, have meant that disparities in perceived access to, or quality of, health services are more obvious and less tolerated.

These external factors have worked to undermine the professional's role of 'manager of scarcity'. The demanding patient is less willing to accept the judgement of the professional as to what is or is not worth doing and when. Yet no significant support for clinicians or alternative mechanisms have been forthcoming. Instead, successive governments have resolutely denied that such judgements have to be made and effectively turned a blind eye to the day-to-day rationing of access to NHS resources, which has always occurred. Instead, they have embarked on a range of coping strategies.

## Coping strategies

Despite the imposition of prescription charges as early as 1952, the options for financing the NHS that have been considered politically feasible have been limited. The Conservatives investigated the possibility of replacing tax finance with an insurance-based scheme in the 1980s but soon rejected it. Instead, they tried to identify extra sources of finance for the NHS by encouraging hospitals to generate income through charges for parking, rents for the provision of shopping facilities, fees from health care provision to the private sector and asset disposals. The overall result was modest: the main coping strategies have, therefore, focused on better use of the available resources.

The list of initiatives taken by the Centre – we use this broad term throughout this book to refer to the Government, the Department of Health, the Treasury and the NHS Executive – to use available resources more effectively is seemingly endless. Since the late 1980s, justification for extra financing of the NHS from the Treasury in each year's public expenditure survey has depended largely upon the ability of the Service to demonstrate improved productivity. Centrally imposed demands for cost savings, initially introduced at a modest level, have been steadily raised.

The organisation of the NHS has been repeatedly changed with the aim of streamlining bureaucracy. In 1974, those services originally entrusted to local authorities were transferred to health authorities and some years later the structure of health authorities was itself transformed. In 1982, area health authorities were abolished. The pace of change quickened in the 1980s and 1990s as district health authorities reduced in number from 146 in 1988 to 100 in 1996, family practitioner committees (and their successors, family health services authorities) were merged into health authorities in 1994, and regional health authorities were abolished in 1995.

The management of the Service has been restructured at the Centre and at local level. The process began with the so-called 'Griffiths reforms' in 1984 – the introduction of general management in district health authorities and hospitals – while at national level the NHS was given its own Management Board, which was later transferred into a separate executive arm of the Department of Health – the NHS Management Executive – in 1990. The 1991 reforms led to further changes at the Centre following the Functions and Manpower Review of the Department of Health and NHS Management Executive. The number of staff in the Department of Health was cut back while the NHS Management Executive became simply the NHS Executive.

A raft of activity has been promoted to increase knowledge of the effectiveness of services provided in the NHS, in order to improve decision-making by purchasers and providers. The NHS Research and Development (R&D) programme was launched in 1992 to direct health and health care research into priority areas for the NHS. Further initiatives followed designed to make the results of existing research more accessible and useful to decision-makers and to encourage clinicians to practise evidence-based and cost-effective medicine.

Successive governments have attempted to improve the performance of the Service by setting explicit performance targets. Again, modest beginnings have led to major change. The early 1980s saw the publication of a range of performance measures, but they were seen as providing information rather than as setting standards to be met. The 1990s saw the introduction of national performance targets for a number of areas, including the main elements of the *Patient's Charter*, such as waiting times for elective care and for the reductions in morbidity set out in the *Health of the Nation* initiative.

However, while the performance of the Service as a whole became more visible, no such spotlight was directed to illuminate the performance of clinicians, other than an unenforceable requirement to audit clinical practice – an activity which was, in any case, led by NHS professionals themselves. The White Paper, *The New NHS*, marked a significant change in approach by advocating a greater central role in monitoring clinical performance through the new Commission for Health Improvement and the publication of a range of indicators of clinical performance. In these ways, clinical practice itself seems set to become open to scrutiny.

Measures such as these can be seen as forming part of a wider programme of public sector reform. Not just in the UK but across the world, governments of all political complexions have been experimenting with new ways of managing and providing publicly financed services. They have done so for broadly similar reasons – to restrain the growth of public spending, to increase efficiency in the use of resources, and to raise the quality, responsiveness and accountability of public sector services.

The UK was a leader in this process. The policies pursued by successive Conservative governments reflected a realisation that the old ways of running the public sector through large semi-autonomous organisations working to national rules were no longer appropriate to cope with wider pressures upon public institutions.

Change in public sector services since the early 1980s has been characterised by at least three main elements: a split of purchasing and providing functions; devolution of responsibility for budgets closer to where services were delivered; and new incentives to increase the efficiency with which resources were used at local or even individual level. The result was a range of policies designed to break up large public bureaucracies into smaller organisations and inject business values by importing new types of incentives, new models of behaviour, and even new methods of financing, from the private sector. As a result, much of the programme designed half a century ago to fight Beveridge's five giants, as well as the massive public corporations such as water, electricity and gas, was dismantled – casualties of both the wider pressures upon them and the solutions designed by governments in response. The nationalised industries bore the initial brunt of these new policies: by the end of the 1990s few remained in public ownership.

The NHS escaped being sold off to the private sector partly because of the high political costs of doing so. But while the NHS escaped, there were massive changes within it, which reflected this wider programme of reform. The idea was to introduce local 'micro-incentives' (rather than rely only on national 'macro-rules') to encourage efficiency, flexibility and responsiveness in public sector organisations, by shifting responsibility for managing finances downwards nearer to where decisions about expenditure were made, introducing competition among providers, and rewarding efficient behaviour, for example through performance-related pay. Following this strategy, the NHS and Community Care Act 1990 imposed a particular set of *incentives* through which *local* services could raise efficiency and quality in response to local problems.

The reforms introduced a split between purchasing and providing functions of the Service, devolved budgets to smaller units such as GP fundholding practices, and encouraged competition between hospitals and other providers. These incentives created a new environment and culture in the NHS, which was reflected in a new nomenclature – hospitals became 'providers' and NHS trusts, and health authorities became 'purchasers' – and in the different ethos injected into the Service by businessmen and women who moved into executive and non-executive management. Furthermore, the boundary between the NHS and private sector became blurred as health authorities and GP fundholders began to purchase services such as pathology tests from private providers, and as NHS trusts successfully competed with private providers to treat private patients in NHS pay beds. Basic and hitherto unheard of questions began to be raised about whether the NHS necessarily had to *provide* care paid for by the State, and even the extent to which it was necessary to use NHS organisations such as health authorities to *purchase* NHS funded care.

These policies not only created, or aimed to create, incentives to encourage efficiency and innovation at local level, but also fundamentally changed the environment within which the NHS operated. In the years immediately after the 1991 NHS reforms were introduced, the political environment was highly charged and hostile. There was fierce opposition by many in the NHS, fuelled by the then Government's own anti-public sector sentiments and its secretive method of policy-making. Doctors and nurses were pitted against the managers charged with implementation.

Other changes were more positive. The reforms in their early days promoted a huge sense of 'can do' in the Service and a new sense of freedom, particularly in general practice where the introduction of fundholding meant that general practitioners were, for the first time, formally responsible for managing a budget for hospital services, drugs and staffing costs. In this way they gained influence over the wider Service, in particular over their hospital-based consultant colleagues. At the same time, hospitals were encouraged to become more self-determining, as NHS trusts. Freed from the direct management control of their host health authority, they were able to innovate as they saw fit in respect of internal management arrangements and the way they delivered care.

In the same spirit, a range of initiatives was introduced to make the NHS more responsive to its users. In theory at least, patients could have a degree of choice over their purchaser of elective care – by signing up with a fundholding practice (which would purchase elective care directly) or a non-fundholding practice (on whose behalf the health authority would purchase care). The Government facilitated this in 1991 by simplifying the process by which patients could change GPs. Through the *Patient's Charter* and NHS performance indicators, through initiatives such as *Local Voices* which encouraged purchasers to involve the public in purchasing decisions, and by simplifying the methods by which patients could complain about the quality of service, the Service was encouraged to be more responsive to the people using it.

## Impact of coping strategies

Although the NHS 1991 reforms and the policies sketched out above that immediately followed them seemed radical at the time, by the late 1990s it appeared that they had succeeded in one main respect but failed in another.

The *success* was that by the mid-1990s, ideas that had once seemed to threaten the notion of a national health service had come to be regarded as compatible with it. There was a growing consensus that some of the reforms, although painful to many in the Service, had been necessary. The need to improve efficiency, quality, and responsiveness was recognised. Consequently the new Labour Government signalled in the White Paper *The New NHS* that it did not intend to undo all the measures introduced by its Conservative predecessors. The split in the structure of the NHS between the purchasing and providing roles would remain, although the boundary would be blurred as annual contracts were replaced by longer-term agreements. Partnership with the private sector through the private finance initiative would continue. Despite the abolition of fundholding, general practitioners would still retain responsibility for managing a budget for secondary care through new 'primary care groups'. Thus the clear message was that change had been necessary, and that there was no going back.

The *failure* was that the 1990 reforms, and subsequent policies, had manifestly not achieved their basic purpose of ensuring that services could be maintained within the resources available from the public purse. Over and above winter crises, GPs complained about their workload, health authorities and NHS trusts continued to be faced with deficits, wards were closed apparently for lack of funding, and waiting lists lengthened. Well-known NHS hospitals such as St Bartholomew's and Guy's in London came under threat of either major reorganisation or closure, as cash-strapped health authority purchasers attempted to 'rationalise' local services to improve efficiency.

A number of health authority purchasers took to identifying services that they would either no longer fund at all, for example infertility treatment or cosmetic surgery, while others did not. There were similar differences between health authorities for a range of drug treatments such as Beta Interferon therapy (to treat patients with multiple sclerosis) and Recombinant Factor 8 (for patients with blood disorders). For example, in 1996 Paclitaxel was available to breast cancer sufferers on the NHS in Taunton but not in Bristol. Similarly, many health authorities virtually opted out of purchasing long-term care, while others continued to ensure its provision. Such differences made a mockery of the claim that treatment in the NHS was based upon equal access for equal need – the principle of fairness that had underpinned public support for the NHS since 1948. The more glaring inequities were seized upon by the media as further evidence that the Service was not coping.

Furthermore, the 'crisis' and the types of policies designed to help alleviate pressures in the NHS – such as an overriding emphasis on efficiency and the promotion of competition – were closely linked in the minds of many NHS staff, the public, and the media. In the atmosphere of mistrust and suspicion that resulted, any changes to the Service were viewed as a fundamental assault on both the institutions and the basic objectives of the NHS. Baffled by this resistance, the Conservative Government set up a 'good news' media unit in the Department of Health, but the success stories put out by the short-lived unit were greeted with derision by much of the Service and cut no ice with the public.

## Why coping strategies have failed

The failure of what were often highly innovative, radical and imaginative policies to avoid crises and funding shortfalls can be explained in three ways. First, in a service free at the point of delivery, the gap between demands on the Service and the level of service available cannot and indeed should not be filled.[3] A gap will always exist. Second, the technical design of the policies introduced in the 1980s and 1990s meant that they did not bear effectively on the fundamental issue facing the NHS – managing the resulting tension between supply and demand – and indeed may have made it worse. Third, too little attention was paid to the external environment within which the NHS must operate to enable solutions to be sought, designed, or implemented successfully.

### The gap

With some exceptions, such as dental charges and prescription drugs, the NHS is free at the point of delivery, and must be, given its objectives. The normal test by which resources are allocated to specific goods or services, that people are prepared to meet the cost of the resources used in supplying them, does not apply. How much should be spent on health must be determined in other ways.

In principle this might be done by judging whether an increment to the health budget would produce more benefit than a similar increment to the education budget or any other spending programme – in rough terms that is what actually occurs when governments determine how much to spend on each. Users seeking treatment, however, have no reason to consider the alternative uses of the resources their treatment would absorb. As they do not have to meet the costs of provision directly, they, like the professionals treating them, will inevitably want to see more or higher quality care provided than the Government, which must consider the alternative uses to which resources can be put, sees fit to finance.

Budgets are of course increased each year and the most pressing of the needs that have previously been denied may be met as a result. But users' expectations are in part fed by what is on offer: as more is provided, so new needs emerge. It follows that the size of the gap is a matter of perception rather than measurement: how keenly it is felt is a subjective matter. Professionals may identify this or that shortfall where existing standards are not those of 'modern health care' but these standards too are subject to change in the light of developments elsewhere in the world and the public's own perception of their importance.

Therefore, the NHS must inevitably manage scarcity: how well it copes is in part how the gap itself is perceived and understood by the public and in part a matter of how well policies – such as those reviewed above – are designed and implemented.

## Technical design

Policies to manage the gap between the supply of services and the demands upon them require action in at least three main areas: raising extra financial resources; increasing effective supply by improving efficiency; and managing demand.

### Resources

Over the long-term, the NHS has enjoyed an average annual increase in resources of some 3 per cent in real terms (that is, after allowing for the change in the general level of prices). This rate of growth continued into the 1980s, and in the early 1990s the NHS received higher real terms increases than usual to oil the wheels of the 1991 reforms. But by the mid-1990s the increments had slipped back to under 2 per cent and only at the very end of the decade were raised to 3.7 per cent following Labour's Comprehensive Spending Review.

The search for alternative sources of finance produced modest results. While user charges were raised, the exemptions were extended in both scale and scope. Not surprisingly, therefore, by the late 1990s, charges still contributed only 2–3 per cent of NHS revenue. The NHS and Medicines Act 1988 allowed NHS providers to raise income to make a profit, for example, through NHS pay beds, but again the amount raised was relatively small. The private finance initiative was designed to raise private financing for capital expenditure, but the process proved slow, complex and cumbersome. By the middle of 1999, only a handful of projects had actually begun, although many more had been approved, and neither the new Government nor its predecessor had provided any convincing evidence of the substantial long-term savings some had claimed it would bring. Thus the NHS still remained dependent on tax finance while the Treasury demanded ever more efficiency savings in return for a higher budget.

### Efficiency

The widely heralded competition between providers that the 1991 reforms were designed to promote, did not in general come about and hence the hoped-for incentive to drive down prices did not materialise. The Conservatives had to acknowledge that local pay bargaining, which they had hoped would lead to lower staffing costs, had not succeeded: the Labour Government has rejected it. The aim of reducing costs through more efficient purchasing remained elusive. The attempts to streamline the organisation of the NHS and cut management costs did produce a reduction in numbers of staff, but there was no evidence as to whether this would help or actually harm the services delivered to patients or indeed that the savings claimed were actually realised.

The new micro-incentives for purchasers – GP fundholders and health authorities – to begin to scrutinise the appropriateness of demands made upon those budgets, were weak. For example, there was little usable information available on the costs and effects of treatments at the beginning of the 1990s. While GP fundholders could keep any savings they made on their allocated budgets, such incentives proved to be too weak to prompt a significant review of the costs and effects of alternative treatments. Furthermore, GP fundholders were unlikely to effect a significant shift of care from secondary to primary care settings where appropriate, since there was little opportunity for substitution of elective surgery – which absorbed the majority of their budgets – in primary care, fundholding offered no significant remuneration to GPs or practice staff for taking on extra work, and the incentives for hospitals were to increase activity as much as possible to secure income. Subsequent policy developments improved matters: for example fundholding was extended to 'total purchasing' (which allowed practices to purchase acute hospital medical care for which there was more scope for substitution) and other initiatives allowed the possibility of greater remuneration for practices in return for extra work. But these remained experiments rather than general policies.

There was very little action to change the pattern of care to improve efficiency or quality. Despite the rhetoric of encouraging a primary care-led NHS, old boundaries between primary care, community health services and hospitals, as well as between professional groups, remained firmly in place. Similarly there was a marked absence of a central lead role in shaping the configuration of services, particularly hospitals. With regional health authorities slimmed down, abolished and then replaced by Regional Offices of the NHS Executive, this responsibility was largely abdicated to local health authority and GP purchasers by default rather than design.

*Demand*

In sharp contrast to the vast array of measures targeted on the NHS itself, there was no serious effort to manage users' demands. Even where, as with elective care, enforced waiting imposed some limits, the Centre's policies directed at the NHS as a whole, such as the NHS efficiency index, may have helped to increase demand. The nature of the measure used meant there was an incentive for NHS trusts to increase activity in the easiest way possible either by treating patients likely to be in hospital for a short period or inflating the measurement of activity itself. Unsurprisingly, demands on the Service actually increased. More patients were treated, but more people were referred. Furthermore, increasing the productivity of hospitals helped to increase stress and reduce morale among the workforce as NHS trusts faced the bleak annual requirement for ever greater productivity.

Finally, there was no obvious central strategy to help purchasers or providers prioritise competing claims on resources. The media spotlight on the seemingly random differences in service availability that resulted contributed to a growing unease amongst the public that the NHS was failing to meet its underlying objective of being fair to all citizens. Successive governments have refused to acknowledge the case for confronting directly the NHS's inability to do everything.

## The NHS environment

The capacity of the NHS to respond quickly to the pressures upon it has been limited by at least four main factors: the trend towards greater openness and accountability; limited availability of intelligence as to what was happening in the Service; the complexity of the management task; and political resistance to change.

## Improving accountability and openness

Efforts were made in the 1990s to improve accountability to Parliament and the public by publishing indicators about NHS performance, requiring health authorities and NHS trusts to publish annual reports, and allowing greater external scrutiny of the NHS by bodies such as the Audit Commission, the Health Service Commissioner and the National Audit Office. This extra information helped to make the Service more accountable, but at the same time also made deficiencies more visible – deficiencies that were seized upon with relish by the media, which devoted more attention to the NHS as the 1990s wore on. So too were the differences in the availability of drugs and other services, emerging from different local purchasing policies, or the apparent cut backs in hospital services that were in fact dealing with more patients. The NHS has appeared to be 'unravelling' before the eyes of the public – the more that was seen, the worse it seemed to get. With numerous interest groups still poised, as Enoch Powell had noted 30 years before, to make the most of these deficiencies, there was no credible counter-voice to explain why it might be justifiable not to provide particular services or to alter the way they were delivered.

## Intelligence

The number of initiatives coming from Government has rapidly increased in recent years resulting in change bordering on 'continuous revolution' in the NHS; what central capacity existed to understand fully the impact of these policies has been swamped by their sheer number. The restructuring and downsizing to which the Department of Health has been subject has created organisational turbulence at the Centre, which in turn has reduced capacity further. The Centre's ability to obtain informal and formal intelligence about the impact of policies locally has been undermined by the abolition of regional health authorities and as more key elements of information, such as basic information by hospital, rather than by NHS trust, were no longer held centrally.

In the early 1990s, an administrative split between purchasers and providers existed within regional health authorities, resulting in a 'Chinese wall' which impeded the sharing of information and hence understanding of the impact of policies. Research effort through the NHS R&D Programme has been directed largely towards evaluation of specific clinical interventions rather than understanding better how the NHS as a *system* was operating in response to policies. Finally almost all the investment into improving the knowledge available to the NHS has been directed towards training clinicians and conducting medical research, rather than improving understanding or capacity to manage the system itself. The NHS is a long way away from evidence-based management or policy-making.

### Complexity of management

Recent policies, and the way they were introduced, have vastly increased the complexity of the central management task. Ironically, attempts to reduce the burden on the Centre have been partly responsible. For example, the policy of devolving responsibility for managing budgets further down the NHS organisational tree has meant that there were many more budgetholders to monitor and influence. Furthermore, policies such as GP fundholding were not imposed fully formed and uniformly upon the NHS. Instead they evolved, largely shaped by the grass roots, for example into community fundholding and total purchasing, and expanded as more volunteers joined. The result has been marked heterogeneity, policies evolving in different locations at different paces, and thus an ever more demanding central management task.

At the same time as devolving budgetary responsibilities, there has been a steady trend towards increasing centralisation as the Centre became increasingly anxious to show that the NHS was delivering efficiently a high standard of care. As we have noted already, throughout the 1990s central directives and guidelines rained down upon health authorities and NHS trusts. The change of government served only to increase the flow, as Labour attempted to meet its election pledges and implement the wide range of initiatives set out in *The New NHS*.

The local NHS must try to deal with this vast range of measures, but the Centre itself is not in a position to assess how they interact with each other, what skills they require if they are to be implemented and what financial or other resources they will absorb. At the same time, the sheer volume of requirements to pursue and guidelines to follow can only have reduced the capacity of the local service to find solutions to its own problems, despite the rhetoric of increasing local responsibility. Furthermore, the danger is increasing that policies being prescribed centrally are inappropriate to local needs and simply ignored by local management.

### Political environment

The fourth factor that has impeded the capacity of the NHS to deal with the pressures upon it is the political environment. A hostile environment breeds mistrust, suspicion and resistance to needed change. In such circumstances, governments have vastly reduced room for manoeuvre because of the potentially high political costs in acting more radically. The result has been the design of policies which are politically more convenient in the short-term, but do not bear on the fundamental issues.

There are at least three reasons for resistance to change in the NHS, resulting in high political costs and thus the tendency towards incremental and timid reform: lack of trust between the key players and Government; a failure to persuade powerful political groups of the need for change; and, failure to engage the public to spearhead change.

First, the lack of trust between the Government of the day and the public and NHS staff was demonstrated *par excellence* under the previous Conservative Government, fuelled by their anti-public sector rhetoric, obsession with privatisation, secretive policy-making during the period of developing and implementing the 1991 NHS reforms, and the very public stand-offs with key political groups inside the NHS such as the British Medical Association. This led to a low-trust environment in which change was resisted and the Government gained little credit for any improvement that was achieved. Little attempt was made to improve trust by developing more open and inclusive methods of developing policies. Only in its last year did the Conservative Government open the process of developing policy by conducting a 'listening exercise', which led to the Primary Care Act 1997. The present Government's approach of lambasting the 'forces of conservatism' in the NHS risks, paradoxically, breeding resistance to change.

Resistance to change is also due to nervousness that change will somehow undermine the principles of the NHS or its institutions rather than strengthen them for the future. Part of this relates to the fact that it has never been clear exactly what the NHS is, and thus any change can be seen as an assault on the Service, especially as little effort is usually devoted to explain the need for change and justify it. In 1997 the apparent failure of the 1991 reforms to resolve fundamental problems drove the Conservative Government to reaffirm its belief in the underlying principles of the NHS. The resulting White Paper, *A Service with Ambitions*, was intended both to reassure the public and NHS staff that despite the apparently radical changes to the NHS, the Service was still safe in the Government's hands, and to demonstrate that it was committed 'to develop the NHS on the basis of these fundamental principles':

- *universal in its reach, available to anyone who wishes to use it;*
- *high quality, applying the latest knowledge and the higher professional standards;*
- *available on the basis of clinical need, without regard for the patient's ability to pay* (p.4).

But these laudable statements rang hollow to many in the Service, partly because they were not subsequently translated into any direct policy, and partly because they were pitched into a historically low-trust political environment, which the Conservatives' had part deliberately, part incidentally, created. Indeed, Labour hardly needed to articulate any policies on the NHS to gain public support.

Second, there has been little real attempt to convince the most powerful political group in the NHS – the medical profession – of the importance of managing economic pressures. As noted earlier, the price to be paid for minimising resistance to the formation of the NHS was the guarantee to the profession of clinical freedom. But in recent years the increasing economic imperative to control costs, coupled with greater scrutiny of performance of the Service, has led to ever more interference by Government and managers. This has rankled with professionals, because they see that their duties are to patients first, rather than supporting the policies of the Government of the day towards the Service. Most have minimal interest or knowledge of management, in part because of a fundamental and widespread belief that the cause of problems in the NHS is inadequate funding, rather than inadequate management of the resources which they themselves are responsible for deploying. In contrast there has been perhaps greater consensus amongst the medical profession of the merits of evidence-based medicine to maximise the effectiveness of treatments offered. However, this was because the initiative, like clinical audit, has been presented firmly as an issue relating to clinical quality of care, rather than one of benefit and opportunity cost.

Attempts have been made to encourage the medical profession to become involved more in managing the Service, for example through initiatives such as GP fundholding, GP commissioning and encouraging doctors to become medical directors in hospitals. However, the doctors involved in management have usually not had sufficient training or professional recognition. This may also be apparent in the new primary care groups, which are now assuming responsibility for spending a significant share of NHS funds. The Royal Colleges have not taken a strong lead to help develop management skills in doctors – undergraduate or postgraduate – or even to justify the need for doing so. For example, almost all the undergraduate training of doctors focuses on clinical medicine – it offers little on the NHS as an organisation, its aims and objectives, developing management skills, or the doctor's role in managing the Service.

Third, there has been no real attempt to appeal directly to the public that the NHS serves, for example by using the public to help lever needed change within the Service, or to articulate better the need for change when it appeared to threaten their services. There are signs this is changing: the new Government for example has established a 'People's Panel' and a new national NHS patient survey has been carried out. Both should help to understand better what the public want. But there has still been no serious attempt to explain the need for change in, for example, the configuration of hospital services.

## This book

This book develops the arguments set out in this chapter and attempts to identify ways in which the technical and political issues that the NHS faces might be better handled. Our starting assumption is that there is no quick fix. A large injection of cash would undoubtedly be extremely helpful to the Service. The share of public spending in gross domestic product is lower than it has been for over three decades.[4] Extra cash could be found for the NHS if there was sufficient confidence that it could deliver enough extra benefits if it received more financial resources.

But even if a large injection of extra cash from the public purse were to materialise, the core issue of how the gap between supply and demand can best be managed would remain. *No* health care system can do everything that is beneficial, nor should it try to.

This simple but fundamental point is consistently overlooked by those who argue that because there is a gap between what a health service can do and what the available level of finance allows it to do, that gap ought to be filled. This view overlooks the value lost in other potential uses of funds. The 'price' or opportunity cost of more health spending would be translated into lower spending on other public sector programmes such as education, or in lower levels of personal consumption of goods and services which lower taxes would allow.

As we pointed out above, to the individual seeking care for him or herself or for others, those costs are not apparent. There is accordingly a fundamental tension that must be managed at national level by the Treasury, at local level by health authority purchasers and at the individual level by clinicians face-to-face with patients. This task, the management of scarcity, cannot be avoided in any health system which insures, or allows the potential user to insure, fully against the need to use health care services, and which thereby eliminates price from the role of bringing demand for services in line with the available supply.

The task of managing the inherent tension between demands on the Service and its ability to meet them is partly technical and partly political. The technical tasks cover issues such as designing services, increasing efficiency and managing demand. The political tasks involve changing the broad environment – the climate of public opinion and user expectations – so that necessary reforms can be made.

The way that technical tasks can be carried out – and the range of options deemed to be politically acceptable – is to a large degree dependent on the environment within which the NHS operates. This environment is discussed in the first section of this book. In Chapter 2, we review the main pressures that together create the external environment within which the NHS must work as well as pressures arising within the Service itself. We argue that the environment is ever more critical and more demanding. It acts as a constraint on what the NHS can do and on the range of policies that governments can propose.

The task of managing and responding to that environment is a political one, not simply in the obvious sense that support for the NHS's broad objectives may have to be consciously sought, but in the less obvious sense that the environment within which it works is at one and the same time part of the problem and part of the solution. It is part of the problem to the extent that it hinders change, part of the solution because, in the final analysis, the NHS, as a major national institution must be organised and financed in ways that are compatible with the interests and aspirations of those who work in it and the society that pays for and uses it. What exactly is compatible with the notion of a national health service is discussed in Chapter 3.

If our analysis of the failure of the technical solutions applied to the NHS in the last 20 years is correct, then a massive range of technical tasks remains to be tackled successfully. The focus of the second section of the book is on the main tasks that the NHS and the Centre must carry out. In the first seven chapters, technical issues relating to managing scarcity are explored: providing finance (Chapter 4); controlling costs (Chapter 5); ensuring an appropriate pattern of provision (Chapters 6–8); and managing demand (Chapter 9). Our aim is to define whether or not the NHS, as it currently stands, is well equipped, technically, to resolve them, and to suggest a way forward.

But, as we argue in Chapter 2, the availability of technical solutions to policy-makers is in part determined by the broader environment within which they work. Technical options can throw up political dilemmas. These chapters also identify the tensions that arise between technical solution and the wider environment. In the chapters that follow, the balance of the discussion changes. While technical questions remain our central concern, the next set of chapters cover areas where these and the NHS external environment are closely related: sharing the available resources between competing uses (Chapter 10); improving the knowledge base required for policy-making (Chapter 11); improving the quality of management and governance of the Service (Chapter 12); and accounting for the Service (Chapter 13).

In the final section of the book, we pull the elements of our argument together. In Chapter 14 we summarise those areas where the NHS appears to be moving in the right direction and then identify those where major issues remain to be resolved. In Chapter 15 we put forward a small number of specific proposals designed to help the NHS 'face the future' with more confidence.

These technical and environmental tasks will in themselves require significant resources – not least time – if they are be tackled properly. But if serious action is taken in these areas then that might inspire the confidence required in the NHS's paymasters to justify a financial settlement that would enable it to become a truly modern Service.

## References

1. Ministry of Health and Department of Health for Scotland. *A National Health Service*. London: HMSO, 1944.
2. Healthcare 2000. *UK Health and Healthcare Services*. London: Healthcare 2000, 1995.
3. Dixon J, Harrison A and New B. Is the NHS underfunded? *BMJ* 1997; 314: 58–61.
4. Office of National Statistics Databank.

Chapter 2

# A changing environment

The notion that the NHS is under increasing pressure is now only too familiar. In considering how the NHS should try to deal with that pressure, it is important to distinguish the various factors that comprise it. Some may be forecastable: others not. Some may be becoming stronger: others less strong. Some may be subject to control or at least influence: others not. Some may influence the level of demand for care: others the way that care is provided and at what cost, and others the overall environment in which the NHS operates. In this chapter, we consider a series of such factors: public finance; demography; morbidity; social change; availability of new technologies; the physical environment; and, finally, the media.

## The supply of public finance

Although the NHS was established at a time of economic stringency, it came to benefit from an economic and political climate that was favourable to the expansion of public spending in general and health in particular. That period lasted until the 1970s when economic growth in the UK and across the developed world began to slow down.

Sluggish economic growth continued across OECD countries into the 1980s. New challenges appeared: increasing competition from the industries in the Far East 'tiger economies'; globalisation of trade; and, increasing flows of capital investment which could be moved around the world in seconds aided by new technology.

The UK has, more than most other European countries, responded to these pressures by deregulation of financial, labour and other markets and restraint of public spending. In practice, the former has proved easier than the latter. Public spending continued to rise during the Conservatives' period of office, but they nevertheless succeeded in bringing down rates of personal taxation, making it impossible in electoral terms for Labour to plan to raise them. When Labour came to office it initially sought to demonstrate its fiscal rectitude by committing itself to the plans left by the outgoing Government, which allowed for virtually no growth in spending on the NHS.

The UK has been in a strong position to exercise such control because nearly all health care financing has come from the public purse. The Treasury has kept a lid on expenditure, through the mechanism of setting a global budget each year. Almost all elements of the NHS budget have been cash-limited in this way, with the exception of prescription drugs (finally cash-limited in 1999) and some elements of expenditure on family health services, which remain largely driven by demand. This method of financing – a single funding stream and a global budget controlled by government – is widely thought of as being the most effective method to contain health care costs.

But while the UK Government has been in a strong position to control directly the rise of health care spending, this benefit has come at a political cost: the Government has been highly vulnerable to attack that the level of expenditure on health care is not enough, almost regardless of the actual level of funding chosen.

Surveys of public opinion, such as the annual British Social Attitudes Survey, consistently indicate that the public think the Government should spend more on public services, particularly health and education. That helps to explain why it has been hard for governments (even the Thatcher administration) significantly to curb public expenditure, especially for programmes that affect most or all citizens directly, and which, like the NHS, are popular.

Furthermore, as noted in Chapter 1, there are powerful stakeholders in health care, such as the medical profession, NHS managers and the pharmaceutical industry, who have a direct interest in securing more funding for the NHS. As time has gone on, they have become increasingly adept at putting their message across to the public through the media. As a result, the very tool – Government control of the purse strings – to help curb expenditure has been exploited by key stakeholders to lever expenditure upwards. Lean years of funding have met with a chorus of complaint within the Service and from a supportive public, and fuelled by stories of 'financial crises' and 'chronic underfunding' in the media.

Thus, despite the compelling economic imperative, it has rarely been possible for the Government to curb real terms growth of health care spending for more than one or possibly two years in succession (as shown in Figure 2.1).

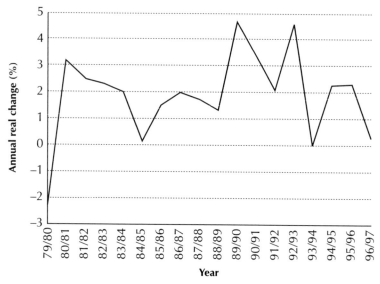

**Figure 2.1:** Growth of NHS resources in real terms

**Source:** Appleby J. Government funding of the UK National Health Service: what does the historical record reveal? *Journal of Health Services Research and Policy* 1999; 4(2): 79–89.

Furthermore, expenditure on the NHS has increased faster than most other areas of the public sector (see Figure 2.2).

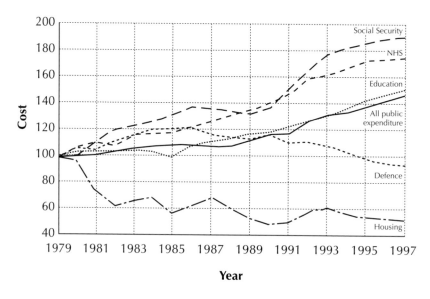

**Figure 2.2:** Expenditure on health relative to other programmes

**Source:** Adapted from Office of Health Economics. *Compendium of Health Statistics.* London, 1999.

This record can be read in different ways. On the one hand, it might be argued that sufficient finance will always be forthcoming from the public purse, once the implications of continuing spending restrictions become clear: this interpretation is in line with the behaviour of the Labour Government since it came to power in 1997, with its special injections of funds over and above the spending plans originally set and the subsequent increases stemming from the Comprehensive Spending Review. In behaving in this way it has been no different from its predecessors. On this view the NHS will always be bailed out eventually – but while the Service waits for that to happen, it will appear to be in crisis and public confidence in it will be undermined.

But 'bailing out' under pressure is exactly the wrong approach. It inflates the sense of crisis in the minds of the public while making it difficult to the Service to plan ahead. What the Service requires is a sustained investment underpinning a long-term agenda. The 'cash for change' principle used by the Government within the Comprehensive Spending Review is along the right lines – provided that the changes are the right ones. What changes are required is the subject of Section 2.

On the other hand, the implication may be drawn that the public purse will never produce adequate finance because of the other demands upon it and the perceived need to run a low tax economy. The crisis, on this view, is fundamental and long-term.

Whichever view is right, however, the immediate implication is the same: that within the existing financial framework, the NHS will always appear to be under financial pressure. It would be a sign of poor Treasury management if it were not. No public funding agency can underwrite every claim on health care resources. As Bevan[1] himself said:

> We shall never have all we need. Expectation will always exceed capacity. In addition the service must always be changing, growing and improving; it must always appear inadequate (p.341).

Furthermore, precisely because it has such a strong hold upon the total budget, the Treasury can seek to impose conditions in terms of explicit indicators of performance which will require the NHS to justify the way the resources made available to it have been used. That, in a nutshell, is what has been happening over the past 15 years. Performance measures such as those in the new NHS performance assessment framework and the national 'public service agreement' between the Treasury and the Department of Health,[2] allied with the increasing use of targeted finance, such as the Modernisation Fund, reflect a growing central desire to ensure that resources are well used. The particular indicators used can of course be criticised and the present set will be modified and even transformed. But the pressure to demonstrate performance will not disappear.

## Demography

Elderly people, along with the newborn, use significantly more NHS resources per capita than the rest of the population (see Figure 2.3).

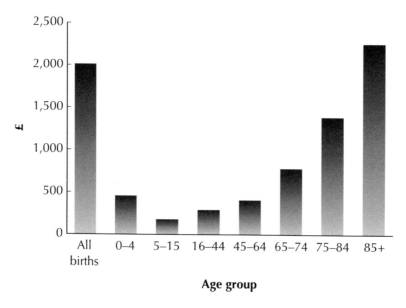

**Figure 2.3:** Expenditure on hospital and health services by age group, 1997/98

**Source:** Department of Health Annual Report.

At the younger end of the scale, higher levels of expenditure can in part be ascribed to the introduction of new medical technologies which have allowed premature babies to survive that would otherwise have died. At the other end, some developments in surgical and anaesthetic techniques appear to have allowed frailer patients to receive treatment, while other newly introduced procedures such as joint replacements are more relevant to the needs of elderly people.

However, most of the increase in hospital activity over the past 20 years can be ascribed to increases in the rate of treatment within each age group rather than changes in the age composition of the population. If rates of treatment are kept constant and applied to the forecast change in the structure of the population, then the pure demographic impact can be estimated. The result is shown in Figure 2.4.

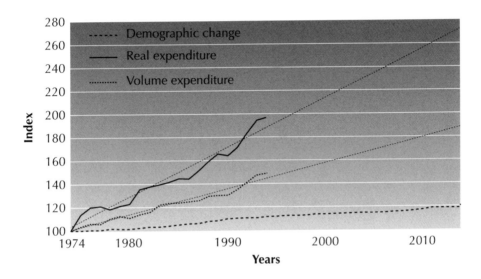

**Figure 2.4:** Demographic change and health spending

Figure 2.4 shows the growth in NHS spending from 1974 to the present day, and a projection to the year 2015 based on a continuation of historic growth over the last 20 years (approximately 3 per cent growth in real terms). In the figure, this projection is compared with the estimated change in growth in costs due to demographic change.

The figure shows that if growth in NHS spending continues on a similar trajectory to that seen in the past, there will be more than enough to cope with the growth in costs from demographic change alone, if rates of treatment remain constant.

## Morbidity: levels of illness and disability

The best available information describing changes in prevalence of overall illness across the population comes from surveys of self-reported health. The largest is the annual *General Household Survey*. Respondents are asked three general questions, relating to acute and long-term illness. Changes in responses to questions about long-term illness by age and sex, since 1979, are shown in the figures below.

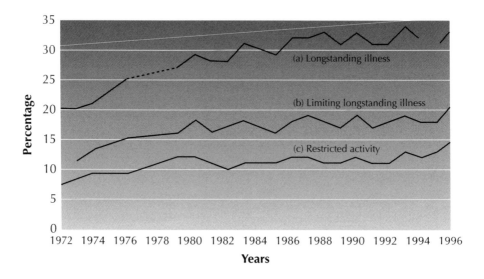

**Figure 2.5:** Trends in self-reported morbidity

The figures indicate that the prevalence of self-reported morbidity is changing very slowly; there has been only a modest increase between 1979 and 1992 across the overall sample population and also, though not shown here, in each age group. If this is an accurate reflection of the picture across the population as a whole, and if this trend continues into the future, it seems unlikely that changes in prevalence of illness or disability will, of themselves, result in significantly higher demands upon NHS resources.

Reflected in the figures above for the oldest age group is the impact of increasing life expectancy on levels of illness. There is unresolved debate over whether elderly people will experience 'extended' or 'compressed' levels of morbidity as a result of increased life expectancy. A recent comprehensive review of the literature[3] suggests that there will be an increase in light to moderate disabilities, but a reduction in the frequency of severe disability. Data from the *General Household Survey* reviewed by Bone *et al.*[4] show that, in elderly people living in private households, there has been very little change in levels of dependency, although there are no comparable data from the survey for those living in communal establishments in which frailer elderly people are likely to reside. Similarly, Bone found that the proportion of elderly people in private households using any of the personal social services hardly changed between 1980 and 1991.

Given the proposals in the Green Paper on public health, *Our Healthier Nation*, and the subsequent White Paper, *Saving Lives*, it may seem possible that illness levels will actually decline. That may well prove optimistic in the light of recent increases in obesity across most of the population and increased smoking, particularly among the young.

However, even if preventive policies do result in a reduction in mortality rates, that will not in itself reduce demand for care. A recent study in The Netherlands[5] estimated that a reduction in mortality from coronary heart disease, lung and colorectal cancer, and chronic obstructive airways disease would actually increase health costs, and that major savings would occur only by elimination of non-fatal disease such as musculo-skeletal and mental disorders. At the moment, such elimination seems unlikely.

On balance, it seems reasonable to conclude that, in the absence of other possible changes, increasing morbidity will not of itself require a more rapid growth in the resources devoted to health care. However, that is far from saying that demands for care and the use of services will not grow since the wider changes we now go on to consider will influence both.

## Social change

Social change may affect the demand for health services in several ways, including the availability and need for lay or non-professional care, particularly for elderly people; increasing wealth and consumerism; and the greater proportion of women in the workforce and changing aspirations of those entering it. We look at each in turn.

### Lay care

Social changes are affecting the need for, and availability of, social care particularly amongst elderly people, which in turn is likely to impact upon the use of health care. The number of elderly persons, particularly those over 75 years, is growing. The proportion of elderly people living alone is increasing – up from 40 per cent in 1973 to 47 per cent in 1996[6] – which is also likely to increase the need for health and social care.

The Royal Commission on Long-Term Care, in its report *With Respect to Old Age*,[7] concluded that the relationship between spending on social care and the use of health services is not well understood, still less the impact of the current pattern of financial incentives facing both public providers and individuals themselves.

On the other hand, the proportion of the workforce who are carers has been growing. By 1990 an estimated 1 in 7 of the workforce reported some caring responsibilities.[8] However, changes in marriage and fertility patterns suggest that, in the longer-term, informal care through family members will be less available to elderly people born after the 1950s. A recent survey of European countries found that there was no evidence to suggest that people were less willing to care for elderly parents and relatives.[9] Elderly people themselves, however, felt less strong ties to their children and increasingly expressed a preference for professional care over family care, especially for conditions requiring a long-term commitment.

Local authorities, responsible for social services and under pressure to contain spending, have responded to the rising demand for personal social services by restructuring their scope, for example by refusing to provide cleaning and other domestic services[10] and by charging patients for certain low level support services which enable elderly people to manage at home, such as home helps and meals on wheels, and shifting costs on to the NHS. Health authorities have responded by raising the threshold for long-term NHS care (which is free at the point of use), and by encouraging the discharge of patients more quickly to social care in the community. It is possible that greater reliance on private finance for social care – not an option favoured by the Royal Commission – might lead to lower use of social care and a resulting increase in the use of NHS care.

Social change is also likely to have affected day-to-day use of health facilities as family networks have loosened. With more single parent families and elderly people living alone, traditional lay networks providing information, reassurance and confidence to individuals in dealing with illness have weakened. Even though there has been a concurrent increase in information about the scope of self-care and in the accessibility of medication, for example, over-the-counter drugs, and of other forms of care (for example alternative therapies), they may not be sufficient to instil the confidence required if people are to deal with their own illnesses without consulting professionals. However, as we argue in Chapter 9, there are ways in which such confidence can be created, and hence possible demands on the NHS, at least for less serious complaints, be reduced.

## Greater consumerism

In the economy at large, expectations of better, more accessible and more flexible services available on a 24-hour basis are growing. Within health, this is likely to fuel public demands for more information, more conveniently provided health services, more choice of how they are provided and a more individualised consumer-oriented service. Consumers not receiving the service they expect will be more likely in future to exercise 'voice' – by complaining or suing – or 'exit' – for example by choosing to buy care in the private sector. Complaints to the Health Service Commissioner rose between 1994–95 and 1998–99 by 60 per cent,[11] although some of the rise may be because the process of making a complaint was made easier. The costs of litigation against the NHS have also risen dramatically. That is almost certainly due to a greater willingness on the part of patients to take legal action rather than an increase in the numbers of incidents of low quality care.

The previous Conservative Government responded to the need for a greater consumer focus in the NHS though policies such as the *Patient's Charter*, *Local Voices*, and requiring NHS trusts, health authorities, and general practices to publish annual reports of their activities. But these efforts to make information more available to consumers may well have also increased expectations among the public, exposed the limitations (and the successes) of the Service more explicitly, and acted to reduce trust in both professionals and the ability of the NHS to deliver adequate care. As we argued in Chapter 1, increasing knowledge of the services that health authorities are unwilling to purchase, coupled with the increasing amount of information in the public and professional domain about new technologies and their availability, are likely to have exposed the limits of the NHS by, for example, focusing on instances where care has been denied or where a new form of treatment is available in other countries but not here.

More fundamentally, the rise in 'consumerism' will tend to undermine the mechanisms that the NHS has used in the past to contain the pressure of demand. The change from patient to consumer implies a reduced tolerance of the various devices that individual clinicians and the NHS as a whole use to defer and contain demand such as waiting lists for elective care and gate keeping by general practitioners to other forms of care. For example, although the NHS has managed to hold the line against direct access to specialists by patients, greater consumerism allied with the wider availability of clinical information could threaten it.

At the same time, however, as we argue in Chapter 9, consumerism, allied with an appropriate NHS response, might lead to greater self-reliance. The initial impact of the recently introduced 24-hour nurse-led telephone advice line NHS *Direct* appears to have been to shift demand from one part of the Service to another and between lay and professional care. As the service is extended, it might succeed in reducing overall demands on the rest of the NHS. In addition, studies of the impact of information on the merits of alternative forms of treatment have found that information can act to reduce the level of active intervention. But this highly structured way of creating the informed patient is a far cry from the rapid and unregulated growth of information that the Internet offers or that which results from international travel or media features that expose the population to what is available elsewhere, both of which might have the opposite effect.

## Changing expectations within the NHS workforce

There is an increasing number of women in the workforce. In the UK, nearly half of married or cohabiting women with pre-school children are in employment. In the NHS, over half of all doctors graduating are now female compared to 36 per cent in 1980,[12] and more are working part-time. Just under 80 per cent of the non-medical workforce (whole time equivalents) are female, and just over 5 per cent are from ethnic minority groups.

This change in the composition of the NHS workforce has created pressure for more flexible working conditions, in part to fit in with child care. For example, in a cohort study of newly qualified doctors,[13] women rated hours worked and working conditions as higher concerns in their choice of career than their male counterparts.

However, some changes apply across the board; in particular, there appears to be a general shift in the way that young doctors perceive their careers. For example, a BMA survey found that older doctors are more likely to see medicine as a vocation than younger ones, and that younger doctors (both male and female) think that medicine must be organised to balance both career and family (see Table 2.1).

**Table 2.1:** Medicine as a career by age

|  | Under 30 | 30 to 34 | 35 to 39 | 40 to 44 | 45 to 49 | 50 to 54 | 50 & over |
|---|---|---|---|---|---|---|---|
| Medicine is a vocation | 0.9 | 1.5 | 3.0 | 4.5 | 10.4 | 18.3 | 17.9 |
| Medicine is a major commitment but doctors deserve a decent family life and leisure time | 40.2 | 50.0 | 50.9 | 58.9 | 50.9 | 49.3 | 61.3 |
| Must be organised to balance career and family | 52.1 | 43.8 | 37.6 | 33.0 | 34.0 | 23.9 | 17.9 |
| Job like any other | 6.8 | 4.6 | 7.3 | 3.6 | 3.8 | 4.2 | 1.9 |

**Source:** British Medical Association. *Core Values for the Medical Profession in the 21st Century.* Health Policy and Economic Research Unit. London: BMA, 1996.

These differences might be the result of changing attitudes to work and lifestyle, for example increasing dissatisfaction at work because of greater job insecurity, or more demanding patients, or a greater intensity of work. It may also reflect the increasing wish of men across the population to be involved in parenting, or of the young to devote time to other pursuits: for example, a recent survey of medical students who graduated in 1995 shows that more than 50 per cent intended to take time out to travel or practice overseas.[14] This wish for greater flexibility also extends into work itself. Young doctors may be less willing to climb a career 'drainpipe' than earlier generations; a recent report from the BMA[15] on the consultant role in future acknowledges that young consultants want, and should have, greater flexibility and choice in their career.

The NHS has already had to respond to pressures of this kind by for example giving a firm commitment to the reduction in the hours worked by junior doctors. Although clearly desirable, the gradual implementation of this policy, alongside other changes in the medical workforce, is making it difficult to maintain the current pattern of hospital services. Many senior hospital consultants, furthermore, believe that the existing level of commitment cannot be sustained in the face of changing expectations among their juniors for an improved balance between work and other pursuits. Similarly, changes in career expectations are making it harder to maintain the current way of organising general practice.

Similar issues arise in other parts of the labour force. A recent survey[16] of the admittedly imperfect evidence on the health of the NHS workforce found that staff in most parts were exhibiting high degrees of illness and stress. If, as seems likely, these are at least in part due to the changes in the way that hospitals and other parts of the NHS work as well as the sustained pressure on the NHS to improve performance and change working practices, then it would seem inevitable that allowances will increasingly have to be made in terms of new working practices – as they have been for junior doctors – which alter the way that services are organised and probably also add to their cost.

## New medical technologies

There has been a vast increase in the number of new technologies available in medicine, from drugs to diagnostic testing to information technology.[17] New technologies can lead to higher expenditure in several ways: by being expensive treatments in themselves; by adding to the cost of, rather than substituting for, existing treatments; by lowering the threshold of care for treatment enabling many more patients to be treated;[18] and by prolonging the lives of patients who require a great deal of support. As noted above, innovations such as minimal access cholecystectomy and fast acting anaesthetics have enabled many more frailer patients to be treated safely. New interventions that save the lives of very premature babies may result in disabled and sick infants and children who are heavily dependent upon health services. Such developments help to explain why costs per capita among elderly people and newborns may be rising at a faster rate than the rest of the population.

However, estimating the future demands on NHS resources from new technologies is not possible. Attempts to do so have typically taken a basket of emerging new technologies, or areas of fast technological change (for example, medical imaging, or genome research), and estimated the potential for each technology to generate costs. But, because of the difficulty of coming to reliable estimates, no serious attempt has been made to estimate the likely overall costs to the NHS. Similarly, in the published literature most evaluations of the costs of new technologies to date have been 'microeconomic evaluations' – estimating the costs and effects of individual new technologies such as minimal access surgery – rather than the impact of a range of technologies on the NHS as a whole.

If it is not possible to attempt forecasts of the impact of new technologies, the pressures they give rise to are obvious enough. With greater media coverage of health issues, pressure from the public, and from the medical profession, to use them is likely to become all the greater. This is particularly true when new and expensive drugs come on the market, for example Beta-interferon (for multiple sclerosis), Aricept (for Alzheimer's disease), Paclitaxel (for breast cancer), and most recently Viagra (for erectile dysfunction). Whereas once such decisions would have been hidden under the cloak of clinical discretion, now they are being opened up to public view. As a result, the pressures of new technologies are becoming ever more difficult to contain.

## The physical environment

The physical environment is in many ways less damaging to health than it was 50 years ago, with better housing and more effective public health measures in place, but in other respects, for example air pollution levels and exposure to new forms of man-made chemicals, it may be getting worse.

At global level, climate change is occurring in part because of the emission of greenhouse gases, particularly from the burning of fossil fuels, which is itself closely linked to population growth. Changes to climate conditions, notably a warming of the world temperature, are likely to have important effects on health, most of which are anticipated to be adverse. McMichael and Haines[19] recently summarised these drawing on the recent report of the Inter-governmental Panel on Climate Change – a multidisciplinary panel set up by the United Nations – and other more recent publications, all of which have been subject to international peer review. The summary findings are shown in Table 2.2.

**Table 2.2:** Mediating processes and direct and indirect potential effects on health of changes in temperature and weather

| Mediating process | Health outcome |
| --- | --- |
| ***Direct effects*** | |
| Exposure to thermal extremes | Changed rates of illness and death related to heat and cold |
| Changed frequency or intensity of other extreme weather events | Deaths, injuries, psychological disorders; damage to public health infrastructure |
| ***Indirect effects*** | |
| *Disturbances of ecological systems:* | |
| Effect on range and activity of vectors and infective parasites | Changes in geographical range and incidence of vector borne disease |
| Changed local ecology of waterborne and foodborne infective parasites | Changed incidence of diarrhoea and other infectious diseases |
| Changed food productivity (especially crops) through changes in climate and associated pests and diseases | Malnutrition and hunger, and consequent impairment of child growth and development |
| Sea level rise with population displacement and damage to infrastructure | Increased risk of infectious disease, psychological disorders |
| Biological impact of air pollution changes (including pollens and spores) | Asthma and allergies; other acute and chronic respiratory disorders and deaths |
| Social, economic, and demographic dislocation through effects on economy, infrastructure, and resource supply | Wide range of public health consequences: mental health and nutritional impairment, infectious diseases, civil strife. |

**Source:** McMichael AJ, Haines A. Global climate change: the potential effects on health. *BMJ* 1997; 315: 805–09.

The table suggests that there may be a serious and far-reaching impact of climate change on health. But none of the potential effects can be predicted with certainty, given the complexity and the likely interactions between them; the assessment of risks to health is based upon scenarios informed by mathematical models that are constantly updated in the light of surveillance data. The consensus is that the populations most vulnerable to the effects of climatic change are those that: are economically underdeveloped; have poor nutritional status; are in locations exposed to rising sea levels; and are subject to cultural or political inflexibility. While the UK population may not be the most vulnerable in these respects, there may be indirect impacts through, for example, disease transmitted by foreign travel.

There are many other uncertainties about the future physical environment which make it impossible to estimate the likely future pressures upon use of NHS funds. For example, more new diseases such as new variant Creutzfeldt-Jacob disease may emerge, or there may be increasing resistance of old diseases to existing treatments, as seen with staphylococcus aureus infection, tuberculosis, and malaria. The pressure to make food production more efficient may mean that risks continue to be taken that may have potentially deleterious immediate or delayed effects on health, for example the production and consumption of genetically engineered crops, or more intensive use of pesticides and fertilisers.

If the health effects of particular environmental features could be identified as clearly as the link between cancer and smoking, then in time no doubt appropriate action will be taken to reduce their impact. However, in many of the areas considered here, such links will be hard to establish because of the complexity of the factors at work. Furthermore, in the case of global warming, the change in the physical environment may be rapid and unanticipated. On this basis, it is hard to come to any clear conclusion, even in qualitative terms, about the future impact of the physical environment, but by its very nature, the relevant action lies almost entirely outside the NHS itself.

## Changes in the news media

The news media as such do not of course place direct demands on NHS services but they have a significant impact on the environment within which the NHS works. There are regular features in most national papers and magazines that highlight the details of specific illnesses and discuss the availability and benefits of new therapies, while usually ignoring the risks of treatment. The wide coverage of these issues, not only in the mass media, but also in relatively new sources of information such as the Internet, will tend to increase demands for new treatments, increase expectations about the quality of care provided, and reduce the threshold for seeking care.

Furthermore, unrelated to new developments in health and health care, attention on the NHS is becoming more intense because of changes occurring in the news media themselves. The NHS has always received wide media attention, partly because the Government of the day is seen to be directly responsible for the performance of the NHS: Bevan's observation that when a bedpan is dropped in the NHS, the sound would reverberate around the Palace of Westminster is, if anything, even more pertinent today.

Increasingly fierce competition between news organisations, whether in the television, radio, or the newspaper industry, has resulted in increasing pressure to cut costs. This, plus the rapid proliferation of TV channels resulting from new technologies such as digitalisation, has meant that there is an increasing demand for short, easily covered, news stories that do not require much research. The NHS provides a ready pool of domestic human-interest stories, and issues covering a number of dimensions, including politics, ethics, biomedical science, economics, religion, and philosophy. Since the NHS is a locally provided service, there is also strong coverage by the regional and local news media. The result has been a rapid increase in the number of health-related news items.

As noted above, it is in almost every group's interest, apart from the Government of the day, to portray the NHS's problems as being a result of inadequate funding. It is very difficult to counter these arguments particularly because decisions on level of funding must be based on value judgements rather than an agreed set of facts. The public is thus fed a fairly unchanging diet of news of underfunding and a Service in crisis, which creates the impression that the NHS is perpetually on its knees.

Any failings in the NHS, however inevitable, can be used to criticise the Government and prompt a reaction from political parties – again resulting in newsworthy material. The politicians responsible for running the NHS are viewed as having a vested interest in good news, and thus appear to have less credibility when countering bad news than the hard-pressed doctors and managers who work at the coal face. Thus, there is little to challenge the impression that the Service is in crisis. Clearly some of the factors at work are outside the control of the NHS. Nevertheless, as we will argue in Section 3 of this book, there are ways in which the NHS can respond to and, to a degree, manage them.

## Conclusion

Our first conclusion is that the main reasons why the tension between supply and demand may grow lie in the environment external to the NHS. Demography apart, the 'market' the NHS serves is not growing. But the environment within which it operates is becoming more critical and demanding.

If the NHS is to continue to command public and professional support in future, it will have to respond to these changes in the external world. To do so may, as we argue in the final section of this book, require some fundamental changes in the way the NHS operates.

Our second conclusion is that change in the external environment influences both demands on the NHS and the way that the NHS responds to, and manages, those demands. The traditional methods of controlling access and utilisation are weakening: new methods will have to be adopted to compensate for this, which rely less on individual professionals.

Our third conclusion is that, with the possible exception of changing demography, it is not possible to quantify with any degree of certainty how these pressures will impact upon NHS expenditure in the future. Some of the pressures identified may be amenable to modification by appropriate and relatively straightforward changes in policy, for example by creating more flexibility in medical career patterns.

But even if some of the pressures on the Service can be modified and even if some of the threats from the physical environment do not materialise, there is no reason, on the basis of the evidence presented in this chapter, to conclude that the tension between what the NHS can provide and the pressure of demand upon it will become less intense than it currently is. On the contrary, there are strong forces at work that will make that tension increase.

## References

1. Foot M. *Aneurin Bevan*. Vol.2. St Albans: Paladin, 1975.
2. HM Treasury. *Public services for the future: modernisation, reform, accountability: comprehensive spending review: public service agreements 1999–2002*. London: Stationery Office, 1998.
3. Robine JM, Blanchet M and Dowd J. *Health expectancy: first workshop of the international healthy life expectancy network*. London: HMSO, 1992.
4. Bone M, Bebbington AC, Jagger C *et al*. *Health expectancy and its uses*. London: HMSO, 1995.
5. Bonneux L, Barendregt JJ, Nusselder WJ *et al*. Preventing fatal diseases increases healthcare costs: cause elimination life table approach. *BMJ* 1998; 316: 26–29.
6. Office of National Statistics. *General Household Survey 1996*. London: HMSO, 1997.

7. Sutherland S (chair). *With Respect to Old Age: a report by the Royal Commission on Long-Term Care*. Cm. 4192-1. London: Stationery Office, 1999.

8. Office of National Statistics. *General Household Survey 1995*. London: HMSO, 1996.

9. McGlone F and Cronin N. *A Crisis in Care?: the future of family and state care for older people in the European Union*. London: Family Policy Studies Centre, 1994.

10. Baldwin S, Lunt N. *Charging ahead: the development of local authority charging policies for community care*. London: Policy Press, 1999.

11. Health Service Commissioner. *Health Service Commissioner for England, Scotland and Wales Annual Report 1998–99*. London: Stationery Office, 1999.

12. British Medical Association. *BMA Cohort Study of Medical Graduates 1995 Third Report*. Health Policy and Economic Research Unit. London: BMA, 1998.

13. British Medical Association. *Core Values for the Medical Profession in the 21st Century*. Health Policy Research Unit. London: BMA, 1995.

14. Allen I. *Committed but critical: an examination of young doctors' views of their core values*. London: BMA, 1997.

15. British Medical Association. *Towards tomorrow: the future role of the consultant*. London: BMA, 1996.

16. Williams S et al. *Improving the Health of the NHS Workforce*. London: The Nuffield Trust, 1998.

17. Geljins AC and Rosenberg N. Making choice about medical technology. *Conference on fundamental questions about the future of health care*. 18–19 April, 1996. Amsterdam: Scientific Council for Government Policy.

18. Legoretta AP, Silber JH, Constantino GN, Kobylinski RW and Zatz SL. Increased cholecystectomy rate after the introduction of laparascopic cholecystectomy. *JAMA* 1993; 270: 1429–32.

19. McMichael AJ and Haines A. Global climate change: the potential effects on health. *BMJ* 1997; 315: 805–09.

# Chapter 3

# A changing Service

Despite the changes – described in Chapter 1 – to the way the NHS is organised, official statements of the NHS's objectives over the years have remained very similar. The central objective has always been that access should be determined by need and not by ability to pay, together with a commitment to equity and to quality of service.

In themselves, these objectives give little indication of what a national health service should actually look like. Some countries, such as The Netherlands, ensure universal coverage through a range of organisations, private and public. Some, such as Sweden, allow local authorities a major role. Others, such as Canada, are content at national level to lay down broad objectives and requirements leaving it to a lower tier of government to interpret their implementation. Yet other countries, such as New Zealand, have radically changed the institutions that comprise their health care system while seeking to maintain the same broad objectives. While few countries have been so radical as New Zealand, most developed countries have, in recent years, reformed and reshaped the means by which they deliver or ensure the delivery of health care services to their citizens.

The initiatives taken have reflected the extent to which the pressures for change have been perceived in each country and the ability of payers of health care, typically governments but sometimes insurance agencies, actually to implement change. Both of these in turn reflect the history, political system, and method of financing and organising health care that has been inherited: in other words, the *environment for policy-making* in each country has been different.

Despite the obvious diversity between countries, the policies they have adopted have the same theme in common – the need to curtail the growth of, or even cut back on, spending on health care, while maintaining coverage and quality of service. They have also drawn on a similar range of policies to achieve this objective. Table 3.1 distinguishes three groups, those directed at the health care system as a whole, at health care professionals, and at users of health care:

**Table 3.1**: Common methods of attempting to reconcile demand with supply in health care systems

---

***Health care system***
- an emphasis on efficiency in the production of health care
- attempts to limit the scope of health care provision by rationing or other measures
- the import of private sector organisations or new forms of public sector organisation or management methods based on the private sector
- the use of financial and other incentives, often with a market, or quasi-market framework, to modify the way that organisations behave
- use of explicit performance measures.

***Health care professionals***
- the use of financial and other incentives to modify the way that health care professionals behave
- other measures to influence clinical behaviour, such as guidelines and utilisation review
- publication of information on costs and effects of treatments.

***Health care users***
- the use of financial and other incentives to modify patient behaviour
- more information about different treatment options
- the promotion of self-care.

---

Some of these initiatives have raised the uncomfortable question of whether they are compatible with the notion of a *national* health service. UK critics of the NHS and Community Care Act 1990 argued, for example, that the measures it introduced undermined the very institution it was purporting to uphold: the very language of incentives, contracts and competition did not belong to *their* concept of a national health service. Supporters of the Act, on the other hand, argued that only if radical measures were taken such as those the Act provided for could a national health service serving its founding objectives continue to survive.

By 1997, however, the White Paper introduced by the Labour Government, *The New NHS*, showed that much of what was once rejected, such as the purchaser–provider split, had become accepted as compatible with a national health service by those who were, out of office, its harshest critics. But other elements of the 1990 Act such as GP fundholding were rejected by the new Government as being incompatible with *its* view of the essential nature of the NHS. *The New NHS* acknowledges the need to strike a balance:

*There are some sound foundations on which the new NHS can be built. Not everything about the old system was bad. This Government believes that what counts is what works* (para.2.5).

What foreign experience and New Labour pragmatism suggests is that the essence of a national health service does not consist of its particular institutions, but rather the objectives it aims to achieve. But while that may be an obvious conclusion to draw in the seminar room, in the real world of policy-making, it may seem completely wrong-headed. In practice, loyalty to what the NHS aims to do is linked in the minds of professionals, users and citizens with the particular forms the NHS takes: ownership of the local hospital, the clinical firm or team, the GP and the district nurse and also with particular forms of behaviour such as emphasis on professional standards and disregard of the financial implications of clinical decisions.

But if the conclusion of the previous chapter is right, that the external environment will become more and more demanding, then pressure for change in the way that the NHS is organised and the way it functions will accelerate. New and as yet unconsidered options for reform will be pressed on policy-makers, some of which may appear to them to be incompatible with a national health service. It will become all the more important, therefore, to be clear as to what is and what is not negotiable with professionals, users and citizens, about the nature of a national health service.

In the rest of this chapter, we consider the notion of a national health service. Does *national* mean uniform? What exactly counts as a *health* service, and does *service* imply provision?

## What is a national health service?

The very notion of a UK NHS is itself a curious one. Although the 1947 NHS Act (which brought the NHS into being) and the 1977 Act (which updated and consolidated the legislation then extant) applied to all parts of the UK, the NHS in the four UK countries is not uniform. While the 1989 White Paper, *Working for Patients*, was signed by the Secretaries of State for Health for England, as well as the Secretaries of State for Scotland, Wales and Northern Ireland, elements from the resulting NHS and Community Care Act 1990 were implemented at a different pace in each country.

The White Papers issued by the Labour Government towards the end of 1997 – *The New NHS* (in England), *Designed to Care* (in Scotland), *Putting Patients First* (in Wales) and *Fit for the Future* (in Northern Ireland) – were the first such series to take the NHS in each country separately. There are some noticeable differences: e.g. while the English White Paper proposed that groups of general practices (primary care groups) should be the main purchasers of health care, in Scotland health boards will have this role. Furthermore, by virtue of the devolution they already enjoy, Scotland, Wales and Northern Ireland spend much more per capita on health than England (see Table 3.2).[1]

**Table 3.2:** Per capita expenditure (£) on the NHS in England, Scotland, Wales and Northern Ireland 1995–96

| | Per capita NHS expenditure (£) |
| --- | --- |
| England | 683 |
| Scotland | 855 |
| Wales | 803 |
| Northern Ireland | 717 |

**Source:** Dixon J, Inglis S, Klein R. Is the English NHS underfunded? *BMJ* 1999; 318: 522–26.

At the same time, many other non-NHS bodies that help to shape the NHS, or represent its workers, have retained a remit that stretches across more than one country, but not necessarily the whole of the UK. For example, the Audit Commission monitors the NHS in England and Wales but not Scotland or Northern Ireland. The NHS Confederation and the British Medical Association cover the UK but the Royal Colleges do not. But as we now go on to see, even within one country, England, the notion of a *national* health service has not been carefully defined, in statute or in practice.

## National?

From its beginnings, the NHS was accountable upwards to the relevant Secretary of State – a line that provided a clear national focus for the Service as a whole. The basis of this line of accountability has been and remains the NHS's source of finance. With minor exceptions, the Service has remained dependent on national sources of revenue: where charges exist, as they do for prescriptions and some appliances, they are set by national scales. These scales, and a whole host of rules relating to spending, access to capital, internal audit and financial reporting, have meant that the NHS has been administratively uniform across the country within the broad elements of service – hospital, community health and primary care. Although administrative structures such as health authorities have changed many times over the years, their roles have been broadly the same in different parts of the country.

But it has always been recognised that in an institution as large as the NHS, some degree of local discretion was inevitable. The Service could not be run on a day-to-day basis from the Centre. The inevitability of delegation was particularly true of clinical services themselves. The 1972 White Paper[2] on the organisation of the NHS explicitly recognised the preservation of clinical discretion as a fundamental organisational principle:

> ... health care professionals should be integrally involved in planning and management at all levels. This involvement must be achieved without infringing the clinical autonomy of medical and dental consultants and without interfering with the professional standards of the health care professions or inhibiting the exercise of professional judgements by members of those professions (para.1.5).

But while clinical freedom may seem both a desirable and an inevitable feature of any health care system, the result has been that there has never been a national health service defined as a common set of services provided in similar ways across the country as a whole.

In the early days of the NHS, variations in the availability of services could be in part ascribed to differences in the resources available in each part of the country. From the 1960s onwards, a series of measures were taken to reduce these disparities. The 1962 Hospital Plan,[3] although later modified in detail, led to the creation of a system of general hospitals in all parts of the country. The 1976 report of the Resource Allocation Working Party[4] led to a sustained attempt, which still continues, to ensure that each part of the country receives broadly the same level of resources for hospital and community health services relative to need. But how those resources were deployed remained a largely local matter, albeit influenced by regional health authorities through their control over capital finance and the medical workforce. As a result, the volume and standard of services varied widely.

As far as general practice was concerned, the Medical Practice Committee (MPC) has, from the earliest days of the NHS, ensured that no parts of the country were without general practitioners (GPs) by 'closing' the more popular parts of the country to new entrants. But respectful of GPs' status as independent contractors, the MPC has never been in a position to ensure a completely equitable distribution of resources, still less to influence what GPs actually did. Not surprisingly as, for example, successive reports on London[5] brought out, standards varied widely. But the mechanisms available to eliminate poor practice and to even standards upwards, have been weak. Indeed until recently, they scarcely existed.

Furthermore, the Department of Health did not have available any routine information on the actual access to services experienced by different groups of the population, or on the quality of care on offer within hospitals or primary care. The Royal Colleges and the General Medical Council, with both a national perspective and responsibility for regulating clinical practice, have been active in developing training for their professions but slow to tackle all but the grossest variations in practice.

Thus up to 1990, the notion of a *national* service rested largely on appearances. Behind the apparent uniformity, there was a diversity that had been allowed to continue rather than one which had been actively promoted. From 1990 onwards, a series of policies has been introduced which simultaneously undermined and promoted the concept of a *national* service. The NHS and Community Care Act 1990 and the rhetoric surrounding it gave explicit support for diversity and local experimentation. The new roles for health authorities and NHS trusts from 1991 allowed significant freedoms to purchase and develop services. A multiplicity of different purchasing models – GP fundholding, total purchasing pilots and locality purchasing – were allowed to develop. The 1996 primary care White Papers, *Choice and Opportunity*[6] and *Delivering the Future*[7] envisaged further diversity in the way that services are provided: the Primary Care Act 1997, passed just before the change of Government, subsequently provided a framework that allowed pilot schemes to be developed outside the financial and other administrative rules which then obtained.

A policy of explicit encouragement for diversity might be, and was in practice, justified in different ways. The NHS and Community Care Act 1990 deliberately enlarged the scope of the discretion allowed to general practice, by giving those GPs taking part in the fundholding scheme the ability to determine directly how a part of the budget for hospital services should be spent, with only minimal accountability requirements. The justification of this measure was that it would create conditions that would put some market pressure on service providers and provide scope for service innovation.

The provision of the Primary Care Act 1997 implied a different case for local variation – it was not clear what the 'best' form of service was and hence new forms should be tried out, but not on a universal basis. The Act responded to the perception on the ground that the existing set of rules governing primary care was too restrictive. But the fact that they had worked to limit variation in the way that services were provided meant there was little experience that would point a clear way to better alternatives. Diversity, therefore, could have been seen as a means of 'collective learning' as to what worked best.

But while diversity was being encouraged on the one hand, the Centre simultaneously became more assertive in laying down requirements to be followed for all parts of the NHS. This was particularly noticeable in the field of corporate conduct and management practice. A series of scandals relating to the use of public funds, for example in the Yorkshire and the West Midlands Regional Health Authorities, resulted in a tightening up of national rules on accountability and standards in public life. These scandals, it might be argued, arose precisely because of the relaxation of controls and the encouragement of local initiative that the 1990 Act had aimed for. Greater local freedom, in other words, led to a greater central role. But this role was primarily regulatory and could be seen as an attempt to make explicit the implicit rules that the Service had generally followed anyway.

More significant was the extension of the central role into clinical areas. Perhaps the first major step was the introduction of the 1990 GP contract, which, for the first time, both prescribed a range of activities that GPs should carry out and created a system of financial incentives to match. Less directive was the rather loose requirement of the 1990 Act that clinical audit should be introduced on a general basis within hospital and community health services – the volume, quality and content of the audit as well as the resulting action was left up to the professions. But this was followed-up by a large number of central initiatives designed to alter clinical practice: some bearing on particular services such as cancer, others on broad activities such as prescribing, and yet others such as the clinical effectiveness programme, on the whole spectrum of clinical work. Others, such as the attempts to reduce waiting times for elective surgery to meet nationally set targets, bore on clinical priorities even though that was not their main target.

The simultaneous push towards local variation and central standards survived the Conservative Government. The Labour Government's White Paper, *The New NHS*, announced measures which could curb further the clinical freedom that professionals enjoy through, for example, its proposal for a Commission for Health Improvement and for 'national service frameworks'. Yet it also contained proposals that would promote diversity by, for example, allowing the new primary care groups the freedom, albeit subject to national priorities, such as reducing waiting lists, to purchase all hospital, community health and primary care services. Furthermore, the new Government has been content to continue the process of implementing pilot schemes provided for by the Primary Care Act 1997, which its predecessor had begun.

Thus overall, we reach the apparently paradoxical conclusion that the NHS is simultaneously becoming a more genuinely national service, in the sense that national standards of provision are beginning to emerge, while at the same time the Government is actively promoting diversity by encouraging experiment and local choices. It would not be a paradox if central and local roles were clearly distinct.

But neither *The New NHS* nor *A Service with Ambitions* attempted to define what the scope of local choice should be and what is properly reserved for national decision. Neither attempted to define systematically the role of the Centre nor the degree to which the local NHS should be free to go its own way.

## Health?

The question of what is, or what is not, a *health* service, was largely taken for granted for most of the post-war period. But a number of responses to budgetary pressures have raised the question of where the boundary between health and other services should be set (and by implication who should pay for these services), and how, and by whom, the definition of the boundary should be reached. We consider here:

- the tendency for the NHS to reduce its commitment to long-term or continuing care
- the gradual drift of dental services out of the NHS
- explicit decisions by purchasers as to what should be purchased including some very expensive drugs.

The provision of long-term (or 'continuing' care) perfectly illustrates not just the question of where the boundary between health and other services lies but also the fuzziness of the central and the local roles. When the NHS was created it inherited a large number of hospitals for elderly people, most of which were gradually closed and their services integrated with district general hospitals as the specialty of geriatric medicine developed. In the late 1970s, however, many elderly people were still remaining in hospital for very long periods. Towards the end of the decade, some local offices of the Department of Health and Social Security (DHSS) began paying nursing and residential care fees virtually automatically (subject to income requirements). This development encouraged hospitals in many parts of the country to discharge patients out of NHS hospitals and into private establishments. This process continued until, through the NHS and Community Care Act 1990, responsibility for DHSS funds for long-term care was transferred to local authorities, and the budget effectively capped in the process. By this time, however, hospitals had become used to discharging patients in this way, and the process continued. It was challenged by a case in Leeds, which was the result of a complaint to the Health Service Commissioner (Ombudsman) on behalf of an elderly man with a range of disabilities who was discharged into nursing home care for which he had to pay.

In response to the Ombudsman's ruling[8] that the discharge had not been justified, the Government set up a process of local decision within a national framework. Meanwhile, monitoring by the National Audit Office revealed that great disparities between different parts of the country existed: some health authorities had ceased to provide continuing care completely, while others had continued to do so.

The national framework laid out a series of general criteria, but as far as the boundary of the NHS was concerned, the critical issue – in the Government's view – turned on the nature of the medical and nursing contribution. Putting it simply, patients requiring *continuing* specialist medical and nursing care were deemed eligible to have the whole of their care paid for by the NHS. If, like most people, they required it only *occasionally*, they were required to pay for all their continuing care costs, including nursing.

Whether this is the right boundary continues, however, to be challenged. The Royal College of Nursing, for example, has argued that any care that needed to be provided *by nurses* should fall within the ambit of the NHS: the Government itself appeared, in response to the Health Committee's report into continuing care,[9] to acknowledge that there might be a case for drawing the boundary at that point. Others have argued that it was less an issue of *who* provided the care, but more the *type* of care provided, since the distinction between care provided by nurses and other staff is often meaningless in practice, as the famous example of the 'health bath' and the 'social bath' – exactly the same service whether provided by the NHS or local authority social services – reflects. Official papers such as *A Service with Ambitions* and *The New NHS* are silent on these issues. The Royal Commission on Long-Term Care[10] however did address them. But the Government appeared to be unprepared for its recommendation that the line should be redrawn so that 'free' care should include health and what the Commission terms 'personal care'. In 1999, the legitimacy of the provision of nursing services by local authorities was tested in the Coughlan case.[11] This purely legal ruling could not by its nature define where the boundary *ought* to be, but no other procedural means of determining it is available.

### Dentistry

In contrast, the place of dentistry within the NHS has changed by a quite different process. Here national rules have been laid down as to who should benefit from NHS care free at the point of service, what the cost for individual procedures should be, who should pay what fraction of that cost and what range of dental procedures fall within the scope of the NHS. Purely cosmetic procedures for example are ruled out explicitly – unlike in general health care where, for example, tattoo removal is not regulated in this way but left to local discretion. Dentists have been paid on national scales, largely determined by a national Pay Review Body.

But while the central role in these respects for dentistry has been very precise, in others it has not. In many parts of the country, for example, access to NHS dentistry for adults has been limited because insufficient dental practitioners have found the terms of service offered to them under the NHS attractive enough. The means available to health authorities for ensuring that enough dental practitioners are willing to provide services within the NHS in their areas have been inadequate to bring about even rough equality between different parts of the country. As a result, the Conservatives' White Paper on dentistry[12] set out proposals, subsequently embodied in the Primary Care Act 1997, allowing health authorities to experiment with pilot schemes to encourage better access to services in their areas. The Labour Government has indicated its intention to ensure the continuation of NHS dentistry by supporting a large number of innovative schemes in areas where dental services and dental health are poor. But the very need to adopt this range of policies reflects the lack of central grip on what was actually available in different parts of the country.

Changes within long-term care and dentistry have been many years in the making. In contrast, financial pressures faced by health authorities during the 1990s led to a number of decisions as to what was on or off the local NHS menu of services. Most of these have involved services that are relatively inexpensive in total, such as tattoo removal or infertility treatment. But, like dentistry and long-term care, these instances have underlined both the vagueness of the boundary between health and 'non-health' services, and the lack of an agreed process for determining it. In contrast, other countries such as New Zealand and The Netherlands, have attempted explicitly to define what is or what is not a 'health service' activity, through the establishment of Commissions.[13] Their deliberations have not resulted in significant reductions in the scope of provision – in effect health services are what health providers provide – but they have generated greater discussion about thresholds of care and also had the merit of representing an explicit consideration of the issues rather than an implicit one.

Similar issues have arisen from the introduction of new forms of treatment, particularly new and expensive drugs such as Beta Interferon. In the UK, the criteria for granting a licence authorising a new drug to be prescribed rests upon whether the drug is shown to be harmful or not. It is not currently necessary for the cost-effectiveness of a drug, or whether it performs significantly better than existing drugs, to be demonstrated. Furthermore, NHS purchasers often have to decide whether to make a new drug available on the basis of very little information. The result has been the widely differing availability of new drugs across the NHS and the emergence of what has been termed rationing by postcode which, as we suggested in Chapter 1, has helped to undermine the NHS's claim to universality.

As these developments indicate, there has been no clear process for determining either what the scope of the NHS should be or at what level such decisions should be made. In *A Service with Ambitions*, the Conservative Government gave a commitment that nothing of therapeutic value would be ruled out of the NHS 'package' of services. However, that still left open the question, particularly relevant to the use of alternative medicine, of who should decide, and on what basis, whether a particular intervention had such value. As with so many of the fundamental issues arising in the NHS, central policy-makers have preferred to leave the question unanswered, leaving it to be solved implicitly in day-to-day clinical practice or by health authorities for their particular area of responsibility. A recent exception was the guidance issued by the Secretary of State on the use of Viagra, which defined the types of patient – by their clinical condition – who could be prescribed it within the NHS. The new National Institute for Clinical Excellence will provide national guidance on whether or not treatments should be available in the NHS, but purchasers and clinicians will not be legally bound to comply with it.

## Service?

For the bulk of the NHS's history, health care has been provided and managed either by full-time NHS employees or by GPs who, nominally self-employed, have in effect been employees as well, albeit enjoying a large degree of discretion. Their private status is almost entirely overlooked in popular perception. In addition, although the NHS never sought to be self-supporting for supplies such as medicines or equipment, the bulk of support services such as hospital maintenance, catering and so on have also been provided by NHS staff. This pattern of provision went largely unchallenged until the early 1980s, when the Government introduced competitive tendering for a range of support services within hospitals. These services were not of a clinical nature and most involved no direct patient contact.

The introduction, in the 1990 Act, of a division between purchase of clinical services and their provision, within hospital and community health services, raised the question of whether the *essence* of a public service lay in the finance *and* delivery of service. In the case of social services, the Conservative Government decided that it lay with finance, not delivery. As a result local authorities were forced, when social security funds were transferred to them, to devote the vast majority to private or voluntary sector suppliers.

In the case of health, private providers have not been encouraged to deliver NHS-funded care in this direct way. Nevertheless, in some areas non-NHS provision has crept in to mainstream services. Many fundholding GPs have turned to private rather than NHS providers for services such as sample testing, and as part of the drive to cut waiting lists in the early 1990s and late 1990s, private facilities were sometimes used. In the case of mental health, the private sector has become a major provider of some specialist services. The private finance initiative (PFI) has further promoted the involvement of private providers – in this case in the provision of physical facilities and their subsequent management. The first tranche of schemes was largely concerned with particular support services such as incinerators, laundry services, combined heat/power schemes or office accommodation, but the most recent have been concerned with whole hospitals. The Conservative Government did not rule out – as Labour has now done – but neither did it encourage, private provision of clinical services as part of PFI schemes, even though there is no formal barrier to health authorities or GP purchasers buying care from the private sector if they so wish.

Other and less controversial changes led to clinical services being provided by voluntary or not-for-profit organisations. This occurred particularly in the field of learning disability and mental health, as part of the switch of hospital care to the community. Groups such as MIND, the hospice movement, and the Terence Higgins Trust have developed services according to their own views of how they ought to be run. The care models developed in this way have sometimes been subsequently adopted as part of NHS provision. Other privately provided services such as homoeopathy and other alternative therapies continue to lurk just outside the boundary of the NHS, sometimes gaining a foothold where GPs are receptive to them.

Unlike some other countries, there is no barrier in the UK to private provision and private insurance outside the NHS, nor to the NHS participating in these private markets. It was part of the implicit contract between the State and the medical profession that NHS doctors should be able to practise privately. Furthermore, the NHS itself has always been a supplier of care to individuals willing to pay privately, whether directly out-of-pocket or using private health insurance. In the early days of the NHS, there were few takers for private insurance, but numbers began to rise from the early 1980s. In recent years the proportion of the population covered by private insurance has remained virtually static at around 11 per cent, but clearly if it grew significantly, the NHS would cease to be a 'one nation' Service.

The Labour Government abolished the tax relief on health insurance offered to people over 60 but this did not form part of a wider consideration of the proper role of private insurance in a country with a publicly-funded national health service. In Canada, for example, it is illegal to provide private insurance cover for a service funded by government. The logic of the one-nation NHS, which *The New NHS* is designed to promote, would have implied such a measure but the White Paper ignores the private sector entirely.

The unwillingness of successive governments to develop a coherent policy towards private provision reflects a political environment both within and outside the NHS that inhibits explicit consideration of the issues even by a

Government with a commanding majority. When changes have been made, as with the private finance and hospital building, their public justification has failed to provide any useful indication of the benefits of doing so. Neither the present nor the previous Government has presented a systematic evaluation of the scope for improving public procurement and how an improved public system might match the private process. In this and other areas such as pharmaceuticals, the political environment appears to inhibit serious discussion of the merits of different public and private roles. When is private provision a threat to the NHS, or a cost-effective partner? The question has still to receive systematic and dispassionate attention across the whole range of NHS activity.

## Conclusion

Over the 50 years of its existence, the NHS has changed its organisational structures and the range of policies deployed within them as it has tried to adjust to the pressures described in Chapter 2. What has remained essentially unchanged is its objectives, at least as applied to services which remain within the NHS.

The innovations of the past 15 years, and the example of other countries, indicate that the very broad objectives of the NHS may be promoted in different ways and through a wide variety of institutional arrangements, and that the relative importance attached to different objectives may change. The emphasis on equity of access, for example, has changed over the years relative to that on efficiency and responsiveness to the public.

The policies adopted and the trends we have described have led to tensions between different views as to what set of institutions are compatible with the values underlying the NHS. They have also served to make explicit what has long been implicit, that the NHS has never been a national service delivered to common standards, that its scope has never been systematically defined nor has the division of roles between public and private providers.

Changes both within the NHS and in the NHS's external environment are forcing these issues out into the open. The round of reforms unleashed by the NHS and Community Care Act 1990 began the process. The harder the new Government presses with its own round of reforms within the NHS and the more it progresses down the path of devolution and constitutional change, the more these underlying issues will emerge.[14] Similarly, the changes in the external environment described in Chapter 2 will tend to make them more apparent, continuing the trend apparent from the 1990s onwards to make explicit what was once implicit in the management and operations of the NHS.

In our view, the Government should respond to this shift by being prepared openly to discuss what it believes a national health service is and explain how the changes it proposes to the NHS relate to that view. *The New NHS*, with its emphasis on the need to reduce variations in access, efficiency and standards of care across the country, addresses these issues only in part. It does not consider the positive reasons for encouraging diversity, nor does it attempt to define the appropriate range of local choice over the range and type of services provided. While ultimately these are political issues, they also turn in part on how some of the technical issues the NHS faces are best approached.

In the next section of the book, we consider a series of essentially technical tasks which the NHS has to tackle in response to the changing environment discussed in Chapters 1 to 3: raising finance, cost control, service design, the organisation of health care delivery, and managing demand. Our aims are two-fold:

- to assess how well the NHS is equipped to discharge these tasks
- to identify how far alternative solutions would be compatible with a 'national' 'health' 'service'.

In Chapters 10 to 13 we consider the broader policy issues that must be addressed, not only to help find suitable policy options for the NHS in future, but also to implement them successfully.

## References

1. Dixon J, Inglis S and Klein R. Is the English NHS underfunded? *BMJ* 1999; 318: 522–26.
2. Ministry of Health. *National Health Service Reorganisation*. Cmnd. 5055. London: HMSO, 1972.
3. Ministry of Health. *A Hospital Plan for England and Wales*. Cmnd. 1604. London: HMSO: 1962.
4. Report of the Resource Allocation Working Party. *Sharing Resources for Health*. London: HMSO, 1976.
5. Acheson D (chair). *Primary health care in inner London: report of a study group commissioned by the London Health Planning Consortium*. London: London Health Planning Consortium, 1981.

King's Fund London Commission. *Transforming Health in London*. London: King's Fund, 1997.

6. Secretary of State for Health. *Choice and Opportunity*. Cm. 3390. London: HMSO, 1997.

7. Department of Health. *Primary care: delivering the future*. Cm. 3512. London: HMSO, 1996.

8. Health Service Commissioner. *Failure to provide long-term NHS care for a brain-damaged patient (Leeds case) – Second report for session 1993/94*. London: HMSO, 1994.

9. House of Commons – Health Committee. *Long-Term Care of the Elderly*. London: Stationery Office, 1999.

10. Sutherland S (chair). *With Respect to Old Age: a report by the Royal Commission on Long-Term Care*. Cm. 4192-1. London: Stationery Office, 1999.

11. Case reference: QBCOF99/01110/CM54. Ms Coughlan, who is severely physically handicapped, successfully opposed a health authority decision to move her into private sector care, funded by the local authority.
    Loux A, Kerrison S and Pollock AM. Long-term nursing: social care or health care. *BMJ* 2000; 320: 5–6

12. Secretary of State for Health. *Improving NHS Dentistry*. Cm. 2625. London: HMSO, 1994.

13. Dunning AJ (chair). *Choices in Health Care – Report by The Netherlands Government Committee on Choices in Health Care*. Zoetermeer: Government Committee on Choices in Health Care, 1992.
    New Zealand Ministry of Health. *Core Services for 1995/96 – Third report of the National Advisory Committee on Core Health and Disability Support Services*. Wellington: NZ Ministry of Health, 1994.

14. Hazell R and Jervis P. Devolution and health: dynamics of change in the post-devolution health services. In: Harrison A, editor. *Health Care UK 1997/98*. London: King's Fund Publishing, 1998.

# Section 2

# Key Tasks

# Chapter 4

# Raising finance

In Chapter 2 we concluded that the environment in which supply and demand in the NHS is managed has become harsher. Not only are there continuing constraints upon the supply of resources and increases in demands for services, but also the way that the gap between them is perceived by the public is changing in a way that makes it harder to manage. In the 1990s, with the split between purchasing and providing in the NHS and with budgets devolved down the NHS organisational tree, for example to GPs, the explicit limits to NHS spending became far more obvious. In turn this only increased the volume of attacks on grounds of inadequate funding. Successive governments have found it hard to counter these attacks, because it has been impossible to identify the 'right' level of funding objectively and uncontroversially. Furthermore, there has been a strongly held belief inside and outside government that it is both possible and desirable to close the 'gap' between the supply of resources and demands on them by increasing the former through additional funding.

In reality, as we pointed out in Chapter 2, successive governments have had to fund the NHS within the constraints set by the country's economic performance and competing demands on the public finances. In 1948, the NHS budget was open-ended partly because it was thought that demand was finite, and that the need for expenditure was likely to reduce as people enjoyed better access to care, thereby forestalling more serious illness. However, in the first year of the NHS, expenditure rose to £402 million, almost 100 per cent higher than that forecast by the Government. From that point on, the need to impose an effective global budget on the NHS was recognised.

How that should be achieved has varied over the years, as the Treasury has struggled to control not only health but also other spending programmes. In the midst of the economic crises of the 1970s, cash limits were applied to the budget for hospital and community health services as part of a general policy of bringing public spending under more effective control. By 1999 cash limits had been extended to practically all areas of the NHS budget, including prescription drugs.

Despite the imposition of a global budget, 'real' and 'volume' expenditure on the NHS has risen significantly over time, as shown in Chapter 2. Furthermore, the NHS has enjoyed a higher rate of growth than other areas of the public sector in the last 20 years, so that in 1996–97 health spending came second only to social security in level of public expenditure (see Table 4.1).

**Table 4.1:** Public Expenditure in the UK, 1999–2000

|  | £ billion |
| --- | --- |
| Social security | 102 |
| Health | 61 |
| Education | 41 |
| Debt interest | 26 |
| Defence | 22 |
| Law and order | 19 |
| Industry, agriculture and employment | 15 |
| Housing and environment | 13 |
| Transport | 9 |
| Other | 41 |
| **Total** | **349** |

**Source:** HM Treasury. *Budget 1999 Leaflet.*

This relatively favourable treatment has arisen for several reasons. There has been a strong political consensus that the NHS is a valuable public service, and worth preserving. The nature of health care has meant that reports of crises, put down to funding constraints, have been very effective in whipping up public concern, and levering more funds for the Service. Failings in the NHS can be linked to particular individuals whose lives may be put at immediate risk by, for example, being left on a hospital trolley or moved from hospital to hospital in search of a bed. The fact that the Service covers every UK citizen, as well as the unpredictable nature of illness, has meant that each individual in the country is potentially vulnerable if the Service is failing. There are powerful and articulate groups in the NHS, particularly nurses, who enjoy significant credibility in the public eye, who have kept up the pressure for more resources, particularly with respect to pay.

However, the steady and continuing increase in the NHS budget has not been enough to stave off financial crises. As a result, the almost complete reliance of the NHS on publicly provided finance has come under repeated attack. In this chapter, therefore, we consider whether there are alternatives that are consonant with the basic principles on which the NHS is based: universal access, based on equity of access for equal need. We begin with alternatives for raising more funds from the public purse, then move into private options.

## Extra sources of finance from the public purse

### General taxation/National Insurance contributions

Currently, general taxation contributes just about 80 per cent of all NHS finance, and National Insurance contributions just over 12 per cent. The most common criticism of the current system of finance has been that it does not produce a large enough budget for the NHS. That criticism would carry more weight if there was an agreed means of determining what that budget should be. Both major independent reviews of NHS spending – the Guillebaud Committee in 1953 and the Royal Commission on the NHS in 1979 – concluded that it was not possible to determine a level of adequate funding for the NHS and that whatever the expenditure on health care, demand was likely to rise to meet and exceed it. The Royal Commission's view was that since extra spending improved the comfort and quality of life of patients, and pay and conditions of staff, it was right the nation should spend more on health care as it grew wealthier. But the Commission was unable to define how much more.

Traditionally the Government has based its annual decision on the NHS budget and that for other public services on a combination of political and economic considerations, together with evidence on the relative 'deservingness' of the NHS put forward by the Department of Health and argued with the Treasury in the annual public expenditure survey round. The relative importance of political and economic factors versus evidence of 'need' in levering extra funds for the NHS has obviously changed over time according to circumstance.

For much of the 1980s, increments to the NHS budget were determined by simple rules of thumb covering allowances for new technologies, for demographic change and additional funds for new Government initiatives. But this arrangement had no real objective basis, and gave a virtually automatic increase in real funding to the NHS. By the late 1980s, the emphasis had shifted from changes in 'need' to estimates of how much the NHS could do with the resources available. As a result, much of the increases that the NHS was 'awarded' consisted of the productivity improvements it was required to make.

This requirement – or more precisely its manner of implementation – was widely criticised, chiefly for the reason given in Chapter 1: use of the NHS efficiency index to measure those productivity improvements skewed incentives by encouraging hospitals to increase in-patient and day case activity, regardless of the impact on the Service as a whole or on the health of the population. Furthermore, many within the Service thought it impossible to extract productivity gains year after year without compromising other desirable objectives such as clinical standards or the welfare of staff.

While from the Treasury, or taxpayer, viewpoint it clearly makes sense to attempt to ensure that extra funds are appropriately and efficiently used, the annual requirement for increases in productivity did nothing to relieve the sense of financial pressure within which the NHS works; indeed it intensified for the reasons outlined above. Nevertheless, the principle of the NHS having to 'earn' increases in funding, rather than receiving them automatically, is the logical consequence of the point made in Chapter 1: that health care benefits are always at the expense of other forms of benefit and hence must be demonstrated rather than assumed.

The Labour Government continued where the Conservatives left off – a direction spelled out in the Comprehensive Spending Review[1] – the fundamental review of public expenditure announced in July 1998 which was used to influence Government allocations to each part of the public sector. There were two main outcomes from the Comprehensive Spending Review – a financial settlement over three years, rather than the usual one, allowing greater stability of funding, and a principle of 'cash for change', in which the type and extent of change was specified by the Centre. This principle underlay policies introduced immediately after Labour came to office such as reducing numbers of people on waiting lists for in-patient care, reducing waiting times for cancer care, or alleviating 'winter pressures'. By setting aside £5 billion for 'modernisation' over three years, the Government developed the logic of this approach, and in effect introduced a further hurdle, this time for individual health authorities to surmount, before they could receive extra funds for modernisation. As far as the Government is concerned, the issue is less 'can't find more' and more 'won't find more unless extra funding has a demonstrable impact'.

The Comprehensive Spending Review allowed, over the three years 1999/2000 to 2001/02, a real terms growth averaging 3.7 per cent, compared to 3.1 per cent over the previous 20 years, although that increase has been offset against the much lower increases for the first two years of Labour's first term in office. But, although Labour has shown that extra funds can be found for the NHS, the winter crisis of Christmas 1998 and the media response to it indicates that the search for additional ways of funding the NHS is never far off the political agenda.

## Hypothecated taxes

When asked if they are prepared to pay more for the NHS, the public consistently indicate that they would. Indeed, the 13th British Social Attitudes Survey reported that health care was the public's highest priority for extra Government spending. Public support for more tax on health, education and social benefits has risen sharply since 1983. Whether this means that the public would be more willing actually to pay higher taxes is another matter. It is a salutary message that even though, as noted in Chapter 3, per capita allocations to the NHS are greater in Scotland (by 25 per cent in 1995), Wales (by 18 per cent) and Northern Ireland (by 5 per cent) compared to England, the public are no less willing to support more spending on health care in the higher spending countries, as Table 4.2 shows.

**Table 4.2:** Public opinion on raising taxation to fund increased spending on health, education, and social benefits

|  | England (n=3072) % | Scotland (n=348) % | Wales (n=200) % | N Ireland (n=1510) % |
|---|---|---|---|---|
| Reduce taxes and pay less | 3.9 | 4.4 | 3.4 | 6.6 |
| Keep taxes and spending the same | 33.8 | 33.8 | 29.2 | 38.3 |
| Increase taxes and spend more | 59.2 | 58.2 | 63.3 | 52.3 |
| None | 2.0 | 2.2 | 2.6 | 1.7 |
| Don't know | 1.1 | 1.5 | 1.6 | 1.1 |

**Source:** Dixon J, Inglis S, Klein R. Is the English NHS underfunded? *BMJ* 1999; 318: 522–26.

In principle, willingness of the public to pay extra taxes could be tested directly if there were an earmarked, or hypothecated, tax specifically for the NHS and if it were possible for the public to vote as to its yield. Advocates of this approach argue that the public would be willing to pay more, if it had that choice, and that funds from a hypothecated tax could be raised outside of the usual political process, and possibly offer some safeguard to the Service.

Despite these apparent attractions, widespread hypothecation is unlikely to be politically acceptable. No government would be likely to relinquish control over public expenditure in this way and indeed it could be argued that the allocation of resources between competing users is precisely the kind of job that governments are elected to do.

But if a government was prepared to set aside a specific source of revenue for the NHS, it would be impossible to find a single tax with a reliable yield through the peaks and troughs of the business cycle and which was more stable than the combination of total tax revenues and the borrowing that the Treasury can resort to if public revenues temporarily fall.

Furthermore, adoption of hypothecation in one area could lead theoretically to a hypothecated tax for all public services, with the result that there would be less flexibility in the funding of each. Perhaps more crucially, from the viewpoint of those who want to see the NHS budget enlarged, the main beneficiaries of the NHS – elderly people – include many non-taxpayers. To make the nature of the transfers between generations that the NHS embodies more explicit could as easily undermine support for it as the reverse.

One variation on the theme of hypothecation was put forward by the Commission for Social Justice which reported in 1994.[2] The Commission suggested that any *increases* in tax should be earmarked for particular services. While the Commission argued that this approach might help to increase public support for tax increases for political purposes, the same drawbacks apply as to those already set out.

## Social insurance

Social insurance-based approaches of funding health care require individuals to make compulsory contributions to cover the costs of health care. Typically this form of contribution is linked to employment in that the contribution is usually made through a payroll tax paid by both employer and employee to a health care financing agency, such as a sickness fund as is the case in Germany. The contributions of those who are unemployed are usually made by the State. Such a system in the UK could be linked to National Insurance contributions.

For this system to be better at raising revenue than the current method of financing the NHS, there should at least be the promise of it raising a higher income. In this respect, increasing the levy to be paid through social insurance would be subject to the same political constraints as raising the level of general taxation. Indeed there could be arguably greater pressure not to increase the level of contributions, since employer organisations would be likely to resist the imposition of a higher payroll tax. Furthermore a payroll tax could be a far more regressive method of raising funds than through general taxation, or if made more progressive, is likely to be more costly to administer. Moreover, such a change would not in itself do anything to tackle the central issue of determining what the level of the NHS budget should be. It is, therefore, difficult to see any advantage in social insurance over the current method of financing the NHS.

## Medical Savings Accounts

The basic idea of Medical Savings Accounts is relatively simple: individuals (and their employers) pay a compulsory tax into a savings account out of which medical costs are paid for that individual. The system allows individuals to use the funds for other purposes, for example to pay for education or to pass unspent savings on to their families. Those who overspend the savings accounts, or who are unemployed, receive care paid for by the State.

This broad arrangement is in operation in Singapore and is being piloted in the USA and in China. In Singapore, 'Medisave' is a compulsory tax-exempt, interest-yielding savings scheme, first introduced in 1984, which covers hospital costs only. Individuals may top up their Medisave scheme if they prefer and are able to. Catastrophic care is covered by a separate insurance scheme, 'Medishield'. The incentives for the individual are not to spend from Medisave, since purely government-funded health care (available for those who use up their account or who are unemployed) is of a different standard to that available to those with medical savings accounts, and, since the funds are not pooled across communities, the savings can be used by the individual for other purposes. Medical savings accounts in Singapore have been combined with fee-for-service payment of providers, and large co-payments for patients.

The potential benefits of this approach are that individuals would have a significant incentive not to use health care, thus reducing the opportunity for inappropriate (although also appropriate) use. Individuals may be more willing to pay extra for health care if they knew that extra funds paid would benefit them personally. Also individuals would be able to choose how much they would be prepared to pay for treatment of various kinds, for example different levels of hotel services, or different lengths of wait for treatment or consultation.

But the drawbacks are significant.[3] The main one is that this system potentially runs counter to the important principle of equity of access for equal need. Those who are unemployed, who cannot pay into a savings account, or those who overspend their account because of a chronic expensive illness, would be likely to have access to a different level of care than those with a medical savings account in healthy balance. If the health care available to those who drew down on, and emptied, their account was the same as those who did not, then there may be few incentives to hold such an account over and above other forms of savings accounts from which individuals could buy private health insurance or meet the direct costs of health care. In Singapore, the medical savings accounts have not curbed costs. On the contrary, per capita costs have risen since they were introduced, although in China the reverse was true. Medical savings accounts do nothing to curb the powerful fee-for-service incentive to providers to generate income and, if combined with co-payments, can result in inappropriate underuse of care by the less well-off. There is significant debate in the USA as to whether medical savings accounts are the way forward to curb costs.[4]

## Health taxes

Taxes on specific goods, such as tobacco, as a method of financing health care, are often mooted as an extra source of funding for the NHS. Such taxes can raise not insignificant sums, for example in 1999, it was estimated that an increase of 3p on a packet of 20 cigarettes would raise £60 million in the following financial year.

In relation to the NHS, there are two main arguments in favour of taxing health-harming products. First, extra taxes are likely to reduce consumption of such health-harming goods, such as tobacco and alcohol, and thus might lead to fewer demands upon NHS resources. But the case for such taxes is the same, however the proceeds are used. Second, taxes from such goods can be used to boost NHS finances directly. In 1999, the Chancellor Gordon Brown announced that any extra tax on tobacco in the 1999 budget would be earmarked for the NHS – potentially raising an extra £300 million across the UK. While these extra funds will help, the drawbacks of this 'earmarked tax' for the NHS are similar to those outlined above for hypothecated taxes. Taxes on goods to pay for health care were rejected by the 1979 Royal Commission because they were thought to be too regressive, and because there were better arguments for putting them into the total pool of tax revenue to allow Government greater flexibility in how they would be spent.

## Increasing funding from local government

Arguments for bringing the NHS more under the control of local authorities are usually rooted in a belief that this would increase the local democratic accountability of the Service. Some argue that there would be greater flexibility to raise finance for the NHS through local taxation, according to the preferences of local people rather than the Government.[5] But while this might be so in principle, in practice, as local authorities have such a limited tax base of their own, any significant level of funding would have to come from central government, as it does now for the existing range of locally provided services.

There may be scope for some extra money being raised locally, if only at the margin. For example, a feature of the recently established Health Action Zones is to pool funding from a number of sources, public and private, to deliver local services. Joint commissioning groups (with members from health and local authorities) already plan and commission services using NHS funds and local taxes. Total purchasing pilots – groups of general practices which were able to purchase almost all types of NHS care[6] – were able to use NHS funds to boost social care of their patients in order to avert the need for admission, particularly of elderly patients. The health improvement plans announced in the White Paper, *The New NHS*, will be drawn up by a panel of local stakeholders including a representative from Social Services and measures announced in *Modernising Social Services*[7] and the subsequent power created by the 1999 Health Act will allow cash transfers across the existing boundary. Thus while the wholesale transference of financing and accountability of the NHS from national to local government seems to be off the agenda, blurring of national and local streams of funding for health care activities looks set to grow.

Constitutional change may radically alter the scope for local funding. The planned Scottish, Welsh and Northern Irish assemblies all have responsibility for health care, although under present plans only the Scottish parliament will have the power to vary the basic rate of income tax by up to 3p in the pound, raising a total of £690 million. Within England, the likelihood of significant devolution of tax-raising powers to regional assemblies looks remote. In the medium- to long-term it could become a reality if the modest changes to local government currently being implemented led to demands for more. But that is a long way off.

## Raising funds for the NHS other than from the public purse

The options sketched above demonstrate that the scope for raising funds from the taxpayer other than through general taxation is currently limited.

Hence the search by governments since 1948 to find non-public sources of funds for the NHS. This has focused on three areas: users, the voluntary sector and the private sector.

## User charges

User charges were first authorised in the NHS in 1951 as a temporary measure to curb demand for specific NHS services. Expenditure on the NHS had soared, and discussion about the apparent rapid rise in costs at the time focused on abuse of health services by over-demanding patients, waste and bureaucracy, rather than a serious search for alternative sources of income. Charges were introduced originally for three specific services: prescription drugs, spectacles and dentures. The Minister of Health at the time, Aneurin Bevan, resigned in protest arguing that user charges conflicted with the principle of equal access for equal need.

Originally charges were meant to be a temporary measure to help curb demand, but the Conservative Government elected in 1952 not only retained but also extended them to dental treatment and surgical appliances. Successive governments have kept, raised, and expanded the scope even further. Recently some services have been redefined out of the NHS completely – for example eye testing (though now re-established by Labour for elderly people), some forms of dental treatment and long-term care – for which patients must pay privately, in effect a 100 per cent user charge.

**Table 4.3:** NHS sources of finance (England)

| | Year ending 31 March | | | | | |
|---|---|---|---|---|---|---|
| **Source** | **1960– 61** | **1970– 71** | **1980– 81** | **1990– 91** | **1995– 96** | **1999– 2000** |
| Taxation – consolidated fund | 81.7 | 85.4 | 88.7 | 77.5 | 82.1 | 79.1 |
| National Insurance contribution | 13.5 | 11.0 | 8.5 | 16.6 | 12.2 | 12.8 |
| Charges to recipients | 4.5 | 3.3 | 2.5 | 4.5 | 2.3 | 2.1 |
| Miscellaneous | 0.3 | 0.3 | 0.3 | 1.4 | 3.5 | 6.0* |

* Mainly capital receipts.

**Source:** Department of Health. *The Government's Expenditure Plans 1999–2000.* London: Stationery Office, 1999.

As can be seen from Table 4.3, the overall revenue raised from user charges has always been small – between 2 to 4 per cent of total revenue, or £783 million in England in 1997. Income from charges in the NHS comes from four main services: hospital (e.g. from private patients and charges to NHS patients for aids and appliances for out-patients); pharmaceutical (prescriptions); general dental (e.g. check-ups); and general ophthalmic (e.g. eye tests), but the bulk is raised from pharmaceuticals and dental care. Table 4.4 below shows the proportion raised in each of these areas over time. The table shows a rise of revenue from dental charges and a decline from prescriptions over time. NHS general ophthalmic services (eye tests) were curtailed in 1988 and reinstated in 1999 – revenue from these sources in the intervening years is thus shown as zero in the table.

**Table 4.4:** Charges to persons using NHS services (England)

| Services | Year ending 31 March – £m (%) | | | | | |
|---|---|---|---|---|---|---|
| | 1960–61 | 1970–71 | 1980–81 | 1990–91 | 1994–95 | 1999–2000 |
| Hospital | 6 (18.7) | 12 (22.6) | 54 (21.6) | 470 (44.4) | 101 (13.1) | 70 (8.0) |
| Pharmaceutical | 12 (37.5) | 15 (28.3) | 71 (28.4) | 207 (19.6) | 287 (37.2) | 379 (43.1) |
| General dental | 9 (28.2) | 16 (30.2) | 92 (38.4) | 380 (36.3) | 383 (49.7) | 430 (48.9) |
| General ophthalmic | 5 (15.2) | 10 (18.9) | 29 (11.6) | - | | 25 (2.8) |
| All | 32 (100) | 53 (100) | 241 (100) | 1057 (100) | 771 (100) | 879 (100) |

**Source:** Health and Personal Social Services Yearbook (various years) and Department of Health departmental reports.

Despite the fact that the level of charges has tended to rise faster than inflation, the overall revenue raised in this way has remained comparatively small. This is largely because a growing and significant proportion of the population – now 85 per cent – is exempt from user charges, including elderly people, children, pregnant women, those receiving social security benefits, together with groups of patients with specific diseases such as diabetes or Addisons disease. Furthermore, as user charges have risen for the 15 per cent of the population that is not exempt, fewer prescriptions have been dispensed, further curbing the revenue raised.

Every government since 1948 has examined the possibility of raising more revenue from user charges, and almost every year there are calls to introduce more and higher charges to raise more funds. Typically these have included hotel charges for patients in hospital, extra amenities for patients in hospital, GP consultations or GP night visits to patients; recently, prescription charges have been mooted for well-off pensioners (those with incomes of over £18,000 per annum).

User charges are costly to administer – and hence are a more expensive way of raising finance than general taxation. But the arguments against user charges rest largely on their effect on service use. From the RAND insurance study in the 1960s onwards,[8] changes have been shown to discourage patients, particularly those on lower incomes, from seeking necessary treatment. The latter may result in adverse health outcomes and ultimately higher costs to the NHS in future years. Furthermore the patients least able to pay user charges are those most likely to have greater needs for care. On the other hand, those exempt from charges use more health care services than the non-exempt. Some have argued that increasing the number of patients who are exempt has pushed up the level of charges for the non-exempt, and that there is a case for reducing exemptions, particularly for elderly people, and lowering the level of charges for all. That policy would be unlikely, however, to raise a great deal more for the NHS as a whole than the existing structure of charges. Charges have also been a weak policy tool to contain costs in countries without a global budget.[9] For all these reasons, the 1979 Royal Commission logically recommended the gradual but complete extinction of charges – a recommendation that fell upon deaf ears.

It is unlikely that any government would willingly forgo, for example, the £400 million or so currently raised from prescription charges, even though the principle may be wrong. But to raise a significant amount of revenue for the NHS, significant expansion of charges would be required, which is unlikely to be acceptable on political grounds alone. However, the public reaction to charges has been mixed. While the public response to raising or expanding charges in general may have been negative, there is evidence to suggest that the public may be willing to pay charges for certain services above others. Furthermore, there has been a notable absence of a public outcry over a reduction of access to NHS dentistry and an increase in the need to pay privately for dental care.

But so far, both the evidence on the impact of requiring users to pay more and the political resistance to doing so have combined to keep a marked expansion of NHS charges effectively off the agenda in the UK. *The New NHS* reaffirms the Government's commitment to the 'historic principle' that access will be based on need alone (para.1.5). Furthermore the Government signalled its intention in the 1998 Comprehensive Spending Review that charges for eye tests for elderly people introduced by the Conservatives were to be abolished, a measure which took effect in April 1999. Any significant expansion of revenue from charges seems therefore very unlikely in the short- to medium-term.

Even if, faced with an economic crisis, the current Government did perform a 'U-turn' on user charges, it is not self-evident that overall NHS resources would increase as a result. As things stand, the yield from charges is described as a 'contribution' to the cost of the NHS. If that contribution rose, it is hard to see the Treasury resisting the opportunity to make offsetting reductions in tax finance.

## Voluntary sector

Charitable donations to the NHS have always been welcomed and encouraged by successive governments. By far the majority of these funds is used to purchase hospital equipment, and fund medical research. The Directory of Social Change[10] estimated that the NHS received at least £370 million from charitable donations or fundraising appeals in the early 1990s. In 1996, charities gave £385 million to fund medical research. The NHS Loto, set up in 1988, raised £3 million between 1988 and 1997, £750,000 of which was given to the NHS.

The arguments for and against raising more charitable funds for the NHS were discussed fully by the Royal Commission in 1979; its conclusions are still convincing today. While charitable funding was welcomed, the Commission thought that the amounts raised were likely to be unpredictable, and there was concern that raising funds for needed but less glamorous projects would be difficult. The arguments for and against starting a lottery for the NHS were examined and the Commission concluded that a lottery was likely to raise only marginal amounts of funds but incur significant administrative costs. Experience with the NHS Loto appears to support this conclusion.

In 1998, however, the Government announced that Healthy Living Centres, heralded in *Our Healthier Nation*, would be financed from National Lottery funds, although the centres are not expected to provide mainstream health services. In 1999, the Government indicated that Lottery funds will be used to boost cancer services but the scale of this contribution seems unlikely to be large relative to the total budget for cancer care.

## Private sector

The NHS has always generated funds from a variety of private sources, on top of user charges described above. However, funds from all these sources currently add up to a small fraction of revenue. The main sources are outlined below.

### NHS pay beds

The Health and Medicines Act passed in 1988 gave extra opportunities for the NHS to generate income through selling specific services to the private sector at a *profit*, rather than at *cost* as previously. The income was to be used to improve health care for patients. As a result, many hospitals set up separate units for patients who paid for care privately (either directly or through private insurance), and income from NHS 'pay beds' steadily increased to £249 million in 1996 (see Table 4.5). The NHS is now the largest single provider of privately funded care in the UK, although the fraction of revenue raised through this route still remains small, and it is not yet back to levels reached in the early 1970s. Most NHS hospitals raise less than 5 per cent of their total revenue from private payers, and only four specialist hospitals generated over 10 per cent of revenue from private payers in 1994–95 – league leaders were the Royal Marsden (53.4 per cent) and The Brompton (25.4 per cent). The profits made, which can be used to fund the NHS, are only a fraction of these figures.

**Table 4.5:** Income to the NHS from private payers 1975–96

| Income from Year beginning (1 April) | private payers (£m) |
| --- | --- |
| 1975 | 22 |
| 1980 | 48 |
| 1985 | 67 |
| 1990 | 113 |
| 1995 | 229 |
| 1996 | 249 |

**Source:** Laing & Buisson. *Laing's Review of Private Health Care 1998/99*. London: Laing & Buisson, 1999.

### Other private services

The 1988 Health and Medicines Act also allowed the NHS to generate income through the selling of other services provided that there was no significant disadvantage to NHS patients, and it was consistent with the goals of the NHS. An estimated £102 million was raised over three years 1989–90 to 1991–92 through a variety of means, for example car park fees, and leasing land.[11]

Since the 1930s hospitals have been able to recoup from insurers the costs of treatment for patients injured in road accidents. This has not been applied systematically as NHS trusts are allowed legal discretion to levy the fee. The current Government has introduced legislation to ensure that the NHS recovers the full £150 million estimated to be available under the rules (£3000 per patient). While welcome, that scale of contribution is clearly insufficient to make a significant difference to NHS finances.

## Private finance initiative

One initiative that has much greater potential to raise private funds for the NHS is the private finance initiative (PFI) launched by the previous Government. Ever since 1948, the capital budget of the NHS has been raided to pay for revenue. Apart from a substantial hospital building programme in the 1960s, the result has been a visible decline in the quality of the NHS estate. Since the public view the NHS very much in terms of bricks and mortar, decrepit hospital buildings and general practice premises symbolise a decrepit and out-of-date health service.

The PFI appeared to offer a way of financing the resulting backlog without a major increase in government borrowing. From the beginning of 1995, all NHS hospitals with plans for capital spending in excess of £250,000 have been required to put the plans out to tender through the PFI. Under these arrangements, private companies or groups of companies can bid to design, finance (with some NHS capital) and build NHS facilities, which are then leased back to the NHS over a period of 20 to 30 years. Only if private funding for capital cannot be found on the right terms can public funds be applied for. Private companies are required to manage non-clinical services in the new facilities, for example catering and cleaning.

As noted in Chapter 1, the PFI was initially slow to take off partly because of the reluctance of the private sector to take on the risks involved. However, since the Labour Government provided the necessary assurances though the NHS (Private Finance) Act 1997, the number of schemes for which final deals have been struck has risen rapidly. Some £3 billion worth of projects are now at some stage of preparation although only a fraction of that sum had actually been committed by the middle of 1998.

The PFI, however, only alters the way that the NHS pays for capital since it replaces a lump sum payment with a stream of payments spread out over 20 to 30 years, and paid through the revenue budget. Whether the NHS will enjoy lower costs overall – that is whether the higher financing costs faced by the private sector will be offset by lower running costs – remains to be seen. Evidence from a recent study by the National Audit Office suggests that the benefits that do result will represent only a small fraction of the total cost of providing hospital services.[12] We look further at the PFI in the following chapter.

## Options for future private income

Although NHS hospitals have been allowed to set up private pay bed units, and are thus encouraged to generate income from privately paying patients, neither hospitals nor NHS purchasers (such as health authorities) have pressed, or been allowed, to set up their own 'NHS insurance'. An 'NHS insurance' could entail charging a premium to the public willing to pay for extra services, such as non-clinical facilities, and cutting out the profit margin of the private insurers. Other similar ideas include offering patients the opportunity to contribute a flat fee, on a voluntary basis, to a 'Saturday Fund' held by NHS purchasers (for example primary care groups or health authorities), again allowing them access to better NHS facilities.

Governments have not offered significant incentives to encourage the public to pay for care privately – for example, to boost the private income of NHS hospitals or to encourage the take-up of private insurance. In fact, tax breaks for health insurance for the over-60s were scrapped when Labour came into office. But with a greater blurring of boundaries between the NHS and private sector, for example through the PFI, these options will continue to be mooted.

Meanwhile the current Government looks set to encourage much greater public–private partnership in health care. What will result – particularly how far it will involve private finance as well as private provision of care – remains unclear. The significant problem with all forms of private finance considered to date (including PFI) is that they run against the basic principle of access to care on the basis of need. As such, they are likely to be resisted by the public and policy-makers, unless the historically strong support for the principle of fairness is eroded. This may happen if the NHS is perceived by a sufficient number of individuals to be providing an equitable but inadequate service, and if a significant proportion of people have the disposable income to be willing to pay for extra care. But that point has not been reached – the proportion of the population with private insurance is rising very slowly and is now about 11 per cent. While those paying for private care out-of-pocket have risen in number, the overall amount of care financed in this way remains small.

## Conclusion

There are three main ways of funding health care: general taxation, social insurance and private insurance. The benefits and drawbacks of each, as evidenced by the performance of health care systems in other countries, are set out in Table 4.6 below.

Since the NHS was established, successive governments have tried to find alternative sources of funding to the public purse, without much success, because alternatives run counter to the equity objective underpinning the NHS. The supplementary sources of finance considered in this chapter contributed only a small fraction of NHS revenue and their potential to raise more is limited. And if they did raise more, the supply of tax finance might fall in response.

Other more radical ideas involving changes to the basis of financing of the NHS altogether, such as the medical savings accounts, hypothecation and social insurance are impractical or inequitable or do not offer any advantages over the existing arrangements. They leave unanswered the core question of how the budget should be determined and how inevitable shortfalls relative to the pressures upon it should be handled.

Taxation remains the cheapest and most equitable way of raising funds. Despite the private finance initiative and blurring of budgetary boundaries at the margins between central NHS and local authority funding of services to improve health, alternative sources of funding for the Service are likely to remain limited and marginal.

How acceptable alternative sources of finance will be in the future to politicians and the public depends upon what principles they think should uphold the NHS, in short what they believe the NHS should be. Up until now,

**Table 4.6:** The performance of alternative health finance systems

| Criteria | General taxation (e.g. UK) | Social insurance (e.g. Germany) | Private insurance (e.g. USA) |
|---|---|---|---|
| • Macro efficiency | • Global, cash limited budgets.- Strong cost control | • Demand-led systems offer poor cost control<br>• Global budgets strengthen cost control<br>• Transparency of payments increases user/payer cost consciousness | • Demand-led and absence of global budget. Poor cost control |
| • Micro efficiency | • Low administrative costs<br>• Work incentives depend upon forms of taxation | • Multiple insurers/sickness funds increase administrative costs<br>• A tax on employment | • Multiple insurers lead to high transaction and administrative costs<br>• Employment-based insurance represents a 'tax' on employment |
| • Equity | • Universal coverage<br>• Payments related to ability to pay as defined by the tax system | • Near to universal coverage<br>• Payments related to ability to pay.<br>• Can be more or less progressive than a tax-based system | • Major gaps in coverage<br>• Contributions based upon risk ratings rather than ability to pay. Higher health risks = higher payments |
| • Choice | • No choice over contribution rates | • Little choice over rates of contribution but generally some choice between insurers | • Considerable choice over insurance premiums (and associated benefits packages) and between insurers |
| • Transparency | • Weak link between tax payments and spending on health care | • An earmarked tax providing a link between payments and spending on health care | • A close link between individual payments and individual health benefits |

**Source:** Adapted from Robinson R, Evans D and Exworthy M. *Health and the Economy.* Institute for Health Policy Studies: University of Southampton, 1994.

no alternative source of funding to the public purse has passed the acceptability test. It may be that, if pressures increase, additional funds will be sought by means such as charges or new forms of private finance that are neither equitable nor efficient but may prove more tolerable to the public than explicit rationing. But in our judgement that day is still some way off. The real question that cannot be ducked is not 'are there suitable alternative sources of finance?' but 'how much public money are governments prepared to commit to the NHS?'. This is especially pertinent now that public expenditure as a proportion of GDP, as we noted in Chapter 1, is at its lowest point for 40 years.

The funding gap will remain and the NHS will have to continue to live almost entirely within the bounds set by its major source of funding, general taxation. In the rest of this section of the book, we consider from a number of different angles how the NHS should respond. We begin, in Chapter 5, with what appears to be the most straightforward approach of all, keeping to a minimum the costs of the human and physical resources it needs to provide services. The more successful it is in doing that, the further the financial resources it receives will stretch.

## References

1.  HM Treasury. *Modern Public Services for Britain: Investing in Reform. Comprehensive Spending Review: New Public Spending Plans 1999–2002.* Cm. 4011. London: HMSO, 1998.
2.  Commission for Social Justice. *Social Justice.* London: Vintage, 1995.
3.  Saltman RB. Medical Saving Accounts: a notably uninteresting policy idea. *European Journal of Public Health* 1998; 8: 276–78.
    Scheffler R and Yu W. Medical Saving Accounts: a worthy experience. *European Journal of Public Health* 1998; 8: 274–76.
4.  See n.3 above.
5.  Hunter DJ. Accountability and local democracy. *British Journal of Health Care Management* 1995; 1: 78–81.
6.  Total Purchasing National Evaluation Team (TP-NET). *Developing Primary Care in the New NHS: Lessons from total purchasing.* London: King's Fund, 1999.
7.  Secretary of State for Health. *Modernising Social Services: Promoting independence, improving protection, raising standards.* Cm. 4169. London: Stationery Office, 1998.
8.  Newhouse J. *Free for all: lessons from the RAND health insurance experiment.* Cambridge: Harvard UP, 1993.
9.  Robinson R and Steiner A. *Managed Health Care: US evidence and lessons for the National Health Service.* Buckingham: Open University Press, 1998.

10. Lattimer M and Holly K. *Charity and NHS Reform – Directory of Social Change Research Report No. 4.* London, 1992

11. National Audit Office. *Income Generation in the NHS.* London: HMSO, 1993.

12. National Audit Office. *The PFI Contract for the new Dartford and Gravesham Hospital.* London: Stationery Office, 1999.

# Chapter 5

# Controlling costs

From its beginnings, but with increasing emphasis since the early 1980s, the NHS has struggled to keep to a minimum the cost of the resources it requires. Like any other provider, the less it pays for each of these resources – labour, drugs, supplies, capital – the greater the volume of services it can make available.

By virtue of the overall limit imposed by the Treasury on the budget available to the NHS, the means for imposing control over what it spends on human and physical resources has been in place since the 1950s. As noted earlier, central control over the NHS budget changed in the 1970s to a cash basis across much of the public sector including health. In principle this meant that once the cash allocation was set for a given service in a given year (and also in principle, the years to come), that figure could not be exceeded. For the last 20 or so years, the bulk of the budget has, each year, effectively been determined at the start of it and not, as happened before the introduction of cash limits, regularly adjusted in the light of actual changes in pay and prices.

Such central control has not been strong in all areas of the NHS budget. Until recently, cash limits were not applied to drug expenditures. Similarly in respect of pay, the situation has been less clear cut, since, in a number of years, supplementary finance has been made available in the light of the pay settlements agreed. But in general, the Treasury has been in a position to hold the line.

But while the overall Treasury-set limit has been critical in creating the appropriate climate for expenditure control within the Service, it has not been sufficient in itself. Each of the main elements of cost has needed a policy of its own, which it has fallen to the NHS to devise and implement.

As the major employer of the human resources and the major purchaser of the goods and services required to produce health care services, the NHS would seem to be well placed to exercise some influence over how much it pays in terms of wages and salaries to staff and the price of goods and services it requires. As virtually all the resources the NHS requires come from the Exchequer, there is a single payer that should be able to harness the potential for effective control.

In practice, the scale of the potential for effective control, for each of the resources required, is limited by a number of external factors including the willingness of people to come and work in the Service in the light of other opportunities, competing objectives such as the promotion of a strong domestic pharmaceutical industry and, in recent years particularly, European Union policies towards public sector procurement. The control of costs, in other words, must always be balanced against other considerations, some of which lie inside the NHS itself and some outside. These trade-offs, as we shall see, can be complex, and hence the task of assessing where the balance is to be struck far from straightforward.

In this chapter we argue that the tasks involved in ensuring that the NHS purchases effectively and produces care efficiently are extremely diverse and becoming more rather than less difficult. We consider the way that the NHS has attempted to control four main cost categories: the workforce; pharmaceutical products; supplies of non-clinical goods and services and support services; capital projects; and, clinical services as a whole.

In doing so, we attempt to identify whether the NHS has the information and expertise it requires to ensure that costs are effectively controlled. We conclude that in many areas it does not. The final section contains some suggestions for improvement.

## Paying the workforce

The NHS must set pay at a level adequate to recruit, retain and motivate its staff and do so in a way that does not seem excessive in relation to pay in other types of employment. From its earliest days, the NHS operated a national system of pay scales and pay determination, known as the system of Whitley Councils, which it inherited on its establishment. These are negotiating forums comprising representatives of staff and management but the scope for real negotiation is limited by the tight financial framework within which they operate. The pay of doctors and dentists (and since 1983 nurses, midwives and the professions allied to medicine) has been determined separately through Pay Review Bodies which are independent and, unlike the Whitley Councils, not subject to the imposition of a cash limit circumscribing what they can recommend. In what follows we focus on the Pay Review Bodies.

Over the years the Review Bodies have been presented with different views as to the proper basis for determining appropriate pay levels by the interested parties, but the central tension has remained the same – between the 'needs' of the national economy and the 'needs' of the workforce. The Treasury evidence to the Review Bodies has regularly stressed the needs of the national economy – variously defined as the need to contain inflation or to control public spending in order to allow reductions in taxation. Against a macro-economic background which has never been favourable enough to justify relaxation of their basic stance, the Treasury and the Department of Health have consistently argued that the key test for pay awards should be adequate recruitment and retention of staff. The following extracts from the 1989 report of the Review Body on Doctors' and Dentists' Remuneration[1] illustrate their approach:

> The Health Departments continued to argue in their evidence that, within the limits of affordability, the main determinant of pay levels for the professions should be what is sufficient to recruit, retain and motivate staff of the right quality (para.16).

The professions, on the other hand:

> … said that they ought, like others, to share in the increasing prosperity of the country. They claimed that many earners had benefited from lower rates of inflation, real increases in pay and lower taxation; and the medical and dental professions should not therefore be singled out for 'modest' pay increases. They laid emphasis on pay comparability as an important factor, particularly against the background of recruitment in the next few years (para.10).

Until recently, the tensions between these different viewpoints were resolved almost entirely at national level. Towards the end of the 1980s however, the notion that pay should be determined more flexibly and that a degree of discretion at local level should be allowed, began to take hold. An official report[2] published in 1989 on NHS staff conditions of employment found that:

> The numerous rules and regulations emanating from Whitley Councils, the Department of Health, professional bodies and trade unions produce a climate antipathetic to innovations. Change becomes more often concerned with process than outcome and the starting point, 'Why it can't be done' not, 'How do we do it?' (p.13).

In other words, the centrally determined rules inhibited local initiative at some – unidentified – cost, in terms of the efficiency of the Service.

A few years later, the Social Services Committee report on *Resourcing the National Health Service: Whitley Councils*[3] supported the case for flexibility and argued that:

> ... *there is a strong case for giving managers at district level some scope for tailoring decisions on pay and conditions of service to their local needs* (para.130).

By the time that the Committee reported, the Conservative Government had embarked on the larger reform set in motion by the NHS and Community Care Act 1990, into which the notion of local pay flexibility fitted very well. NHS trusts were given new freedoms, including the negotiation of staff contracts – in particular, contracts for medical staff were transferred to them – with the expectation that at some stage, NHS trusts would become the effective pay bargaining units.

However, even though local pay determination received wide, though not universal, endorsement, in practice its introduction proved difficult, even under the Conservatives. Doctors remained effectively outside its scope altogether, while only a small fraction of nursing pay was determined in this way, even before the decision made by the Labour Government in 1997 to abandon it completely.

Despite this failure, most NHS trusts have persuaded at least some of their staff to sign local contracts. Some have stripped out features of national agreements where these impeded flexibility or represent 'bad value for money' such as provisions for payment of travelling expenses or shift premia. Furthermore, many have come to local agreements on job definitions and roles such as 'generic' support workers who can be moved from one kind of work to another so as to provide greater flexibility.

The main obstacle to the development of greater local discretion has been the opposition of those representing NHS staff, particularly the Royal College of Nursing and Unison (which represents both nurses and manual workers), to the very notion of local pay, and their continued support for national pay scales. This opposition was sufficiently strong to force the Conservative Government to accept a catching up mechanism which meant that if staff in some NHS trusts gained a pay advantage in any one year, staff in others would broadly catch up the following year.

A second factor making it hard to develop local pay has been the level of expertise required both to negotiate new pay structures and to run bargaining machinery on a year-to-year basis. The Social Services Committee acknowledged in 1989 that the local management role would be demanding if local discretion were allowed. Its Recommendation 15 ran as follows:

> We recommend that the NHS Management Executive ensure that managers have the necessary training and skills to be able to make local pay bargaining effective (p.4).

Despite these warnings, the need for such expertise was persistently neglected. As recently as 1997 the Nurses Pay Review Body report[4] recommended that funds should be set aside for improving local expertise – effectively echoing the Health Committee – in the belief that the level of expertise at NHS trust level was insufficient to implement local bargaining properly.

> We therefore recommend that separately identified funds be made available within the Health Departments that Trusts might draw on, as and when they can demonstrate that they have a viable strategy for restructuring remuneration, to the benefit of the service offered to patients and the nursing staff who provide it (p.3, para.14).

A third factor impeding the development of local pay has been the limited ability of the Centre to understand the labour market within which NHS staff are recruited. The Nurses Pay Review Body has consistently pointed to the fact that the labour market is changing, as a result of the development of the private sector and also the increasing desire of women to combine career and family, and that the information available to it about the state of the labour market is weak. In its 1989 report[5] it complained:

> We said last year that it was difficult for us to draw firm conclusions about recruitment and retention from the evidence available to us. This remains our position (para.34).

Ten years later the Pay Review Body made a similar complaint when the evidence presented to it by the Department of Health and by staff representatives came to diametrically opposed views on the state of the labour market. While that in itself might be only to be expected, each side having its axe to grind, the continuing lack of comprehensive information or in-depth local analysis is not.

In February 1999, the Secretary of State told the Health Committee that he intended to ask the NHS to conduct a survey of staff shortages, a belated response to the weaknesses the Pay Bodies had been complaining of. In itself, this will not redress all the weaknesses they identified, but it reflects belated recognition that 'a lot of the data at the Centre is quite inadequate to the task' (para.321),[6] is a step forward. The question is: why should it have taken so long for the Centre to acknowledge this inadequacy? One possible explanation is that while the Centre was attempting to introduce local pay during the 1990s, the need to improve information about the workforce at national level did not seem important since central responsibility was to be reduced. Whatever the reason, the net result has been that neither the Centre nor the local NHS possesses accurate and comprehensive information about the NHS's main labour markets.

Although the Labour Government has set its face against local pay determination, *The New NHS* nevertheless supports the general concept of 'decentralising responsibility for operational management'. In respect of pay it states that:

> *In a national health service, the current mix of national and local contracts is divisive and costly. The Government's objective for the longer-term is therefore to see staff receive national pay, if this can be matched by meaningful local flexibility, since current national terms of service for a multitude of staff groups are regarded as inequitable and inflexible. Exploratory discussions on these issues are already under way with staff organisations and NHS employers* (para.6.28).

The no-doubt studied ambiguity of this paragraph is itself recognition of the tensions between two incompatible objectives – uniformity and flexibility. The paragraph fails to acknowledge a further source of possible tension, the scope that its proposals for primary care groups will create for differences between general practitioners – and any others working with them – both at individual practice level and more widely. In late 1997 the NHS Executive put out a consultation paper on pay determination, setting out in very broad terms an agenda for discussion with staff representatives. But its very lack of precision only served to underline that the Government has not found a way to provide meaningful local flexibility while retaining national bargaining.

In February 1999, *Agenda for Change: Modernising the NHS Pay System* was published.[7] In the introduction, the Secretary of State denounced the 'confusing mix of national and local pay systems' inherited from the previous Government, but nevertheless the paper itself recognised that 'pay modernisation has to strike the right balance between national and local decision-making' (para.8). That balance has yet to be struck. Although the Government's expectation was that the main elements of the new arrangements would be agreed by September 1999, the implications of whatever is agreed will inevitably take a long time to work through. Thus the central issues – the weight to be given to comparability with workers elsewhere as opposed to productivity and recruitment within the NHS and the precise balance between local flexibility set against national control – still remain to be fully resolved.

The first of these conflicts is unlikely to disappear: there is an inevitable tension between the aspirations of staff and the goal of cost control. In 1998, the Government attempted to tie the Review Bodies into its view of how pay should be determined, i.e. by reference to national economic criteria and the needs of the Service. Although their terms of reference were re-drawn, both insisted, in their 1999 reports, that they would continue to consider fairness alongside the economic imperatives urged on them by the Government. It remains possible therefore that they will recommend in future awards greater than the Government would like to see.

In 1970, members of the then Pay Review Body for doctors and dentists resigned because the Government did not accept the full range of their recommendations. When a new body was subsequently set up, the Government accepted that its recommendations would not be rejected unless there were 'compelling reasons' for doing so. Although its recommendations have never been rejected outright, in several years, pay awards have been staged – that is, some of the recommended increase has been deferred to half way through the financial year – which effectively reduced their value. But this is the only significant area of flexibility that the Government now has for these staff groups, short of calling on 'compelling reasons'.

On a year-by-year basis, therefore, it might seem that the two Review Bodies have not been as tough in keeping staff costs down as a Government prepared to face down its labour force might have been. Taking the longer view, however, the Pay Review Body system appears to have been effective in the 1980s and 1990s at finding a balance which, while not fully satisfying the aspirations of NHS staff, has avoided major industrial conflict on the one hand and widespread shortages on the other.

The second conflict, the balance between local flexibility and national rules, will take a long time to get right. Leaving union opposition to one side, finding the right balance between the various objectives that the process of pay determination has to deal with, would involve an estimate of the gains in terms of potential cost reductions to the NHS from being able to match pay better to local conditions, to create new pay packages both to respond to tight labour market conditions for some staff and to design new job definitions and roles. To be set against these potential benefits, is the risk of local bargaining leading to higher than 'required' increases in pay where unions manage to outwit local management or to play one NHS trust off against another, where, for example, staff with particular skills are scarce or where pay is set inappropriately in relation to the demands of particular jobs.

Whatever the appropriate current balance is, it is likely to become more rather than less difficult in future to strike the best overall compromise, whether pay and conditions are primarily determined nationally or locally. As we noted in Chapter 2, the market for doctors is becoming more like a conventional labour market, as career expectations change in response to broad social developments. As noted already, the private sector is growing in importance as an employer of nurses, thereby reducing the NHS's influence over pay and making it harder to monitor the nursing labour market. In both cases, the influence of the wider European, and indeed world, markets for clinical skills will grow. Furthermore, as we argue in the following three chapters, the way that the NHS will provide care in the future is difficult to predict but will almost inevitably change in the light of new technologies and treatment methods.

The knowledge base for responding to these challenges is weak and the skills required at local level in short supply. Because of the failure of the previous Government to get its way and an apparent lack of decisiveness on the part of the new one, the situation is that neither the Centre nor the local NHS is well equipped, in terms of knowledge, information and expertise, for its responsibilities. We have already cited continuing Pay Review Body complaints about lack of information at the Centre. Similarly, the Health Committee's conclusions about local expertise in the 1980s are echoed in the Audit Commission study of management of staff turnover, *Finders Keepers*.[8] This found that few NHS trusts had carried out an analysis of staff turnover even though that was the basis of an effective employment policy and even though their information systems allowed them to do so.

As a recent review by Alastair Gray and James Buchan[9] confirms, there is 'a lengthy agenda for future theoretical and empirical research work on the complex issue of local pay bargaining in the NHS'. That remark in turn reflects the very limited amount of information directly relevant to the UK that their review was able to call on and that in turn reflects a fundamental bias, which we refer to throughout this book, against investing in research and information about the broader context within which the NHS works.

Announcing the plans for a new pay structure, the Secretary of State stressed the scope for flexibility that they would create and that the changes would be fair – equal pay for equal work – precisely the principle which underlies staff-side support for national scales. How these two different interests will be met simultaneously neither the Secretary of State nor the consultative document issued at the time, managed to explain. But it is clear enough that if greater local discretion is created than under the Conservatives, the gaps in information and expertise identified by the Audit Commission and the Pay Review Bodies will prevent local discretion being used effectively. It is therefore hard to conclude that the NHS has, as of now, the means available to it to ensure that it finds the best compromise between the conflicting objectives that any system of pay determination has to resolve.

## Pharmaceutical products

The cost of drugs to the NHS depends on the price and the volume that the Service uses. We begin by examining policies targeted on the former – the supply side – and then consider briefly measures bearing on the latter – the demand side. Demand-side issues are discussed further in Chapter 9.

### Supply-side

The principal direct means of influencing the price of the pharmaceutical products the NHS requires is the Pharmaceutical Price Regulation Scheme (PPRS). The Guillebaud Committee[10] identified the basic dilemmas and difficulties, which remain today:

> *The whole problem is obviously one of great complexity and difficulty. On the one side, the Departments must be able to feel satisfied that reasonable, and not excessive, prices are being paid out of the public purse for the pharmaceutical products which are being consumed by the National Health*

*Service. The Service is a very large buyer of these products (in some instances virtually the sole buyer) and it is clearly right that the taxpayer should have a voice, through the Departments administering the service, in the prices which are to be paid. On the other side, account has to be taken of the present position and future development of the pharmaceutical industry of this country* (p.169).

The PPRS was introduced on a non-statutory basis in 1957. It was most recently negotiated with the industry in 1999.

In 1995, the Health Committee[11] investigated the PPRS – the first time it had been systematically reviewed since its inception – and concluded that it should be maintained. However, the Committee strongly criticised the way PPRS had been implemented. Its main concern was a lack of transparency as to how it was applied, which in the Committee's view led to:

*an unhealthy climate of suspicion and misunderstanding amongst those who seek to understand the Scheme, and undermines the principle of public accountability* (p.xxii).

It, therefore, recommended that the Department of Health should publish an annual report into the way the PPRS worked.

The Department of Health published the first ever report on the PPRS in 1996. This did little, however, to reveal the way the interests of the NHS and the industry were reconciled or the true impact of the PPRS. The Committee had proposed that the two roles of promoting the industry and securing low prices for the NHS were distinguished so as to allow a proper evaluation of the trade-offs involved. In response, the organisation of the Department was modified so as to reflect better the two roles. An internal division was created corresponding to the objectives of industry promotion and cost control – but that of course revealed nothing about the relationship between them in the real world.

There is little doubt that if control over the price of pharmaceutical products is to continue in its present form, it must be exercised centrally. Thus two questions arise:

- is the PPRS the best way of achieving control?
- if it is, is the Centre able to use it to best effect?

The Department's first report on the workings of the PPRS did not argue the case for a scheme of profit regulation nor did it examine systematically the alternatives. In fact, there is a wide range of options for controlling both the price and the use of drugs at national level. Other countries including those with substantial pharmaceutical industries adopt different approaches. Proposals for reform range from complete abolition of control to the development of a more sophisticated form of regulation and profit formulae drawing on the now extensive experience of such schemes within the field of the privatised public utilities such as water and electricity, where policy-makers also have to balance commercial and non-commercial objectives.

As Alan Maynard and Karen Bloor have pointed out,[12] the logic of the current situation is that the NHS should have some degree of control over the content of the R&D that the industry carries out. In line with this view, the Health Committee recommended that:

> ... the Department of Health take steps to monitor more effectively that research for which companies are claiming costs under the PPRS. Research which is aimed at duplicating drugs within a therapeutic category in which sufficient products are already available to meet all therapeutic needs or which is simply disguised promotion, should be disallowed as a cost under the Scheme in order to divert funds to more pressing areas of research (para.90).

The Government response[13] was cool:

> The Government does not accept the Committee's suggestion that there should be Government interference in or direction of the research programmes of the pharmaceutical industry. There is no evidence that these programmes are wasteful or unproductive. There is a competitive imperative for every company in such a research-based industry to get the best results, in terms of therapeutic advance, from the large sums it spends on them. The company's [sic] future in the world market ... depends on those results (p.7).

This reply misses the central point that commercial and health objectives may not be identical. Nor, despite the prodding of the Health Committee, has the Government shown why it considers that the present system of regulation produces the 'right' type and amount of research and development, that is one which best serves the interests of the NHS. The issue is not addressed in the Department's second report on the PPRS published in 1997[14] which simply records the level of spending by the UK pharmaceutical industry on R&D – some £2.1 billion in 1996. As we note in Chapter 11, this spending is far greater than that of the NHS R&D Programme and the Medical Research Council combined and hence is of critical importance to the standard of care the NHS provides as well as how much it has to pay out for drugs.

Although the Department has now published two reports on how the PPRS works in response to the Select Committee's concerns, the central issue of whether a better deal could be obtained for the NHS remains unresolved. The second report indicates that the prices of branded products within the scheme's ambit have fallen in recent years: overall, UK prices remained higher than those obtaining in Italy and Spain but lower than in the USA, Germany and The Netherlands (see Table 5.1).

**Table 5.1:** Relative drugs costs in selected countries: 1996

| UK | 100 |
|---|---|
| France | 105 |
| Germany | 125 |
| Italy | 93 |
| Spain | 89 |
| USA | 191 |

**Source:** Department of Health. *Pharmaceutical Price Regulation Scheme: second report to Parliament.* London: DoH, 1997.

Although these data give some assurance that UK prices are not excessive, it is still not clear that the NHS gets the best deal available from the PPRS, consonant with the other declared objective of the Scheme of supporting a UK-based drugs industry. The Select Committee's verdict was that 'if the Scheme does result in an unfair tilting, there are grounds for supposing that this may be in the direction of the industry rather than the NHS'. The official reports on the PPRS that have appeared since have done nothing to undermine that broad-brush conclusion. Equally, the merits of alternative strategies have not been convincingly demonstrated either. These might comprise not only alternative forms of price control, but also demand-side measures, to which we turn next.

## Demand-side

There is already a large number of measures in place designed to reduce spending on drugs by individual clinicians. These include limited prescribing lists at both national and local level, pharmaceutical advisers and the use of prescribing data for purposes of comparison and (informal) peer review. The work of the newly created National Institute for Clinical Excellence and the Commission for Health Improvement will also have an impact. More important, the introduction of cash limits for drug expenditures which follows from the creation of primary care groups will in itself limit total NHS demand and also create an environment in which GPs and other prescribers will become more cost-conscious.

As far as patients are concerned, charges, for the reasons set out in Chapter 4, can have only a limited role, but other micro-level measures are available such as therapeutic reference pricing which requires individuals to pay top-ups if they choose a drug which is not the cheapest in a therapeutic band. In principle, the better informed and tightly constrained purchasers that these measures will tend to create should be able to exert some downward pressure on prices, which might offset the need for a global form of control.

The Centre has never, at least not for public eyes, considered the actual and potential interplay of measures such as these on the prices of individual drugs as well as the quantity purchased and hence the need for price controls. As we argue in Chapter 9, measures to reduce the demand for drugs are still in their infancy and hence their potential as an alternative to price controls undeveloped. The NHS Act 1999 gives the Government new powers to control drug prices – but it will not know how best to use them until this potential is fully explored. The renegotiation of the PPRS, the results of which were announced in July 1999, appears to have taken place within the traditional framework, i.e. between industry and government.

As with pay, the task of finding the right balance between competing objectives is likely to become more complex as the number of ways through which the Centre tries to influence the use of pharmaceutical products – and their rate of introduction – grows. International considerations such as the development of a European Union-wide pharmaceutical market, which will limit the scope for purely national policies, also come into play. Although the

Centre did go some way to responding to the criticisms of the Health Committee by, for example, making changes to its internal organisation to keep NHS and industry interests distinct, it has yet to attempt systematically to explore all the policy options, including demand and supply side measures, taken together. Whether the NHS gets the possible deal from the PPRS in its current form remains therefore very much an open question.

## Supplies and support services

### Supplies

Purchasing the goods and services the NHS requires may seem one of the more straightforward tasks it has to discharge. The NHS should, it might be thought, be able to combine market power and expert knowledge in such a way as to ensure it could purchase at the lowest possible cost. In fact, attempts to improve purchasing go back to its very early days. The Guillebaud Committee[15] reported that is was 'left with the impression that hospital authorities generally have not yet taken full advantage of the enormous volume of knowledge and well tried practices in supplies purchasing which are already common to all large undertakings in this country' (para.425). Accordingly it believed there were substantial savings to be made. Subsequently the Messer Committee, appointed 'to investigate and report on the organisation of all forms of hospital supplies',[16] i.e. medical supplies such as bandages and dressings as well as everyday items such as crockery and furniture, made a large number of recommendations designed to achieve these savings.

Despite this long heritage, the efficient purchase of supplies has remained difficult to achieve. In 1991, the Committee of Public Accounts[17] found that:

> *Nearly all the readily available management information about NHS supplies relates to the 10 per cent by value of items, such as bandages, which pass through NHS stores depots and are classified as 'stock'. There is virtually no usable management information about the 90 per cent classified as 'non-stock', which include specialised equipment and services. For example, most regions were unable to provide the National Audit Office with a list of the top 50 items by value purchased in the last two financial years or the top 30 suppliers to each region* (p.vi, para.5).

It went on to conclude not only that better information was required but also that:

> ... *the NHS could learn from the private sector about using management information as a basis for strategic oversight* (p.vii, para.11).

Against this background it is scarcely surprising that the National Audit Office study[18] which led to this report found that there were wide variations in the prices paid for the same goods, and hence scope for lower prices for at least some parts of the NHS.

In autumn 1997 the Public Accounts Committee returned to the subject on the basis of a further report[19] from the National Audit Office. The NHS Supplies Authority had been established in 1991, taking over responsibilities from regional health authorities, with the expectation that a single body at arms-length from the NHS would be able to deploy greater expertise and buying power.

Although the Committee acknowledged that progress had been made on a number of fronts, it found overall progress had been slow, and that the savings made by the NHS Supplies Authority had been largely eaten up by the cost of running the organisation. Against this background, it was surprised to find the NHS Executive had relaxed efficiency targets on the Authority and suggested that it should 'take a hard look at the scope for further saving'.[20]

While progress at the Centre appears to have been modest, at local level, an Audit Commission report on purchasing[21] found that NHS trusts did not take these matters seriously:

> *All trust boards face demanding agendas, and they need not discuss supplies matters frequently. But they have two important responsibilities: supplies strategy; and establishing a system of accountability* (para.98).

According to the Commission, these responsibilities are not being discharged systematically. Not surprisingly it concluded that there remained scope for improvement, particularly by modifying relationships with suppliers in ways being pioneered outside the Service. Its report also pointed out that there was a wide range of consortium arrangements which existing organisational structures hindered:

*It is generally accepted that competition between trusts has discouraged some forms of co-operation. For example, joint hospital committees which used, among other things, to consider new products, now rarely exist. Similarly, many major hospitals have discontinued their roles in providing smaller units with advice on specialist areas and products (for example, tissue viability, intravenous therapy) (p.68, para.140).*

Arrangements such as these are more likely to emerge in the light of *The New NHS*'s emphasis on co-operation rather than competition but it remains to be seen whether they will.

The Treasury Minute which responded to the Public Accounts Committee report on NHS Supplies largely accepted the Committee's findings; indeed it stated on four occasions that 'The Executive notes the Committee's concerns'.[22] But essentially the message the Minute conveys is the familiar one: a mixture of promised organisational change and (new) tough targets. In May 1998, the NHS Executive announced that the purchasing of supplies would be subject to an efficiency review, but not one that would question the position of the Supplies Agency. The announcement of another review confirmed that even in this apparently straightforward area, it is not clear that arrangements designed to minimise the cost of NHS supplies are yet in place. The resulting report[23] made a large number of recommendations for improvement, having identified six themes that ran through successive purchasing reviews:

- *Fragmented purchasing – a need for more joint contracting.*
- *Lack of common specifications – a reluctance to agree standards of regular use items, a precursor to joint contracting.*
- *Incomplete management information – a lack of reliable data on usage, lines purchased, supplier performance and price levels.*
- *Insufficient management attention – procurement tended to be of peripheral interest to senior management.*
- *Inadequate storage facilities – stores were small, disparate and poorly controlled.*
- *A need for specialist well trained supplies managers (para.1.8).*

Against that background, it is clear that there is some way to go before NHS purchasing of supplies is carried out satisfactorily. There appears to have been a great deal of progress, after a long period when improvements seemed particularly slow in coming. But there remains a lot to do before it is possible to be confident that the NHS obtains its supplies at the lowest possible cost.

In the light of the weaknesses identified in the Cabinet Office report, it is likely to be some time before such confidence can be enjoyed.

## Support services

Unlike supplies, most support services such as catering and building maintenance have been provided by NHS employed staff. In 1981/82, just before the Conservative Government introduced competitive tendering, only £17 million out of £1000 million spent on support services was contracted out to the private sector. Compulsory competitive tendering opened up what had hitherto been local monopolies to competition from the private sector – and in some cases other parts of the public sector. The 1983 policy, extended over the following years, brought about sharp changes in the way that support services were provided and in the level of wages paid both by the NHS and private suppliers, and hence their cost. Department of Health figures produced in the 1980s suggested that substantial savings had been made. A critique[24] of those figures claimed that the savings might not be as large as claimed – the costs of achieving the savings for example were not included.

The compulsory system was later relaxed but the NHS was encouraged, in a White Paper *Competing for Quality* published in 1991,[25] to continue with 'market testing' all support services:

- *all those new areas and existing contracts to be market tested in the current and forthcoming financial year;*
- *an account of the outcome of market testing for the year of the report* (p.21).

The White Paper claimed that market testing had saved the NHS over £626 million over the previous seven years, but the approach it proposed for the future was encouragement rather than direction. It was particularly supportive of the use of contracts to manage NHS facilities, i.e. buildings and their services, which, as we see in the next section, became the object of a further initiative encouraging private finance of hospital building. This financial mechanism, in effect, transfers contracting for hospital support services to the private sector.

In recent years, the Department of Health has not published an estimate of the gains from tendering in response to the annual round of questions from the Health Committee. A recent review[26] of tendering for catering services found that it had little impact, in part because competition failed to develop and in part because NHS managers were reluctant to change fundamentally their approach to industrial relations by putting greater pressure on their staff to become more efficient. In many areas however, including administrative functions, such as IT or legal advice, NHS trusts have turned to competitive tendering in order to meet their annual efficiency savings target.

Within the field of local authority services, the Government has a new approach termed 'best value' described in *Modernising Local Government: improving local services through best value*.[27] The new approach is intended to provide a more flexible framework than the previous system of compulsory tendering, which the Conservatives had imposed. The paper describes compulsory tendering as being inflexible in practice and as over-emphasising cost at the price of lower quality. In its place it proposes that effectiveness and quality should be given greater emphasis and that new national targets, standards and audit procedures should be introduced.

Within the NHS, there is as yet no parallel development. The NHS Procurement Review notes the purpose of best value is 'entirely appropriate for the NHS' (para.1.17), emphasising 'that the quality of services as well as their cost matters, and although there is no compulsion to put services out to tender, there should be no presumption that services should be delivered directly, if other more efficient and effective means are available' (para.1.17). The clear implication is that the current arrangements for providing support services offer scope for further improvement, but the report does not identify how large that potential is.

## Capital projects

Until the introduction of capital charges following the NHS and Community Care Act 1990, capital was 'free' to its users, who therefore had no incentive to plan schemes economically nor to use the assets they had at their disposal in an efficient way. The Audit Commission found in 1991 that the NHS had a huge maintenance backlog and substantial savings could be made from utilising the existing capital stock better. The incentives to do so however were then weak since capital assets, once in place, were effectively free to the NHS.

It had been recognised before the 1990 Act that a means had to be found for bringing home to the local NHS the opportunity costs of the assets it employed. The process of converting NHS provider hospitals into quasi-commercial enterprises, NHS trusts, provided the occasion for introducing charges for the assets they took over. The process involved the valuation of the whole NHS portfolio, itself a massive and time-consuming task. That done, the assets each NHS trust took over were subject to a charge that reflected their estimated value which in turn had to be met out of income earned from purchasers. In this way an incentive to the disposal of under-used assets was automatically created.

How effective the introduction of capital charges has been remains hard to determine. The new arrangements took time to establish since they required a valuation of all the NHS land and buildings: accordingly although the system of capital charges is no longer new, the scope for evaluating its impact is limited. No systematic monitoring was put in place as to the impact of the change in England, but as noted in Chapter 4 asset disposals have been running recently at a high level.

In Scotland the Centre did commission a programme of external research. Drawing on its results, Professor David Heald observed[28] that:

> *Experience over five years shows that NHS capital charging is a useful but imperfect tool. There should be no illusion about the possibility of quick results; the history of NHS budgeting reform shows that much patience over the long-term is required to effect changes in managerial attitudes and behaviour. Success in refashioning the NHS estate can only be assessed over the medium term, and capital charging will be only one of the causative factors. Nevertheless, the survey evidence shows that the message that assets must be managed more systematically and effectively is being digested* (p.139).

As this makes clear, there remains a long way to go before it could be confidently claimed that the costs to the NHS of using capital assets are as low as they could be. However, just as the capital charges system was bedding down, a new policy – the private finance initiative – was introduced through the public sector.

The private finance initiative (PFI) was designed as a means of escaping the squeeze on public sector capital funding by in effect converting capital spending to a current cost and shifting the burden of financing it to future years. However, the true test is whether PFI offers a more cost-effective means of purchasing capital assets and the services that go with them.

In principle, the initiative may reduce building costs through better design and/or better procurement, or lead to lower running costs again through design or better managerial incentives. Savings in these areas must outweigh the likely higher financing costs of the private option. But because the potential sources of benefit are limited to the non-clinical areas which have already been subject, for the most part, to competitive tendering, the potential for reducing costs this way is inherently small since it only bears on about 30 per cent of hospital running costs. Clinical services remain outside the scope of the PFI.

Evidence presented to the Health Committee[29] relating to some of the first schemes approved suggests that they are producing sufficient benefits from this narrow base to offset the higher capital charges which the private operators must meet. The first detailed examination by the National Audit Office of a major hospital project[30] found that the private finance route did offer cost savings relative to the public but the calculations offered in justification of the scheme had overstated their extent.

What seems clear from this report and other assessments of individual schemes[31] is that this form of hospital procurement does not offer major savings and may, if all the criticisms prove valid, do the opposite. Furthermore, whether the savings claimed are greater than could be achieved by improving public sector procurement is unclear since no effort appears to have been made to do so. The previous method of hospital procurement had been characterised by delays and cost-overruns such as those identified in the National Audit Office report on Guy's rebuilding but, as the report points out, there were obvious ways to improve it.[32]

Furthermore, the way that the private finance initiative was introduced for major schemes was itself inefficient. The process of preparing schemes was almost entirely left to individual NHS trusts. The result was that many of the same problems were 'solved' several times over: for example, each NHS trust and its private sector partner had to resolve a set of common issues relating to the division and definition of risk. The Labour Government made it clear in 1997 that it intended to ensure that the costs of the negotiation process would be reduced through the introduction of standard forms of agreement.

While useful, changes of this sort do not bear directly on the nature of the schemes themselves. In particular, they will have no impact on the degree to which schemes embody new ideas, fully reflect the risks of clinical change to the public sector and take into account the strategic context, i.e. changes in the health care sector as a whole across all providers of service. In particular, as we note in the following two chapters, a number of factors are leading to the development of systems of care running between hospitals in different locations and between hospitals and community services.

If these issues are to be taken seriously then the existing focus on the individual NHS trust and the individual scheme must be modified in favour of a regional purchaser. The new Government has partly recognised this weakness and established a national Committee to prioritise projects. But such a Committee can only judge the schemes submitted to it. It is not designed to act as a strategic hospital building agency.

As we argue in the following chapter, the Centre has not yet provided a strategic framework for service planning in general and hospital planning in particular. Furthermore, as the volume of research on the economics of running hospitals remains tiny, there is virtually no way for the Centre to be sure that the best possible deals, taking running costs alone, are emerging from the existing process. For example, some of the new schemes embody views about the way that wards will be staffed in the future and how work will be organised. These views cannot be checked against any existing systematic body of evidence on current practice or informed speculation about the impact of changes in working practices in future. Furthermore, there are grounds for believing that the hospitals being built through the private route do not have sufficient capacity. It was only in the second half of 1998 that the Government announced it was setting up a National Bed Inquiry to review long-term requirements for hospital beds by which time a number of major schemes had been committed with more in the pipeline.

Our conclusion must therefore be that it is impossible to be confident that the NHS centrally or locally is in a position to ensure that the capital and running costs of the new estate in which it is investing unprecedented amounts of money are at the lowest achievable level nor are there sufficient grounds for confidence that the schemes currently being built are appropriate for the demands they will have to meet. This lack of confidence stems, as we argue in the following chapter, from a persistent neglect of the wide range of issues which hospital development presents.

## Clinical services

If the cost of each of the factors discussed above – pay, drugs, supplies, support services and capital – were effectively controlled that in turn should control the cost of clinical services. The task would remain of combining those factors in the most efficient way. Here again, we find that from the Guillebaud report in the 1950s onwards, official reports have expressed concern about the costs of providing services, but the task of ensuring that services are provided at lowest cost remains.

Despite the early concerns, it was not until the 1980s that an attempt was made to reduce costs by explicitly making efficiency in the use of resources a central government objective backed by quantitative targets. The approach initially adopted, the so-called 'Rayner' scrutiny into particular parts of the NHS and the broader ranging cost improvement programmes (CIPs), was indirect, in that it required regional health authorities to find quite modest levels of savings from the areas they administered but did not specify what the source of savings should be. How effective that process was is unclear. A King's Fund report[33] published at the end of the 1980s suggested that the reported figures for savings were overstated:

> The evidence we collected indicated that little effort was made within districts to establish whether individual savings were indeed recurrent. More significantly, even where it was clear that savings were not recurrent, the district CIP figures were not adjusted. The best example of this concerns competitive tendering. While the original tender may have yielded a saving that is recorded as a CIP, renegotiated contracts are often more expensive. The additional costs are not offset against earlier savings (p.27).

As a result, whether or not the recorded savings represent the true picture was open to doubt. The report goes on:

> In fact this is a general conclusion which applies to all aspects of CIP valuation: the imprecision surrounding them makes the certainty with which cumulative savings are cited at the national level a source of concern (p.29).

After the introduction of the purchaser–provider split, the modest targets that characterised the 1980s became more demanding. Separate if related measures were directed at the two 'sides'. For purchasers, as we have noted earlier, target increases in the so-called 'NHS purchaser efficiency index' (a measure of the number of care episodes bought for a given quantum of finance) were set by the NHS Executive. Providers on the other hand have been required to provide cost releasing efficiency savings, the level of which has varied from trust to trust. It is the achievement of such savings that should allow purchasers to buy more care per £ spent. For most of the 1990s, the improvement required has been around 3 per cent per annum.

At the same time, the internal market was itself intended to create competitive pressures directly on the cost of clinical services by allowing purchasers to obtain the services they required from the lowest cost suppliers. In principle therefore this process should have encouraged not simply a search for lower unit costs for each resource required, but also a search for better ways of combining or managing those resources by, for example, substituting cheaper for more expensive inputs or redesigning services so that total resource requirements were reduced.

In the event, clinical services have rarely been put to competitive tender. Some competitive pressure resulted from GP fundholding but that applied to a relatively narrow range of services such as pathology and the cheaper elective surgical procedures. In contrast, the application of the efficiency indices does appear to have had an impact. Unlike the competitive process, the NHS Executive absorbed the indices into its management processes so that there was a management link between the centrally determined target, via regional offices and district health authority purchasers, to providers.

Nevertheless, it remains unclear whether the policies adopted during the 1990s have had the intended impact. First, the central weakness of the measure of activity used, the finished consultant episode, means that the appearance of gain may have been illusory. Providers may have 'created' episodes by changes in recording of clinical practice. Second, gains for one provider may have been at the expense of another – if, for example, hospitals cut back on lengths of stay but NHS community trusts or GPs had to provide more community care as a result. Third, many of the cost-releasing savings that NHS trusts have made were indistinguishable from reductions in service quality – there were no measures or monitoring systems available which would distinguish between them. Fourth, since the NHS efficiency index did not apply to general practice or other family health services, there was not even a broad brush indication of whether or not costs in these services as a whole had been effectively controlled and efficiency in their delivery increased. Finally, the incentives inherent in the index encouraged providers to increase episodes of care regardless of the clinical appropriateness of doing so.

*The New NHS* indicated that the Labour Government did not intend to encourage competitive pressures. At the same time, the previous NHS efficiency indices were abandoned although a general requirement to improve efficiency remains. But there is now no direct mechanism for extracting efficiency gains from providers over and above the general pressure exerted on all parts of the Service by the tension between demand for care and the limited resources available.

However, *The New NHS* announced a 'programme which requires NHS trusts to publish and benchmark their costs on a consistent basis'; the first National Schedule of Reference Costs has now been published,[34] more than 40 years after the need for such information was identified in the Guillebaud report. As the NHS Executive acknowledges, high costs do not equate with inefficiency, but even if they did, how NHS trusts – no longer faced with competitive pressures – will respond remains unclear.

The White Paper goes on:

> *Where the schedule indicates poor performance, Health Authorities, Primary Care Groups and NHS Trusts will need to investigate why, sort out plans to tackle inefficiencies and build these into long-term agreements. Primary Care Groups will be expected to bear down on NHS Trust costs over time so as to achieve the best possible value for their local community. Where NHS Trusts prove unable to make satisfactory progress over a period of time, the Regional Office will investigate and, if necessary, intervene* (para.9.21).

While this is a start, the White Paper did not indicate what measures were to be taken to support the Regional Offices if they do decide to address the persistence of high costs. Experience with the nationalised industries – towards which the sponsoring departments had what was in effect a similar role – suggests it is far from being a straightforward matter. It is likely to be all too easy for NHS trusts to explain away high costs in terms of special local factors.

The competence to distinguish the justifiable from the non-justifiable variation from the 'norm' does not widely exist – indeed it will require considerable development before satisfactory norms are established which properly allow for the genuine range of variation that the NHS, given its diversity, is likely to exhibit. Attention will probably focus initially on 'outliers' – those far above the average – but even the proper identification of outliers will be in doubt until there can be confidence that the costing methods used in different NHS trusts are strictly comparable.

Those working in the NHS might in any case argue that, after so many years of cuts relative to increases in activity, there is no further scope for improvement in efficiency. What evidence there is from detailed studies of how the Service works in practice suggests otherwise. Reports from external auditors such as the Audit Commission inevitably identify ways in which costs can be reduced at NHS trust level for example in the supplies function as noted above, or more typically because they identify variations in performance which are hard to explain by reference to differences in workload.

In principle, the scope for cost reductions identified in such reports should be achievable by effective local action, supported by local auditors, provided that enough management attention could be focused on such issues. But that, as we noted in relation to procurement, cannot be taken for granted: the competing pressures on NHS trust boards and senior management are immense. Furthermore, procurement is a relatively straightforward task. Much less straightforward is the task of ensuring that clinical services running across NHS trusts are efficiently provided.

Measures announced in *The New NHS* such as the national framework for assessing NHS performance, have the great merit, compared to the efficiency index, of containing a focus on outcomes of care and other Service objectives. These too will require a great deal of work to implement and to enforce but they still represent only the first step in the direction of measuring how well the NHS is doing. Furthermore, these measures, like the National Schedule of Reference Costs, fail to mesh with other parts of the Government's agenda, particularly the national service frameworks and the development of systems of care. These require measures that take into account the relationships between providers in both secondary and primary care and hence the costs arising as a patient moves along a care pathway comprising contributions from different providers. The financial framework to bring the costs of the various elements of a care pathway together does not exist. The Schedule of Reference Costs is therefore best seen as the first step in a long process of making available and learning to exploit accurate cost information for clinical services. Again, therefore, our conclusion is that we cannot yet be confident that the NHS has available to it the means to ensure overall efficiency in the delivery of care.

## Conclusion

The tight central control over NHS spending, together with explicit efficiency targets, has provided the essential backdrop to controlling NHS costs. But within the specific areas covered in this chapter, there is no consensus as to the best way the NHS should be organised to ensure that its component costs are kept to the lowest possible level consistent with its broader objectives.

In no area is there an established system for delivering cost savings that is clearly producing the maximum gains possible. In some areas, particularly drugs, the full range of options has not been examined. In others, particularly pay and supplies, there is a muddle between central and local roles which has meant that neither has the knowledge and intelligence available to it that is required. In both these areas, new initiatives have been announced: for these to be successful, some of the NHS's long standing failings in respect of expertise and information will have to be addressed.

The basis of any long-term strategy to ensure that resources are purchased effectively is a greater level of understanding and intelligence as to the way each of the relevant markets works now, the factors affecting how they will work in the future and the options available for new policies and the creation of the skills required within the Service to use and respond to better information.

These requirements cannot be met quickly. In the areas discussed in this chapter and in subsequent chapters in this section of the book, the weaknesses we have identified reflect decades of neglect of the need to understand, on the basis of research or wider intelligence, the issues which cost control poses. That in turn reflects the enduring bias against 'system' or 'management' knowledge that has been inherent in the NHS since its foundation. Against this background, there is no quick road to improvement.

At the moment, because of the extensive private sector involvement and the international nature of the industry, only in the areas of drug costs is there an existing body of analytic expertise outside the NHS and much of this has a clear interest in reducing the impact of price regulation. In other areas such as pay and hospital development, there is expertise within parts of the NHS and associated organisations, but no substantial external organisation with the ability to comment authoritatively on whether existing arrangements are 'the best possible' and if not how they might be amended. In some of the other areas considered here, particularly purchasing, the external auditors of the NHS, the Audit Commission and the National Audit Office, have made substantial contributions to identifying what is wrong and what might be done. But by virtue of their terms of reference, neither explores in detail the full range of policy options nor is it their responsibility to ensure the availability of the appropriate expertise.

The NHS requires a clear focus for taking seriously the issues discussed in this chapter. Initially this might be provided by a Costs Inquiry or Commission mirroring the Guillebaud Committee of the 1950s. This might, as that Committee did, identify more systematically than we have done the gaps in information and understanding in each of the areas reviewed and on the basis of that, programmes of research could be defined and commissioned.

But it also requires the capacity, throughout the Service, to improve information systems bearing on staffing, pay, and other costs, and to use effectively the data they produce. The Schedule of Reference Costs represents a step in the right direction but it will only work properly if the data it embodies are regarded as reliable, and if the capacity to interpret and apply what it reveals exists. How these broad requirements should be met – whether by strengthening analytic expertise inside the Service, centrally, regionally, or locally, or outside it – is an issue we shall return to in later chapters in this part of the book. All this requires substantial investment but unless it is made, any future review of the NHS's attempts to control its costs will reach the same conclusion as this.

## References

1. Review Body on Doctors and Dentists Remuneration. *19th Report*. London: HMSO, 1989.
2. Warlow D. *Review of the Conditions of Employment of Staff Employed in the National Health Service (England, Wales and Scotland)*. London: Department of Health, 1989.
3. House of Commons Social Services Committee. *Resourcing the National Health Service – Whitley Councils Volume 1*. London: HMSO, 1989.
4. Review Body for Nursing Staff, Midwives, Health Visitors and Professionals Allied to Medicine. *Fourteenth Report on Nursing Staff, Midwives and Health Visitors*. London: HMSO, 1997.
5. Review Body for Nursing Staff, Midwives, Health Visitors and Professionals Allied to Medicine. *Sixth Report on Nursing Staff, Midwives and Health Visitors*. London: HMSO, 1989.
6. House of Commons Health Committee. *Future NHS Staffing Requirements – Volume 1: Report and Proceedings of the Committee* and *Volume 2: Minutes of Evidence and Appendices*. London: Stationery Office, 1999.
7. Department of Health. *Agenda for Change: Modernising the NHS Pay System*. London: Department of Health, 1999.
8. Audit Commission. *Finders, Keepers: The management of staff turnover in NHS Trusts*. London: Audit Commission, 1997.
9. Gray A and Buchan J. Pay in the British NHS: a local solution for a national service. *Journal of Health Services Research and Policy* 1998; 3: 113–20.
10. Guillebaud CW (chair). *Report of the Committee of Inquiry into the Cost of the National Health Service*. London: HMSO, 1956.
11. House of Commons Health Committee. *Priority Setting in the NHS: the NHS drugs budget. Volume 1: Report, together with an Appendix and the Proceedings of the Committee*. London: HMSO, 1994.

12. Maynard A and Bloor K. Regulating the Pharmaceutical Industry. *BMJ* 1997; 315: 200–01.

13. Department of Health. *Government response to the Second Report from the Health Committee Session 1993/94: Priority Setting in the NHS: the NHS drugs budget.* Cm. 2683. London: HMSO, 1994.

14. Department of Health. *Pharmaceutical Price Regulation Scheme: second report to Parliament.* London: DoH, 1997.

15. See n.9 above.

16. Ministry of Health Central Health Services Council. *Final Report of the Committee on Hospital Supplies.* London: HMSO, 1958.

17. House of Commons – Committee of Public Accounts. *42nd Report – National Health Service Supplies in England.* London: HMSO, 1991.

18. National Audit Office. *NHS Supplies in England.* London: HMSO, 1991.

19. National Audit Office. *NHS Supplies in England.* London: HMSO, 1999.

20. House of Commons – Committee of Public Accounts. *1st Report – NHS Supplies in England.* London: Stationery Office, 1997.

21. Audit Commission. *Goods for your Health: Improving supplies management in NHS Trusts.* London: HMSO, 1996.

22. *Treasury Minute on the first to fourth reports from the Committee of Public Accounts 1997–98.* Cm. 3880. London: Stationery Office, 1998.

23. Cabinet Office. *NHS Procurement Review – November 1998.*

24. Key T. In: Maxwell R, editor. *Reshaping the NHS.* Hermitage: Policy Journals, 1988.

25. HM Treasury. *Competing for Quality.* Cm. 1730. London: HMSO, 1991.

26. Kelliher C. Competitive Tendering in NHS Catering: a suitable policy? *Health Manpower Management* 1997; 23: 170–80.

27. Department of the Environment, Transport and the Regions. *Modernising local government: Improving local services through best value.* London: Stationery Office, 1998.

28. Heald D and Scott DA. NHS capital charging after five years. In: Harrison A, editor. *Health Care UK 1995/96.* London: King's Fund, 1996.

29. House of Commons, Health Committee. *Public Expenditure on Health and Personal Social Services.* London: Stationery Office, 1997.

30. National Audit Office. *The PFI Contract for the new Dartford and Gravesham Hospital.* London: Stationery Office, 1999.

31. Gaffney D, Pollock AM, Price D and Shaoul J. PFI in the NHS – is there an economic case? *BMJ* 1999; 319: 116–19.

32. National Audit Office. *Cost Over-runs, Funding Problems and Delays on Guy's Hospital Phase III Development: report by the Comptroller and Auditor General.* London: Stationery Office, 1998.

33. Schocket G. *Efficiency in the NHS: a study of cost improvement programmes.* London: King's Fund Institute, 1989

34. NHS Executive. *National Schedule of Reference Costs.* Leeds, 1998.

# Chapter 6

# Designing systems of care

The NHS is most visible as a provider of health care services. It is this task which above all it must do well. But what exactly is the task?

For the individual patient seeking care, the prime requirement is that the professionals they consult diagnose their condition accurately and treat it effectively. Our concern in this chapter, however, is not with the specific clinical intervention, for which the skill and knowledge of the individual professional or team of professionals is critical to the delivery of effective care. Rather, our focus is on broader questions, in particular:

- how best to *group* clinical facilities usually found in hospitals as between larger and smaller units, and between hospitals and other facilities. This requires the balancing of the advantages to be gained from locating clinical activities in large but distant sites, which means balancing any quality advantages with the disadvantages in terms of access or cost that this may bring

- how best to *link* clinical services provided by different professionals in different locations. This involves ensuring that all the elements required for an effective system of care are in place and that the various elements work efficiently together so that, for example, patients whose needs do not require the expensive facilities of the hospital are cared for in lower cost environments while those who do are routed effectively to the specialised facilities they require.

These tasks, which taken together we term 'designing systems of care', are closely linked. In the case of cancer care for example, the service can only be designed properly if the right elements are present within the hospital system – in this case, the right numbers of clinical staff with the right level of expertise serving populations large enough to enable their clinical staff to develop and maintain high levels of expertise – and their roles are properly linked to community-based clinicians, primarily general practitioners, community nurses, social services and voluntary agencies.

Clinical matters are central to system and service design, but they are not the only matters to be taken into account. Wider considerations are involved, comprising economic and financial factors as well as the determinants of access to services, which include geographical and transport factors as well as the personal, economic and social characteristics of users, or potential users. In addition, the training requirements of professional staff and the research capacity of the institutions concerned may also have to be taken into account. To assess these factors and weigh the options available requires considerable analytic expertise, and significant management and implementing skills are required to ensure that those chosen are run effectively. Designing systems of care represents, therefore, a huge challenge.

In the first part of this chapter, we argue that the NHS has not tackled this challenge effectively. As a result, there are shortfalls in its performance as a deliverer of care. We then go on to describe some promising recent developments which are beginning to address these shortfalls. We conclude however that these are not sufficient and hence make recommendations designed to address the weaknesses that remain.

## Early developments

Prior to the establishment of the NHS, blueprints such as the Dawson report[1] in the 1920s proposed a pattern of provision based on primary and secondary health centres and went so far as to set out which services and facilities should be found in each. These recommendations had little impact. Instead, the pattern of provision continued to be influenced by a wide range of local factors and, as a consequence, was extremely diverse. In some parts of the country, there were, for example, a number of small hospitals carrying out different functions; in others, these were largely grouped together into one large hospital. How services were provided, be it for accident victims or cancer sufferers, varied enormously, as did the balance of work between hospital and community-based services.

### Hospitals

The first NHS document to address systematically the way that hospital services should be determined was the 1962 Hospital Plan.[2] This, and the subsequent modifications to it, set out the concept of a district general hospital, serving around 100,000–150,000 people and meeting the majority of the health care needs of that population. It also recognised that some services had to be provided at regional or even national level, while others could remain in smaller hospitals. This hierarchy reflected the type of illnesses to be treated: treatments for rare conditions were likely to be better provided for larger catchment populations, for example a region comprising perhaps two to three-and-a-half million population with a teaching hospital at its centre; treatments for common conditions but which required the physical facilities and human resources of the hospital were suitable for district general hospitals, while continuing care and other services might be provided in smaller local institutions such as community hospitals.

The model of the district general hospital supported by specialist units in larger hospitals and, in some parts of the country, small or community hospitals has continued to this day. However in practice there are still significant variations between different parts of the country. Acute hospitals in all parts of the country contain broadly the same range of services, but the precise mix varies a great deal, as does the way they are staffed and organised. Furthermore, since the 1962 Hospital Plan was formulated, specialisation within medicine has grown rapidly, so nowadays a general hospital with medical and surgical staff in all the major specialties is necessarily a much larger institution than its predecessor of 30 years ago.

Thus the 1962 Hospital Plan did not turn out to be a blueprint – indeed revisions to it were made very soon after its publication. But for more than 30 years, the basic idea underlying it, that the majority of hospital services should be grouped together into a single institution, has been applied, albeit in accordance with local circumstances – such as the availability of finance – and with developments in medical technology and knowledge. There remain some exceptions to the Plan's underlying principles, for example, the small but significant group of single specialty hospitals. Nevertheless, the 1962 Plan has provided a generally accepted approach to the development of hospitals in most parts of the country.

Since the 1960s, however, there has been remarkably little official analysis of the structure of hospital services or concern about whether they are appropriately organised. The Royal Commission on the National Health Service[3] reporting at the end of the 1970s did not attempt the task. Between 1980, when a consultation paper on hospital services[4] was published by the Government, and 1990, there was no concerted or centrally directed attempt to determine the role or functions of hospitals.

That remains true for the country as a whole. London is a partial exception; two reports, one from the Tomlinson Inquiry[5] and the other from the 1997 London Review Team,[6] made a series of specific suggestions for the way in which London's hospital system should develop and a series of studies of specialised services was prepared for the London Implementation Group, which was established to promote change in the capital's health care services and its medical education and research facilities in light of the Tomlinson report.[7] But neither report had available to it any systematic analysis of the role and functions of hospitals as a whole nor of the appropriate way to group together their various functions. Such 'blueprints' had been proposed in, for example, reports from the South East Thames and Oxford Regional Health Authorities[8] but they were not widely adopted.

The broad structure of hospital services has changed since the 1962 Plan, in favour of larger hospitals carrying out a wider range of functions. This trend has occurred in part as a result of technical innovations, for example in diagnostic techniques, and in part as a result of changes in medical education and the impact of growth of clinical knowledge on medical specialisation. But there has been no process designed to ensure that the overall structure of the hospital service was changing in the right direction, from the viewpoint of the Service as a whole. There has been no nationally organised attempt to determine whether for example the changes in accessibility arising from a reduction in the number of hospitals was harmful to patients' interests or not.

## General practice

There was no equivalent for general practice to the 1962 Hospital Plan. The merits of a local, neighbourhood service with its promise of continuity of care and easy access have largely been taken to be obvious and indeed general practice has always received strong public support in opinion surveys, most recently in the National Patients and Users Survey.

The Medical Practices Committee – working at national level – has aimed to ensure that all parts of the country enjoyed reasonable access to general medical services through influencing where new practices could be set up. But the GPs running them have been left to determine their own ways of working both with regard to the range of their services and way they are provided. The definition of general medical services has in practice been whatever GPs choose to do. The consultation paper, *Primary Health Care: an agenda for discussion*, published in 1986, was described as the first comprehensive review of primary care services in the life of the NHS.

It contained a large number of ideas for better services, but it did not attempt to specify how these services should be provided. Only with the introduction of the 1990 GP contract has a part of the GP's role come to be defined by a centrally determined requirement. The same has been largely true of community health services, the pattern of which has continued in many areas to reflect its origin as a local government service and the wide discretion enjoyed by local authorities as to what they provided.

## Balance of care

The 1962 Hospital Plan took it for granted that services that did not need the special facilities of the hospital should be provided outside it. But how that division should be achieved in practice was unclear then and remained so for the subsequent decades.

Since the beginning of the 1990s, however, there has been a series of broad policy statements about a shift of care away from the hospital and into the community. In the case of London, for example, the Tomlinson Inquiry suggested that there should be a major boost for primary care, in part to relieve the load on London's hospitals. The emphasis on community-based options reflected the perception that within a provider-led NHS, the professionally dominant institution, the hospital, had been too powerful, with the result that alternative forms of provision had been systematically ignored. But while there was merit in this argument, it was adopted too uncritically.

The assumption that improvements in primary care would lead to a fall in hospital use was not based on any real understanding of the way in which primary and secondary care interact. In fact, while there is some evidence which suggests that access to good quality primary care can reduce the workload of the hospital, the relationship can work the other way if better primary care leads to identification of more people who can benefit from access to hospital-based service, or it can be neutral, for example, where extra resources devoted to primary care result in entirely new services not provided previously by either primary or secondary care, for example, counselling services for the 'worried well'.

In the event, there has been very little shift of whole services from hospital to community, with the exception of patients in long stay hospitals. In London and elsewhere the scope for shifting specific functions from secondary to primary care has been demonstrated in experimental projects in small areas of the capital,[9] while the development of local GP purchasing has stimulated other changes, for example consultants giving out-patient clinics in local surgeries and efforts to reduce hospital admission and length of stay for elderly patients in particular.[10] In general, however, hospital services have continued to expand and their share of medical resources to grow. Despite the vast range of case studies and local experiments bearing on the overall balance of care between hospitals of different kinds and between hospitals and other forms of provision, no substantial analysis of the whole care system has emerged from the Centre since the 1960s.

One result has been that the NHS has not been in a position to ensure that all the elements required for effective services are in place and that they are of the appropriate scale. Such a lack was revealed by the London Implementation Group reports into specialised services, including cancer, burns, paediatrics and renal services, referred to above. Although their specific conclusions differed, they all found that the existing structure of hospital services was not as clinically effective as it could be.

Parallel to this, there has been a persistent failure to ensure that the various elements required for the effective care of a client group such as elderly people properly relate to each other. In its report on community health services, for example, the Clinical Standards Advisory Group[11] found:

> The provision of community health services for elderly people is characterised by fragmentation (and) confusion (p.32).

This finding echoes those of many other reports on services for elderly people and others requiring care from several providers. In a series of reports,[12] the King's Fund identified, for example, the lack of intermediate and rehabilitation facilities which inhibited the development of a fully integrated system of care for elderly people. The Audit Commission concluded, in respect of care services for older people[13] that:

> Older people often experience care services that are poorly co-ordinated (p.17).

These are just two examples from a large number of reports at both national and local level bearing on the failure of hospital and non-hospital services to link effectively – not to mention similar failure at the boundary between the NHS and local authority social services.

The reasons underlying the persistent failure of the NHS to link appropriately the various elements required for an effective system of care from within the

NHS itself and also between the NHS and social services, lie partly in the organisational, professional and financial frameworks within which individual parts of the Service work – their significance is considered in the following chapter. But it also stems from a persistent reluctance, at all levels of the Service, to consider whole systems of care for specific groups of the population and to ensure that all the components required are in place. Instead, as we argue in Chapter 11, the vast majority of the resources going into research and development as well as professional training have been devoted to the specifics of delivering care to individual patients rather than the broad system or service of which it forms part. That however is at last beginning to change.

In the case of cancer care, a national committee was appointed in 1993 chaired by the Chief Medical Officers for England and for Wales, which concluded[14] that for both countries the existing pattern of services had to be radically changed if an effective service was to be provided. Unlike the reports prepared for the London Implementation Group, it did not make specific recommendations bearing on individual hospitals. Instead the Committee set out the broad concepts which it concluded should guide the development of cancer services, from primary care through to specialist centres. As we go on to see, the present Government has decided to extend the approach adopted for cancer care to other important services.

## Recent developments

In part, the lack of strong central direction over the broad pattern of care provided in the NHS reflects the nature of the political settlement between the medical profession and the Government at the time the NHS was founded. As noted earlier, clinical matters were left firmly in the hands of the professions. In part, it also reflects the belief that in a large organisation such as the NHS, providing services in a wide range of geographical settings, a single blueprint would be inappropriate. The 1962 Hospital Plan could be seen as an exception, but only a partial one since it did not specify how hospitals should function or the range of services they should provide. No system of national accreditation or monitoring was established to check whether the model of the district general hospital was indeed more effective than what it replaced, or whether it still remained appropriate in the conditions of the 1980s and 1990s.

The NHS and Community Care Act 1990 might, in principle, have made it easier to address the task of system and service design. It was promoted at the time as an attempt to end provider, particularly hospital, domination of the

Service through the creation of free-standing health authority purchasers, independent of them. Health authorities were originally tasked to purchase services in the light of assessments of the needs of their populations. In principle this opened the way for purchasers to determine both what treatments were offered and also the manner of their delivery – in short, to design services as well as buy them.

In the event, these objectives have not been realised: the impact of health authorities on system and service design has been limited. While in principle purchasers could specify the services they wanted to buy and the way they should be provided, they did not in general have the knowledge, the data, or the clinical expertise required to redesign them. For example, the Audit Commission report[15] on the treatment of elderly patients with hip-fracture found:

> *Purchasers are clearly responsible for ensuring that care is provided that meets the needs of people who have fractured their hips. But few are in a position to discharge this responsibility* (p.55).

Most of what expertise existed was to be found within providers. But that expertise was itself also deficient: most comprised detailed knowledge of particular treatments or processes rather than knowledge of how they related to each other. While purchasers might have been in a better position to identify and encourage more effective links between providers and to take a dispassionate view of what the balance of work between them should be, in practice they did not. Not only did they generally not have the required expertise, but they also faced substantial barriers, particularly the division between finance for hospital and community services on the one hand and primary care services on the other.

The alternative to purchasing by health authorities, purchasing by GPs in the GP fundholding scheme, was also designed to challenge the provider domination of acute hospitals by giving other clinicians – GPs – the incentive and the leverage to change the way that services were delivered. There have been successes at the margin, as the Audit Commission study[16] found:

> *The most common changes have been improved communications with hospitals and consultants; kick starting or speeding up specific local changes that had been difficult to achieve in the past; more rational prescribing; and making budget savings. The least common have been wholesale switching between providers (whether for lower prices or other reasons); seeking*

*increased day surgery; planning future developments with the health authority and providers; agreeing with consultants that the GP should manage the waiting list for non-urgent operations; and introducing guidelines designed to make healthcare more effective* (p.37).

But, overall, the Audit Commission found that change had been limited:

*While there is wide variation in application of individual actions, there is even more variation in the extent to which individual practices achieve change across the whole spectrum. In the Commission's experience, a few fundholding practices have achieved change in many of the areas listed. The majority, however, have focused on achieving one or two significant gains for their patients. It is therefore important to ask what it is about the way fundholding practices are organised, and the environment in which they operate, that could account for such differences* (p.40).

This may have been partly due to lack of experience which could have been overcome in time, or it might have been due to the lack of purchasing clout by GPs buying care on behalf of relatively small numbers of people. But it might also be due to lack of the relevant expertise. While GPs may be judged to perceive clearly the needs of their own patients, this is not the same as being able to perceive the best way of providing a given service such as emergency surgery or cancer for the local population as a whole. To do that requires a perspective extending beyond the individual practice population and a range of knowledge which few individuals in the country as a whole can command.

In the last two years, however, two significant initiatives have been taken bearing on the design of services, the formal acknowledgement of the need for experiments with different forms of provision and the introduction of a service design function at national level.

The first bears on primary care. The Conservative Government recognised in its White Paper, *Choice and Opportunity*,[17] that the existing ways of providing general medical services did not always work well. The framework created by the Primary Care Act 1997 – passed just before the General Election – allows experimental changes to the rules governing the provision of general medical services and for new ways of providing primary care to be developed on a pilot basis – known as Primary Care Act pilots or PCAPs. The pilot programme started under the Conservatives has been extended by its successor.

This experimental approach is a sensible way of filling gaps in knowledge and trying out new ideas. It is highly relevant to primary care – including dental and medical services – since the rules governing primary care have been restrictive since the establishment of the NHS, making innovation difficult. Not surprisingly, therefore, there were a large number of applications for pilot status.[18]

The piloting approach may have a wider relevance since there are other areas, including many hospital services, where experiments with new forms of services are the only means of finding out what the best way of providing services is. One such example was the establishment of a Trauma Centre in the North Staffordshire Hospital in response to a critique from the Royal College of Surgeons[19] of the existing pattern of accident and emergency services. However, such examples of nationally promoted experiments are rare.

---

**Box 6.1:** National service frameworks

These will comprise the following elements:

- a definition of the scope of the framework
- the evidence base:
  - needs assessment
  - present performance
  - evidence of clinical and cost-effectiveness
  - significant gaps and pressures
- national standards, timescales for delivery
- key interventions and associated costs
- commissioned work to support implementation:
  - appropriate R&D, inc. through the NHS R&D programme (inc. Health Technology Assessments (HTAs))
  - appraisal
  - benchmarks
  - outcome indicators
- supporting programmes:
  - workforce planning
  - education and training
  - personal and organisational development (OD)
  - information development
- a performance management framework

**Source:** Department of Health. *A First Class Service: quality in the new NHS.* London: HMSO, 1998.

The second, the notion of a national service framework, bears on the design of systems of care for client groups. These are described in *The New NHS* as follows:

> *The new approach to developing cancer services in the Calman-Hine report, and recent action to ensure all centres providing children's intensive care meet agreed national standards, point the direction. In each case, the best evidence of clinical and cost-effectiveness is taken together with the views of users to establish principles for the pattern and level of services required. These then establish a clear set of priorities against which local action can be framed. The NHS Executive, working with the professions and others, will develop a similar approach to other services where national consistency is desirable. There will be an annual programme for the development of such frameworks starting in 1998 (p.56).*

During 1998 and 1999, the Centre announced plans to devise frameworks for mental health, coronary heart disease, diabetes and care for elderly people (see Box 6.1, above).

In contrast to the approach of the 1997 Act, the creation of national service frameworks is a top-down process. It clearly makes sense if reliable information is available to define a single best system design. In principle, this approach should, as far as major services are concerned, lead to a situation where most major services are consciously designed. In the light of the criticisms set out above, this represents a major step forward.

However, there are risks with the client group by client group approach the Government has adopted for the development of national service frameworks. The early frameworks may skew the system inappropriately to favour certain services. Any such biases should be overcome in time as more frameworks are developed. But, the more national service frameworks are determined, the greater the need to consider the broader system questions – the structure of hospital services and the balance between hospital and community care taken as a whole – and how financial incentives and other factors bear on the linkages between these services. Furthermore, the national service framework approach cuts across other service divisions, principally that between planned and unplanned (emergency) care, a distinction that is critical to the design of hospital services. *The New NHS* ignores these broader issues – indeed it makes no significant mention of hospital services and the overall balance between hospital and community.

The need to consider that balance has, however, been recognised by the Centre. During 1997 to 1999 the Centre put out a mass of advice[20] designed to help the Service cope with winter pressures and the task force set up to report on how they were handled – the Emergency Services Action Team – collected a great deal of information about service innovations which was disseminated throughout the Service. However, this process fell short of attempting to define how the NHS should be organised so as to provide emergency care services as a whole, taking hospital and community services together. While official papers[21] refer to a 'whole systems' approach combining hospital and community and emergency and elective care services, the phrase has remained largely rhetorical. The capacity to consider all the elements of effective service at one and the same time does not exist, a point we return to below. In principle, the process of developing local health improvement plans will both require and help to create this capacity, but it will take substantial investment in human and other resources if that potential is to be realised.

## Knowledge gaps

While the White Paper proposals seem set to improve the NHS's capacity to design care systems, the empirical basis for doing so remains weak. As the attempts to implement the Calman-Hine proposals have shown, much of the information required to do this is not available, some of it the most basic kind. The Committee's report contained very little information on the costs of implementation, staffing requirements, or on the current pattern of access to care. A study by the King's Fund[22] identified a large number of information gaps, and also pointed to a number of areas where action was needed, either at national or local level, to ensure that the necessary staff were available. In brief, the Calman-Hine Committee could not demonstrate rigorously that the care system it proposed would be the best that could actually be achieved within the NHS.[23] The result was a set of general proposals rather than a blueprint, based on consensus rather than conclusive evidence. While those proposals seem likely to improve the quality of care on offer, they may nevertheless be undermined by subsequent additions to clinical knowledge.

One central issue considered by the Calman-Hine Committee is the relationship if any between the size of the hospital (or a particular specialty) and the quality of its clinical performance. Research on these issues has been summarised by the NHS Centre for Reviews and Dissemination (CRD)[24] in the following terms:

*The evidence is inadequate to offer guidance on the possible causes of any positive relationships which may exist in particular procedures between volume and outcome, and this is a significant problem in interpreting the evidence in a policy context (p.11).*

This tentative conclusion reflects the very modest effort that has been devoted to issues of this sort since the foundation of the NHS. In general, specialisation has been taken to be a *sine qua non* of improvement and very little research has been done on it within the UK – the CRD review relied very heavily upon studies from the USA as to the most clinically and cost-effective scale for the specialties which a general hospital comprises as well as the hospital itself. Not surprisingly, therefore, many of the recommendations put forward in the London Implementation Group service reviews were based primarily on professional judgement rather than systematic evaluation.

What the optimum balance is between specialists and generalists within the hospital service remains moot, as a recent report[25] from the Royal College of Physicians recognised:

*There is little firm evidence about whether [patients] have a better outcome when they are treated by a specialist physician or a general one (para.4.24).*

This gap reflects a general lack of research linking the way that hospitals are staffed and the results they achieve in terms of outcomes for patients. There has been some work in the USA[26] on the links between nurse staffing at hospital level and outcomes for patients but none has been completed so far in the UK although some is underway. Recent work on medical staffing levels[27] has suggested that higher levels of staffing are linked to better outcomes for patients admitted as emergencies. But precisely because this work is focused on one profession at a time, it cannot reveal what the best mix of professional skills may be.

Given this uncertainty, it is hard to define the best way of providing hospital services, particularly for the admission and management of acutely ill patients. But the basis on which decisions have to be made about the way services should be provided is itself changing as we showed in Chapter 2. Some factors, such as demography, are slow moving and relatively well understood. Others, such as the implications of information technology or advances in genetic testing for new forms of service delivery, the implications of social and economic change for recruitment and retention, or the impact of an ever growing volume of clinical knowledge are not.

These forces pull in different directions. For example, currently the growth in medical knowledge and the specialisation which it produces, together with changes in junior doctors' hours and the reforms of medical staff training are pushing in the direction of making hospitals ever larger. So too are concerns about quality of decision-making and care by relatively inexperienced staff. On the other hand, developments in medical and information technology are making new forms of work clinically feasible by allowing those in small hospitals or in the community to access specialist advice at a distance. These, together with the development of new professional roles, mean that new options are developing. For example, effective IT links may allow ambulance staff to make decisions which they could not make unsupported as to whether and where someone needs hospital care. This may in turn allow them to seek other sources of help than the hospital itself such as district nurses or even social carers.

Thus the current situation, as far as the overall health care system is concerned, is one of considerable uncertainty and change. There is no substantial body of knowledge on which to base a firm view as to what the division of work should be between hospitals of different sizes, between hospitals and community-based services and between different skills within both. Although a great deal of detailed research and practical experimentation has been done which bears on these issues, there is currently no one place where all the elements are brought together. This is particularly true of emergency medical care, which recent experience at times of winter peak demand suggests is not well designed as a care system in its own right to meet unexpected pressures upon it.

In this situation, planning of future hospitals is extremely difficult. Searching for reduction in the costs of hospital provision, the present Government has, as we saw in Chapter 5, largely committed itself to the private finance route. However, the schemes, which have been developed and accepted via this route, have been designed largely in a vacuum. Furthermore, *The Capital Strategy for the Department of Health*,[28] published in 1998 – the first of its kind for the NHS – failed to link the capital programme with the factors making for changes in the way that health care is delivered.

This gap reflects the fact that there is no substantial source of expertise at the Centre on such issues as likely future activity levels, particularly in emergency medical care, the implications of new technologies for hospital services and the interrelationship between physical design and the level of clinical costs and outcomes and the practical scope for appropriately shifting care from hospital to community – and vice versa.

There are some glimmers of light. The report of the National Bed Inquiry from the Department of Health, published in early 2000, represents the first official attempt to consider the role of the hospital for 20 years. Furthermore, a new R&D programme, Service Delivery and Organisation, has been launched recently which is likely to look at some of the issues considered in this chapter.

## Central and local roles

The gaps in knowledge described above and the implication of technical and other change undermine confidence in any single view of the future and any attempt to devise a national blueprint such as that set out for hospitals in the 1960s. However, if change is inevitable but its nature is unclear, how should the task of designing the broad pattern of services be tackled? In particular, what should the roles of the individual NHS trust or primary care group be at local level and what should be the role of the Centre, in working out how best to provide care given the lack of information on which to base decisions?

As things currently stand, there is a confusion of roles as to which level of the NHS is meant to shape which services. This emerged clearly from the Audit Commission's study of specialised services:[29]

> In the NHS, there are inconsistencies in the relationship between the Centre and local health authorities. Recent policy statements have emphasised the responsibility of clinicians and commissioners locally to make decisions about priorities for healthcare and the general approach has been a 'light touch from the Centre'. But at the same time, the NHS Executive has been prescriptive in a few high-profile areas, such as the number of beds that health authorities fund for paediatric intensive care (p.99).

The New NHS envisages an enlargement of the central role in relation to the major service areas to be covered in national service frameworks as well as in the narrow range of services covered by the National Commissioning Advisory Group but leaves unresolved how these frameworks should relate to each other and what the scope for local variation should be in these and other parts of the Service. Instead, different parts of the White Paper make a series of different and apparently unrelated proposals as to how services should be designed. In some places it emphasises the scope for experimentation and the involvement of local NHS organisations, for example through health improvement programmes, in others it emphasises the national role.

Given the inevitable lack of a single agreed vision of the future pattern of services, some division of roles should continue. If the Centre cannot be confident what the precise pattern of future services should be, because of the vast range of factors bearing on service delivery and the range of local circumstances which the NHS has to deal with, then the task must in part at least pass down to the local NHS, as it does now, to experiment and learn from those experiments. Where such lack of confidence extends to whole services because the evidence is weak, then it is appropriate to organise larger scale experiments by deliberately encouraging and evaluating different service designs in different parts of the country.

While it might seem desirable to define a precise division of roles between the Centre and the local NHS, in practice that is very hard to do: as in other policy areas, the boundary is likely to prove flexible. The critical requirement therefore is that the NHS has the capacity at the Centre or within the local NHS to make reasoned judgements on future patterns of provision. In the final section of this chapter we make some suggestions designed to enhance that capacity.

## Conclusion

We have shown in this chapter that the tasks of system design and service have been persistently neglected. The recent introduction of national service frameworks represents an important first step in making good this deficiency and there are signs of progress within the NHS R&D programme. But as the National Bed Inquiry has shown there is a long way to go before the Centre has available for its own use or for use by the local NHS, a sound evidence base for tackling the questions set out above (p.121): how best to group clinical facilities and link the elements together into integrated systems of care.

The range of factors to be considered is enormous and the way they interrelate highly complex. There is no quick route to defining with confidence a single best health care delivery system. Nevertheless, some progress can be made towards improving the NHS's capacity to handle this central task. We suggest:

- an enhanced national and regional capacity to monitor the full range of developments bearing on the broad pattern of service delivery. This might require a new NHS Executive body combining the roles of the Emergency Services Action Team and the National Patient Access Team (which focuses on waiting lists and elective care) which would have at its disposal all the available data whether routinely collected or not. At the moment, even the most elementary kinds of information about, for example, the changes taking place in the way hospital services are provided are very poorly described in official statistics and what data exists is poorly integrated. This national and regional capacity would provide localities with guidelines and technical support on how to plan local services

- an enhanced capacity for learning from local experience through better exchange of experience between different parts of the NHS. A start has been made here with the work of the Emergency Services Action Team and the National Patient Access Team but a general capacity needs to be systematically developed. The formation of the NHS Learning Network[30] is a useful start

- a requirement for the Centre to develop the capacity to take account of the links between the policies it develops which bear on service delivery, e.g. the links between changes in junior doctors' hours and the roles of consultants and the structure of hospital services and the incentives facing primary care providers and purchasers

- development of a capacity to design, implement and evaluate major national experiments, i.e. at hospital or whole service level where there is major uncertainty as to the best way to provide a service or where new ideas can only be tested 'on the ground'

- a greater emphasis in the NHS R&D programme on the large-scale aspects of service delivery and issues such as the appropriate degree of specialisation within the medical profession and the corresponding degree of specialisation within the hospital.

## References

1. Ministry of Health – Consultative Council on Medical and Allied Services. *The Dawson report on the future provision of medical and allied services 1920: an interim report to the Minister of Health*. London: King Edward's Hospital Fund for London, 1950.
2. Ministry of Health. *A Hospital Plan for England and Wales*. Cmnd. 1604. London: HMSO, 1962.
3. Merrison, Sir Alex (chair). *Report of the Royal Commission on National Health Service*. London: HMSO, 1979.

4. Department of Health and Social Security. *Hospital Services: the future pattern of hospital provision in England: a consultation paper.* London: HMSO, 1980.

5. Tomlinson, Sir Bernard (chair). *Report of the Inquiry into London's Health Service, Medical Education and Research.* London: HMSO, 1992.

6. Turnberg L (chair). *Health services in London: strategic review ('the Turnberg report').* London: Department of Health, 1998.

7. London Implementation Group. *Reports of an independent review of specialist services: cancer, neurosciences, plastics and burns, cardiac, renal and children.* London: Department of Health, 1993

8. South East Thames Regional Health Authority. *Shaping the Future: a review of acute services.* Bexhill-on-sea: SETRHA, 1991.
   Dixon P, Gatherer R and Pollock A. *Hospital Services for the 21st Century: a report to Oxford Regional Health Authority.* Reading: West Berkshire Health Authority, 1992.

9. Fulop NJ, Hood S and Parsons S. Does the national health service want hospital-at-home. *Journal of the Royal Society of Medicine* 1997; 90: 212–15.

10. Audit Commission. *What the doctor ordered: a study of GP fundholders in England and Wales.* London: HMSO, 1996.

11. Clinical Standards Advisory Group. *Community health care for elderly people.* London: Stationery Office, 1998.

12. Vaughan B and Lathlean J. *Intermediate care: models in practice.* London: King's Fund Publishing, 1999.

13. Audit Commission. *Coming of Age: improving care services for older people 1997.* London: HMSO, 1997.

14. Department of Health. *A Policy Framework for Commissioning Cancer Services: a report by the expert advisory group on cancer to the Chief Medical Officers of England and Wales (Calman-Hine).* London: HMSO, 1995.

15. Audit Commission. *United they stand: co-ordinating care for elderly patients with hip-fracture.* London: HMSO, 1995.

16. See n.10 above.

17. Department of Health. *Choice and opportunity: primary care: the future.* Cm. 3390. London: HMSO, 1996.

18. Jenkins C. Primary Care Act Pilots. In: *Health Care UK 1999/2000.* London: King's Fund Publishing, 1999.

19. Royal College of Surgeons. *Report of the Working Party on Head Injuries.* London, 1986.

20. Department of Health – Emergency Services Action Team. *Emergency Services Action Team 1998 Report.* London: Department of Health, 1998.

21. NHS Executive. *Additional Resources in 1998/1999 for whole systems action to support sustained reductions in NHS waiting lists* (HSC1998/096).

22. Cancer Collaboration. *The Workforce and Training Implications of the Calman-Hine Cancer Report.* London: King's Fund Publishing, 1997.

23. Harrison A. National Service Frameworks. In: Klein R. *Implementing the White Paper: Pitfalls & opportunities.* London: King's Fund Publishing, 1998.

24. NHS Centre for Reviews and Dissemination. *Relationship between volume and quality of health care: a review of the literature 1995.* York: University of York NHS CRD, 1995.

25. Royal College of Physicians. *Future Patterns of care by general and specialist physicians: meeting the needs of adult patients in the UK*. London, 1996.

26. Aitken LH, Slone DM and Sochalski J. Hospital organizations and outcomes. *Quality in Health Care* 1998; 7(4): 222–26.

27. Jarman B, Gault S, Alves B *et al*. Explaining differences in English hospital death rates using routinely collected data. *BMJ* 1999; 318: 1515–20.

28. Department of Health. *Capital investment strategy for the Department of Health*. Leeds: Department of Health, 1999.

29. Audit Commission. *Higher Purchase*. London: Audit Commission, 1997.

30. Langlands A. Learning the Steps. *NHS Magazine* 1999; 17: 16–18.

# Chapter 7

# Organising systems of care

In the previous chapter, we argued that the NHS has not devoted enough attention to the key function of designing systems of care. This failure can be in part explained by professional and cultural barriers such as those between hospital- and community-based doctors or between different clinical professions. But it also reflects organisational boundaries between the various elements that a broad service such as care for elderly people requires. Such boundaries have been reinforced by the way that finance has flowed down in separate streams, e.g. one for hospital and community services and one for general medical services, with separate rules governing each and, because finance and accountability are so closely linked, separate lines of accountability.

In this chapter we take a closer look at some of the barriers preventing effective linkages between NHS organisations and thus preventing an effective 'whole system of care' from operating. As we show in the first part of this chapter, the fact that the various elements which comprise the NHS have not always worked well together has been a constant source of concern to policy-makers. But the approaches adopted have changed radically in recent years. From the 1950s through to the 1980s, successive reorganisations aimed to bring about administrative unification of the *supervision* of provider organisations but not the providers themselves. From the 1980s onwards, the emphasis switched in two ways. First, the functions of purchasing and providing care were distinguished and put into new and separate forms of organisation, health authorities and NHS trusts, and second, primary care providers were able, within bounds, to create their own organisational forms such as out-of-hours co-operatives in response to local circumstances. The second part of this chapter describes these developments in more detail.

The final section argues that although these changes have led to a more flexible NHS, better able than its predecessors to adapt to the changing requirements of health care delivery, they have not fully removed the organisational barriers to integrating whole systems of care. Moreover, the recognition of the need to design services nationally – which we argued in the previous chapter represented a significant improvement – remains hard to reconcile with the structure and responsibilities of locally-based organisations. We conclude with some recommendations.

## A divided service

As noted in the previous chapter, throughout the life of the NHS, two questions have remained difficult to answer:

- which elements of the Service should be grouped together in the same organisations?
- how should the different elements that it comprises link to each other?

Historically, the bulk of health care services have been financed and administered in three large service groupings, hospital, general practice and community services, each with its own different geographical focus and administrative identity. One result has been that the organisation – for example the hospital or the GP practice – has been taken to be synonymous with a particular group of services. Within each, particularly hospitals and community services, groupings have been based on the professions providing care such as health visiting, on the patient group such as paediatrics, on broad service category such as general surgery, or on a particular disease or part of the body such as cardiology.

When the NHS was established, the three broad groups – the hospital service, general practice, and community health services – each had their own distinct organisation and roles. With some exceptions, each had a geographical focus – it was assumed that each administrative grouping should serve a particular area. However, the services themselves embodied different geographical concepts – the practice served a registered mainly local population while hospitals served a wider catchment area. Community services, still the responsibility of local authorities, focused on the geographical areas which these authorities represented.

This tripartite structure reflected the way in which responsibility for health care had developed in the first half of the 20th century and also the deep divisions within the medical profession between hospital and community-based physicians and between medical and other clinical skills such as nursing. These divisions were in effect confirmed by the organisational structures within which each worked.

Not only were the three groups of service embedded in separate organisations, but the organisations were of different types. General practitioners remained quasi-independent, working almost entirely in small, sometimes one-person organisations, and were to be found in large towns as well as villages in rural areas. Hospitals on the other hand were relatively large scale, employing large numbers of professionals on a small number of sites: teaching hospitals had their own boards of governors and in this sense were quasi-independent too: other hospitals reported to hospital boards. Community health services came in-between these two. Their units of organisation were normally much larger than a practice and smaller than a hospital.

The administrative supervision of the three main elements was itself originally divided between different organisations (see Figure 7.1). That division was perceived in the early days of the NHS as providing a fundamental obstacle to an efficient service. Indeed, for much of the NHS's existence, issues of organisation have largely been seen in terms of the need to bring together the disparate parts of the Service both at local level and within the supervisory structure at national or regional level within a unified supervisory structure.

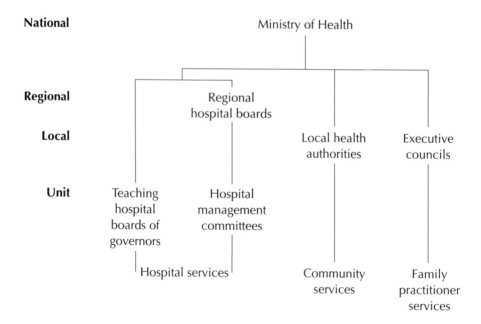

**Figure 7.1:** The NHS 1948–74

The Guillebaud Committee[1] in the 1950s concluded:

*Many people, both before and after the Appointed Day, have criticised the tripartite structure of the National Health Service because of:*

*a) the difficulty of integrating the services provided by the three branches of the National Health Service, particularly in relation to the maternity and child welfare, tuberculosis, mental and aged sick services;*

*b) the danger of duplication and overlapping between the three branches of the Service;*

*c) the difficulty of adjusting priorities within the Health Service, when three separate administrative organisations – two ... financed wholly by the Exchequer and the third ... partly by the Exchequer and partly by the local rates – are responsible for the provision of the services;*

*d) the danger that the Service may develop into a National Hospital Service, with all the emphasis on curative medicine, instead of a National Health Service in which prevention will play as important a part as cure* (p.54).

Despite what appears to be a damning critique of the then current pattern of organisation, the Committee concluded that organisational change was premature in what was then a young Service. But the issues it identified continued to worry those concerned about the efficiency of the Service. In the next decade, a series of essays[2] edited by David Owen and published in 1968 argued:

*What gives cause for more concern is the persistent evidence that because of the system's inherent inefficiencies, patients themselves suffer, falling victims to the divided responsibility and isolation that all too frequently reduces the concept of community care to an illusion. It would be extraordinary for any major industry, whether manufacturing or service, to retain unchanged its administrative structure for over 20 years. Yet this is exactly the situation which has existed within the NHS* (p.8).

The solution he and his colleagues put forward would have led to a unification, in administrative terms, of all clinical services, i.e. a merger of hospital and community clinical staff, and with other support and welfare services under the same broad umbrella (see Figure 7.2). This distinction between clinical and support services found no favour, although it was to re-emerge, albeit in a partial form, within the private finance initiative some 30 years later.

|  | **Functions** | **Personnel** |
|---|---|---|
| **Clinical services** | Treatment and prevention | Doctors<br>Nurses, in-patient and community<br>Ancillary medical staff:<br>Physiotherapists<br>Pharmacists<br>Pathology technicians, etc. |
| **Administrative services** | Residential accommodation, facilities for clinics, equipment, etc. | Managerial, maintenance clerical, etc. |
| **Welfare services** | Social work and welfare, welfare for sick, aged and disabled in the community and their families | Social workers, including those now hospital-based, and those in local health authorities |

**Figure 7.2:** An alternative structure for local services

A Green Paper, *The Administrative Structure of the Medical and Related Services in England and Wales* published by the Ministry of Health[3] in 1968 accepted that services needed to be brought together:

> ... *a new administrative structure is required. The authorities of the future should have wide scope to bring together the related services* (p.12).

A second Green Paper *The Future Structure of the National Health Service*[4] continued in the same vein, arguing that '...more could be achieved if the service were not still divided into three parts' (p.2). The proposals it went on to set out were designed:

> *To unite the National Health Service. Not only must the different branches be controlled by the same authority but the separate services must be integrated at the local level* (p.2).

The subsequent White Paper, *National Health Service Reorganisation: England*[5] accepted these objectives:

> *The National Health Service should be a single service. Its separate parts are intended to complement one another, and not to function as self-sufficient entities* (p.1).

In the event, the goal of a single service was not achieved by the 1974 reforms. The health services that had hitherto been the responsibility of local government were brought together with the hospital service, but primary care remained distinct in administrative terms. As a result (see Figure 7.3) the NHS became a bipartite service.

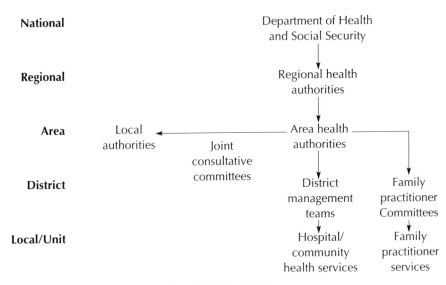

**Figure 7.3:** The structure of the NHS in 1974

Although the 1974 changes were designed to improve the linkages between services, at the same time, they were also aimed at reducing what were seen as inappropriate supervisory structures. Richard Crossman,[6] when Secretary of State, referred in evidence to the Royal Commission to:

> *... the insensitivity of the health service to local feeling and patient criticism, the remoteness of the service, its bureaucratic nature, its refusal to understand local needs, the setting up of hospitals with no transport to them, the creation of great marble palaces and the closing down of well-loved and small hospitals* (p.312).

The Royal Commission agreed with this view, arguing for the removal of one administrative tier, the area health authority – which the Conservatives carried out in the 1980s – and for the integration of Family Practitioner Committees (responsible for the administration of general practices) with health authorities, which they carried out in the 1990s (see Figure 7.4).

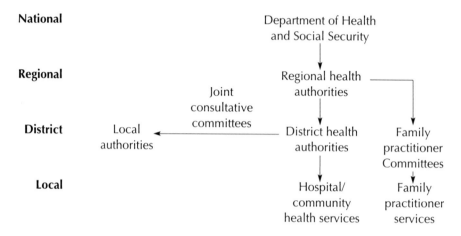

**Figure 7.4:** The structure of the NHS, 1983–1991

As this brief account suggests, for most of the life of the NHS, the main focus of concern about organisation of health care delivery was primarily on its administrative structure – in particular whether there should be a single or several hierarchies, how many tiers each hierarchy should have, the size of the areas which each element of the hierarchy should be responsible for, and whether the areas they covered should be geographically similar, and finally the appropriate groupings within those hierarchies, for example whether primary care should be part of the same hierarchy as hospital services or not. There was less focus on the incentives to link the services offered by different NHS providers – a fact which goes a long way to explaining why the links between them were typically poor.

Neither the papers from the DHSS nor the Royal Commission considered whether the basic structure of general practice was appropriate to the Service of the future, nor whether the changes already apparent at that time in the way that hospital services were provided could be accommodated in the administrative structures they proposed. In the official papers cited above, getting the links between services made effectively and avoiding duplication were assumed to follow from getting the administrative organisation of the Service right in terms of groupings and hierarchies.

Resolving all these issues was almost entirely a central matter, since only the Centre could change administrative structures, boundaries and responsibilities. Localities enjoyed some degree of freedom over internal administrative arrangements – though even here the 1972 DHSS guidance *Management Arrangements for the Reorganised National Health Services*[7] set out in fine detail the way the new authorities should be structured. The way clinical services were provided in hospitals was not set down in this way. Similarly, GPs were free to make whatever arrangements they wanted for their own 'businesses'. But responsibility for the broad structure of the NHS, as well as the roles governing the framework within which GPs operated – the famous 'red book' – was almost entirely a central matter. This way of thinking about the organisation of the NHS started to crumble with the introduction of the NHS and Community Care Act 1990.

## New directions

The 1990 Act changed the emphasis on hierarchical structures in three ways. First, two separate hierarchies were introduced, based on a division of functions between purchasing and provision which, within the NHS, had not been perceived as an option until shortly before the Act came into effect. Second, new provider organisations were established – NHS trusts – which were intended to enjoy substantial day-to-day independence of the supervisory hierarchy. Third, a new function, general practitioner fundholding, was introduced to general practice. This offered direct control, to the practices volunteering to participate, over part of the hospital and community health services budget, thereby creating a link between primary and secondary care based on contracting rather than the integration of the administrative structures supervising general practice and hospital care.

At the same time, the supervisory structure was itself altered. Although the process was not carried out immediately, by 1996 an entirely new structure was in place, which finally brought together the three elements of the old tripartite structure (see Figure 7.5). In particular, family health service authorities merged with health authorities to create a unified administrative structure. However, while the new supervisory structure looked simpler than its predecessor did, the opposite was true for the provider organisations that were to be supervised. Here the new arrangements introduced diversity rather than uniformity and they increased the number of organisations to be supervised, with each district health authority being divided into two or more providers and GP fundholders effectively becoming, at least for their purchasing roles, organisations in their own right.

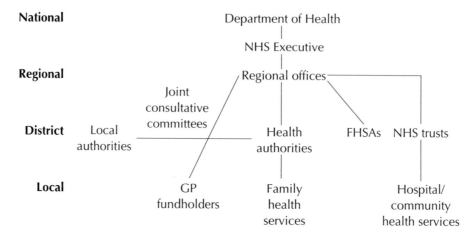

**Figure 7.5:** The structure of the NHS 1991–96

Furthermore, although this restructuring, as before, was a central responsibility, the pace and the precise pattern of change allowed some local variation. Although it rapidly became the norm, NHS trust status was initially sought and offered to only a small number of providers of secondary and community health services. By the time that Labour came to power in 1997, GP fundholding had established itself in only half the country. Although there were strong incentives and pressures for GPs to become fundholders, the pace of change depended critically on their readiness to 'sign up'. Not only was the pace different across the country, but in some areas fundholders began to create new forms of organisation by merging management functions in so-called 'multi-funds'. In other areas, non-fundholders began to form locality commissioning groups, advising health authorities on commissioning but not holding a budget directly. And in others they formed co-operatives to provide out-of-hours services. So although the process was managed centrally, the pattern of organisation on the ground – the division of purchasing functions – and to a lesser extent the pattern of provision, was strongly influenced by local circumstances.

In introducing these changes, the then Government did not explicitly abandon the quest to link together the various elements comprising the NHS. A pamphlet issued by the NHS Executive in 1991, *Integrating Primary and Secondary Care*,[8] emphasised the same themes as had Guillebaud decades before:

- seamless patient care
- an effective balance between prevention and treatment

- an effective balance between primary, community and hospital-based care
- better collaboration between health professionals, and between professionals and managers
- more effective use of resources.

This brief paper described in summary terms a wide range of measures that would promote integration of services, including developing information systems and greater joint working between district health authorities and FHSAs encouraged by joint appointments.

However, the Government's emphasis on other objectives, specifically greater efficiency in service delivery in the individual parts of the Service, clearly worked the other way. This was particularly true of NHS trusts, the advantages of which were described, in the Working Paper[9] published before the Act was implemented, as follows:

- a stronger sense of local ownership and pride
- encouragement of local initiative
- an increase in choice
- greater competition
- improved quality of service
- increased efficiency.

The main emphasis was clearly on the effectiveness of NHS trusts as quasi-autonomous organisations rather than their role in the larger NHS and their links with other services. The independence and freedom of that status would, it was hoped, promote service innovation and encourage competition rather than collaboration between providers.

What limited evidence there is[10] suggests that these aims were achieved only to a very limited degree. Whatever the merits of trust status, however, it seems clear that the creation of NHS trusts worked to harden the boundaries between different parts of the NHS and hence work against effective linking of services such as those for elderly people where, as noted in the previous chapter, contributions from a range of providers have to be combined. The financial and other incentives facing trusts, particularly those providing acute care, were more tightly defined than those facing their predecessor organisations and indeed intentionally so. Not only were trust boards charged with meeting specific financial targets, they were also required to meet activity targets set by national policy on waiting times for elective care and make their locally determined contribution to meeting the requirements of the NHS efficiency index. This created a series of incentives that did not necessarily coincide with the needs of the local Service as a whole. For example, they created a disincentive to transfer activity to other settings, however suitable those might be, and a positive incentive to increase activity in terms of episodes, a currency which, as noted elsewhere, few could have total confidence in.

In principle, however, the creation of free-standing purchasers – health authorities and GP fundholders – might have worked to overcome these pressures. However, the scope for purchasers to determine the way that services work across boundaries has in practice been limited. As noted in the previous chapter, purchasers have not been able in the face of powerful providers to impose themselves by designing services to their own specification. In effect it is arguable that the distinction between purchasing and providing, although apparently clear, in practice was not. The system and service design functions identified in the previous chapter fell somewhere between the two: purchasers may have had the responsibility but the providers had the knowledge. And as the evidence cited in the previous chapter indicated, the resulting gap has been only partially filled. Furthermore, financial, professional and cultural barriers to working across the secondary/primary/community organisational interface remained.

However, the introduction of a separation between purchasing and providing did open the way for new ways of managing services, through contracts rather than administrative integration. In some parts of the country, health authority purchasers used providers to manage contracts which themselves ran across more than one provider (see Figure 7.6).

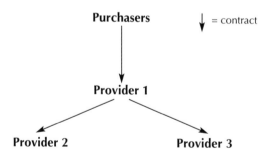

**Figure 7.6:** Providers as purchasers

This form of 'provider–purchaser' emerged for services such as paediatrics, maternity and elderly care, which ran across the boundaries of NHS trusts. In some cases, its use led to changes of ownership of hospital assets through transfers to community trusts. In others, they have been arranged through contracts under the control of community trusts without transfer of assets.

Such arrangements were far from universal, but they demonstrate that the structures created by the 1990 Act created the opportunity for a unified management structure, which did not rely on change in organisational boundaries in provider or administrative structures, and which stem largely from local initiative. The general point that follows is that contracts and organisational change are to some degree a substitute for each other, as means of integrating systems of care. Paradoxically, the 1991 reforms encouraged fragmentation – by encouraging hospital trusts in particular to promote their own objectives – and integration – through the contracting mechanism.

Thus, even if the introduction of the purchaser–provider split did not have a fundamental impact in terms of its original objective of promoting competition and reducing provider domination, viewed from another perspective it can be seen as part of a broader revolution in the way that health care services are structured and managed. It is, in other words, a piece of new administrative technology that allowed new thinking about organisational structures which were not part of the NHS's mental tool-kit up to the 1980s. *The New NHS* explicitly acknowledged that the purchaser – provider split was worth keeping even though the evidence for its value is, like that for trust status, limited. As a result, the NHS retains a much greater range of options for organising and managing service delivery than it has ever had.

## From competition to collaboration

The Labour Government came to power committed to the abolition of competition. Instead, *The New NHS* emphasises co-operation and partnership within the NHS and between the NHS and other agencies and backs this rhetoric up with the introduction in the Health Act 1999 of a statutory duty for health and local authorities to work together. The annual contracting framework of the 1990 Act was to be replaced by long-term service agreements. Furthermore, the Government has introduced new mechanisms such as health improvement plans, which offer an administrative framework for integrating care across organisational boundaries (see Figure 7.7). But they do not bear on some of the key organisational obstacles to service integration noted above.

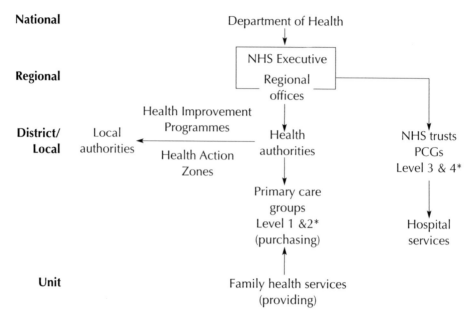

**National**

Department of Health

NHS Executive
**Regional**       Regional
offices

Health Improvement
Programmes
**District/**   Local                                 Health              NHS trusts
**Local**   authorities                           authorities            PCGs
Health Action                                    Level 3 & 4*
Zones

Primary care
groups
Level 1 &2*                            Hospital
(purchasing)                           services

**Unit**                      Family health services
(providing)

\* The levels represent stages in the development of primary care groups from
advisers on commissioning to independent primary care trusts responsible for
both commissioning and providing.

**Figure 7.7:** The structure of the NHS 1998–

## Trusts

*The New NHS* supports the continuation of NHS trusts and indeed proposes
their extension into primary care in the form of primary care trusts. But it fails
to address the tension between the effective management of the parts – trusts
and general practices – and effective working across the boundaries of those
parts which the design and implementation of systems of care requires.
This tension will grow as the number of national service frameworks increases
and the strength of the interconnections between the parts of the Service grows.

The nature of the difficulties involved in providing services that run across
trust boundaries emerged from the report into the failure of the cervical
screening programme at the Kent and Canterbury Hospitals NHS Trust[11]
which brought out the difficulty of running a nationally determined structure
within a local form of organisation. The report argued that:

> A national screening programme requires special organisational arrangements
> to ensure the integration of the various elements of the programme, to set and
> monitor standards and to achieve adequate quality assurance. These requirements sit
> uneasily with the recent NHS emphasis on devolution, local priority determination
> and the separation of responsibility for different bits of the programme (p.39).

It went on to suggest that:

> *National consideration should be given as to whether the existing accountability of senior NHS trust managers is sufficiently clear and properly exercised* (p.39).

The screening programme is well defined and highly focused but, as this investigation brought out, how it should be run was not clear to those nominally responsible for it in each locality, and the central direction of the programme was weak at the time the failures were identified. Screening is, however, a much simpler area of activity than cancer care or any other major disease or client group, for which national service frameworks are to be designed. The latter will involve close links between professionals in what are now different organisations and within both secondary and primary care. national service frameworks imply a strong central role in the design of services, and also in their monitoring. Internal and external clinical audit will also have to follow the service and hence be carried out across existing organisational boundaries.

As we showed in the previous chapter, the notion that services should be designed and hence managed as 'systems of care' comprising elements from different parts of the hospital service, as well as the community is gaining general acceptance. In *Future Patterns of Medical Care*,[12] the Standing Medical Advisory Committee recognised that these developments had organisational implications:

> *For some clinical services Trust boundaries are an obstacle to the efficient and effective delivery of specialist care. The present competition for contracts discourages collaboration between Trusts and encourages inappropriate developments to meet unsustainable ambitions. Greater collaboration will be required if the right balance is to be struck between accessibility of the service to patients and availability of good quality of care 24 hours a day. There are several models for practical collaboration including hub and spoke and network. The choice depends on which model is most appropriate for the particular task. Commissioners of secondary care have a crucial role in the local implementation of this policy and should be encouraged to facilitate integrated care management, particularly for emergencies. Clinicians from primary, secondary and tertiary care must be involved in this process* (para.3.1).

If systems of care do develop in this way, the question arises as to whether NHS trusts in their present form are the appropriate organisational form for managing and accounting for them. The proposals in *The New NHS* for a new legal duty for quality to be placed on trust chief executives do not deal with the effective *interdependence* of trusts which a nationally defined service implies and hence the possibility of competing lines of accountability.

As things currently stand, some of the clinicians contributing to a service such as cancer care, for which a national service framework exists, perform other functions within their hospitals as well. It may not make sense to introduce a new organisational boundary for this one service. But the greater the emphasis on the specific system of care, the greater the pressure will be to create a 'hard' or organisational boundary round the service itself, for which its clinical managers would be accountable. The logic of the arguments that lead to services running across trust boundaries suggests that they might be self-organising, contracting for the specific hospital and other resources they require, and accountable at national level for their clinical and financial performance.

Recognising this, *The New NHS*[13] states:

> *Efficiency will be enhanced through incentives at both NHS Trust and clinical team level. Many NHS Trusts already devolve budgetary responsibility for clinical teams and involve senior professionals from them directly in the management of the NHS Trust … Increasingly, clinical teams will develop and agree the new longer-term service agreements with Primary Care Groups. Clinician to clinician partnerships will focus service agreements on securing genuine health gain. The efficiency incentives that come with budgetary responsibility will be reinforced by longer-term service agreements that allow a share of any savings made to be re-deployed by the clinical teams, in a way consistent with the NHS Trust's priorities and the local health improvement programme (para.6.21).*

The final sentence of the paragraph hints at opportunities for clinical teams to become budgetary units in their own right – as some groups of hospital services did during the experiments in the 1980s with resource management. But it also highlights the tensions between the interests of clinical teams, those of the Service – as defined within a health improvement programme – and existing trust structures, on which both financial and clinical governance requirements rest. Reconciling them will require more sophisticated costing and contracting arrangements than are currently the norm, a point we return to below.

## Primary care

While the NHS and Community Care Act 1990 radically changed the organisational structure of hospital and community services, it left the organisational structure of primary care provision fundamentally unchanged. Instead a new function was grafted on to it, that of purchasing secondary care, at the practice level. The introduction of GP fundholding in the NHS and Community Care Act 1990 was intended to 'improve the quality of services on offer to patients, to stimulate hospitals to be more responsive to the needs of GPs and their patients and to develop their own practices for the benefit of their patients'.[14] However, the working paper which set out these benefits did not propose change in the organisation of general practice. Throughout the 1990 reforms general practice therefore continued to be based on partnership between doctors, with other professions generally not directly involved in the management of the small-scale 'business'.

However, as noted above, fundholding led to a number of developments for which the 1990 Act had made no specific provision such as 'multi-funds' sharing management and other services, or co-operatives, to deal with the pressure of night time calls. Many of these were not formally part of general practice 'organisation' but developed locally because the practice was not an efficient size or organisational unit for these activities. Furthermore, where fundholding did not develop, a variety of ways emerged for linking GPs into the purchasing role through locality commissioning and a series of similar arrangements.

None of this significantly changed the nature of the basic organisational unit, the practice, or its medical governance, but in contrast to the creation of NHS trusts, most of these changes came about as a result of local initiative. The Centre confined itself to setting a lower limit to the size of practice that could fully participate in fundholding and the scope of the services to be purchased, while maintaining the 'red book' rules for practice finance and administration.

The 'listening exercise' noted in the previous chapter led to the White Paper *Choice and Opportunity*[15] which embodied the recognition that the existing structure of general practice and the constraints and incentives it faced was not appropriate to the future, in particular:

- incomers to the profession often did not want principal status since they did not want the lifetime commitment it required

- the hierarchical practice structure based on leadership by the medical profession role did not allow other professional leadership roles to develop.

*Choice and Opportunity* and its successor *Delivering the Future*[16] argued for what was in effect a deregulation of general practice, with the express aim of allowing for new organisational forms to develop and for new professional roles to emerge. The Primary Care Act 1997 provided the basis for such a deregulation, albeit on a pilot basis. As the pilot approach implies however, what should be put in place of the existing structure was far from clear: there were no models tried and tested by previous research. Not surprisingly therefore, a number of different types of organisation have emerged from the 'bidding' process for support under the Act, including nurse-led primary care organisations and locally determined contracts for GPs. The new Government has continued these experiments and announced further waves of pilot schemes.

We suggested in the previous chapter that this approach represents a sensible response to lack of knowledge or even experience of different ways of providing services. But although the Labour Government accepted the experimental approach for the provision of primary care and pressed ahead with the 1997 Act pilots, *The New NHS* did not adopt the pilot approach for its proposals on purchasing in primary care. Instead it laid down that primary care groups would be established throughout England on the basis of 'natural communities' of some 100,000 population. However, it explicitly provided for stages in their development at local level particularly for the nature and pace of development of primary care trusts. Hence, despite the apparently blanket approach to the organisation of purchasing which the White Paper embodies, it is possible that in five years' time the NHS will continue to display a variety of purchasing and providing structures within primary care. The same might be true of the management structures administering primary care groups, some of which might contract out for these services or make shared arrangements with other groups.

Given that the form of primary care provision typified by the GP surgery is overwhelmingly local and small scale, diversity and experiment would seem an appropriate way forward. However, national service frameworks will involve a substantial primary care component, which may not fit well either with the nature or current organisation of general practice or the experimental approach typified by local pilots.

One possible implication of nationally defined systems of care running across primary and secondary providers is the development of local specialists in care for particular diseases such as diabetes, who might be contracted to the particular service and work for most of their time outside hospitals, another is the development, possibly stimulated by NHS *Direct*, of a community-based emergency medical service – in effect a 24-hour version of the out-of-hours service offered by many groups of practices already. But logical as this form of development may seem from the viewpoint of a system of care for a particular patient group or of a particular category of need, it runs counter to what many see as the essential value of general practice as it now stands – its generalist nature and the potential for continuity of contact between patient and doctor. Furthermore, it remains to be seen whether the existing divisions within primary care groups – i.e. the separate practices that form them – can effectively work together. Here too new forms of contract and incentive structure may need to be devised – as we note in Chapter 9.

Even if primary care groups do create an environment within which genuine co-operation can flourish at local level, many, by virtue of their size, will have to work on a partnership basis particularly for specialist hospital services which serve much larger populations. The trend, as we have noted, is for hospital services to serve ever-larger population groups so, with the exception of those services that are nationally commissioned, the level of partnership working will tend to rise.

The creation of primary care groups based on 'natural communities' and their potential development into primary care trusts represents in effect a primary care version of the Conservatives' approach to trust creation after the 1990 Act. That emphasised, as we noted above, the advantages of NHS trusts as quasi-autonomous bodies. Furthermore, they were established largely on the basis of existing organisations rather than on an explicit consideration of the best fit between organisational structure and the requirements of delivering whole systems of care. Similarly, new organisational structures are being created for primary and community-based services without any apparent consideration of how whole systems of care shall be delivered.

These issues are already emerging from developments in emergency care designed to deal with winter pressures on the hospital service. Winter pressures require effective working between the different elements of the local health economy. As noted in the previous chapter, the Centre has issued a large amount of advice to influence service delivery. Furthermore, with NHS *Direct*, it has introduced a new form of service, which operates largely independently of other local services and which opens the way for designing a system of emergency care that spans the entire local health economy.

But there is no obvious organisational framework within which that system could fully develop. Such a framework might emerge from the kind of local co-operation that the process of devising health improvement plans is intended to promote. But for it to work effectively will require not just clinical but also contractual and financial agreements running across the different providing interests. In turn these will have to be based on accurate and up-to-date information about the way that patients use the different services, how they might respond to service change and the financial consequences of that happening. But precisely because the NHS is still taking only tentative steps towards developing an emergency care system on these lines, this kind of information and understanding is in short supply – a point we return to in Chapter 11.

## Conclusion

Despite the large amount of change that the 1990 Act generated, the organisational structure of the NHS in the late 1990s would still be recognisable to those that created it in the 1940s, even if specific procedures and treatments provided have changed radically. The central feature of the UK NHS – the GP as gatekeeper to the hospital service – has remained virtually unchanged. This structure has been regarded as the main organisational method of managing demand and hence sacrosanct. Similarly, hospitals continue to be the major provider organisations, largely independent of the rest of the Service. The impact of the role of purchasers of whatever form, has, so far, been extremely small.

Nevertheless, the situation towards the end of the 1990s is very different to that at the end of the previous decade. The tripartite supervisory structure has at last been unified. Moreover, the way has been opened up for innovation, experiment and diversity and many of the changes that have occurred have been the result of local initiative rather than national directive. This, we believe, is entirely appropriate.

In the past, designing the organisational structure of NHS provider organisations has been almost entirely a central matter and the rules governing all NHS providers has been uniform. The same has been true for non-provider organisations, such as health authorities. That dominance was undermined by the changes resulting from the NHS and Community Care Act 1990 such as GP co-operatives and multi-funds, which happened largely spontaneously and hence in different ways, and in different parts of the country. The Primary Care Act 1997 pilots add to that diversity.

Furthermore, the introduction of contracting between health care purchasers and providers, and between providers themselves, has opened the way for a range of relationships that were undreamed of in the first three to four decades of the life of the NHS. As a result, the Service is potentially much more flexible than it has ever been, with greater scope for responding to change in the way that services should be delivered and combining different elements of service into a care system.

But at the same time, other developments such as national service frameworks and long-term service agreements are taking place, which are tending to cut across existing organisational boundaries. In the new environment that will emerge as these mechanisms come into operation, the relationships set out in Figure 7.7 will be a pale reflection of the situation on the ground. Its relative simplicity will be replaced by a complex web of systems of care based on strong contractual links between existing provider organisations.

This complexity will be the direct result of taking seriously the need to link the various elements required for effective service delivery together. But it brings in its wake new and demanding tasks – the formulation of appropriate contracting relationships – as well as tensions between alternative ways of organising the delivery of health care. The key point is that the identification noted earlier in this chapter between health care organisations and a specific group of services is beginning to break down. As *Commissioning in the New NHS*,[17] the draft guidance issued by the Centre on long-term service agreements, notes:

> *The move to a care pathway approach requires that Long-Term Service Agreements should be increasingly client/service based, rather than based on institutions* (p.13).

It goes on to say that long-term service agreements:

> *... will be dynamic, incorporating incentives for improving quality and cost-effectiveness, and as part of this, they will reflect clear responsibility for risk management, ensuring activity does not get out of kilter with funding* (p.12).

But it is far from precise as to how such agreements will be devised and what information and expertise is required to frame them.

These developments reveal a series of tensions – inherent in any way of organising health care provision:

- between preserving scope for innovation at local level and equity of provision between different areas
- between promoting innovation through incentives for particular organisations and the need for linkage between services
- promoting accountability of services run to national models within current, locally-based organisations.

These tensions present a series of difficult trade-offs, on which existing information and knowledge shed little light. As with system and service design, this gap stems from a long-standing failure to give sufficient priority to the pursuit of knowledge about, and understanding of, organisational structures and of the relative merits of different ways of linking the diverse activities that make up a system of health care delivery. Clinicians have been active in developing care protocols and guidelines for systems of care, but they have generally not concerned themselves with financial and contracting issues. But all these must be got right if effective systems of care are to be developed.

The conclusions we draw from this analysis represent an extension of those of the previous chapter.

First, the issues discussed in this chapter require greater attention from national R&D programmes than they have attracted so far. The central question of inter-organisational relationships needs to be considered in its own right, including the tensions between the development of service delivery systems based on client groups or specific service needs and the main existing organisational structures, hospitals and general practice.

Second, while the development of contracting relationships between existing organisations represents a major gain, a great deal remains to be done to find the best way of devising financial incentives which harmonise the interests of those providing a system of care for a particular group or need and those of the rest of the Service.

Third, the piloting approach allowed for in the Primary Care Act 1997 is appropriate for organisation as well as for service design but it should be far more extensive. The general requirement is that the rules governing the organisational framework for the NHS should allow new structures to emerge, at local or service level, in line with new forms of service delivery and management. This might mean that services embodying elements from a range of trusts might themselves gain a form of trust status but not necessarily under the same rules as those which apply now. For example, it might make sense for a local emergency medical service to develop, based on elements from existing providers, and with its own lines of accountability. Such trusts might be led by clinicians, provided of course that they took on the same range of duties in respect of finance, accountability and corporate governance as existing trusts. And as with any other form of innovation, their implementation should be accompanied by appropriate evaluation and dissemination of findings.

## References

1. Guillebaud CW (chair). *Report of the Committee of Enquiry into the Cost of the National Health Service*. London: HMSO, 1956.
2. Owen D (MP), editor. *A Unified Health Service*. London: Pergamon Press, 1968.
3. Ministry of Health. *National Health Service: the administrative structure of the medical and related services in England and Wales*. London: HMSO, 1968.
4. Ministry of Health. *The Future Structure of the National Health Service*. London: HMSO, 1970.
5. Ministry of Health. *National Health Service Reorganisation*. Cmnd. 5055. London: HMSO, 1972.
6. Merrison, Sir Alex (chair). *Report of the Committee of Inquiry into the Regulation of the Medical profession*. Cmnd. 6018. London: HMSO, 1975.
7. Department of Health and Social Security. *Management Arrangements for the reorganised national health service*. London: HMSO, 1972.
8. NHS Management Executive. *Integrating Primary and Secondary Health Care*. London: Department of Health, 1991.
9. Department of Health. *Self-governing hospitals – NHS Review Working Paper 1*. London: HMSO, 1989.
10. Mays N, Le Grand J and Mulligan J, editors. *Learning for the NHS internal market: a review of the evidence*. London: King's Fund Publishing, 1998.
11. NHS Executive South Thames. *Review of cervical screening services at Kent and Canterbury Hospitals NHS Trusts*. London: South Thames NHS Executive, 1997.
12. Department of Health – Standard Medical Advisory Committee. *Future patterns of medical care: a paper by the Standard Medical Advisory Committee*. London: SMAC, 1997.
13. Secretary of State for Health. *The New NHS*. London: Stationery Office, 1997.
14. Department of Health. *Funding general practice: the programme for the introduction of general practice budgets*. London: DoH, 1989.
15. Secretary of State for Health. *Choice and Opportunity*. Cm. 3390. London: HMSO, 1997.
16. Department of Health. *Primary care: delivering the future*. London: Stationery Office, 1998.
17. Health Service Circular. *Commissioning in the new NHS – Commissioning Services 1999–2000* (HSC 1998/198). London: Department of Health, 1998.

Chapter 8

# Ensuring the supply of human resources

The ideal process for determining how many staff are needed by the NHS, what their roles should be and how they should be trained would start by defining, in the light of patient needs and the nature of the services required to meet them, the knowledge and skill requirements most likely to meet those needs effectively. In other words, service and human resource planning should go hand in hand.

In practice this conjunction has proved difficult to achieve. Nearly two decades ago, a House of Commons Select Committee[1] found that:

> *Although Department of Health and Social Security guidelines clearly ask health authorities to assess the manpower implications of their service plans and to ensure that the bids they place for additional staff are related to the service developments they are planning, the two aspects of planning do not seem to mesh as happily as they should. For instance, in the Northern region, the Committee was told that Districts (health authorities) often have to change their plans because the Region has received an allocation of consultants in quite different specialties to those required for locally determined service developments (p.1).*

This extract illustrates a point that recurs later in this chapter and, indeed, in other chapters: the Centre can see in general terms what ought to be done but cannot give guidance to the local NHS in specific terms as to how to do it.

The process of linking service planning to workforce planning would be a demanding one even if conducted against the background of a clear view of the future demand for care and of the best means of meeting it. But as we showed in Chapter 6, no such view exists, nor is it likely to given the massive potential for change in the NHS's internal and external environment. Not surprisingly, therefore, the training needs of the NHS have never been systematically defined in relation to an agreed view of what the Service requires. Instead, for most of the life of the NHS, providers have worked with, in the case of medical staff, the numbers of staff allocated to them and the specific bundles of skills that have emerged from the professions themselves, while non-professional skills have been relatively neglected.

Each profession has had, and still largely retains, its own training system. The boundaries between the professions have been determined largely by internally defined criteria as to what constitutes medical or nursing work and how specialties should be defined, rather than by the nature of the work that the Service itself requires or the most efficient way of meeting a particular service need. Equally, service requirements for particular skills or combinations of skills have only rarely been systematically examined with the same rigour that applies to the determination of the appropriate intervention for a clinically defined need.

Nevertheless, over the years, attempts have been made to determine how many professionals the NHS requires. We begin this chapter by reviewing some of these – focusing particularly on doctors and nurses – and then go on to describe some recent changes in the way that the need for particular kinds of NHS staff is identified. We conclude that existing arrangements still fall short of what is required and therefore put forward a number of suggestions for improvement.

## How many?

The extract from the Select Committee quoted at the beginning of this chapter reflected the fact that as late as the 1970s, the NHS had hardly started to get to grips with the task of taking a systematic approach to defining the human resources it required. A review of workforce planning in the NHS in the late 1970s[2] recognised that it should be 'at the heart of the NHS management process' and went on to ask: 'Why has such an integrated approach to manpower planning taken so long to materialise?' (p.101).

In the authors' view: 'The answer to this question must lie primarily in the virtual absence of effective health service planning generally until the 1970s' (p.101).

In fact neither effective service planning nor integrated planning for human resources materialised in the years following this survey. The professions continued to be planned for in isolation of each other and the methods used inspired little confidence. A review by the Department of Health and Social Security Operational Research Service[3] published in 1983, of the methods available for planning the number of nurses the NHS should be training, pointed to the broad range of factors which should, in principle, be taken into account:

> ... Both recruitment and wastage in nursing are affected by national economic, educational and demographic factors. Decisions are also affected at district [i.e. health authority] level by local labour market factors such as transport, schools, the availability of alternative jobs and relative pay and conditions, and also by the geographical location of hospitals (in relation to housing areas) and of basic and post-registration courses (p.8).

But it had to recognise that the amount of information bearing on any of these was very limited:

> Due to the lack of a comprehensive information base on nurses, little is known about flows between the NHS and the independent sector or the potential supply of qualified nurses who are not currently working for the NHS, or the impact of career structures within the NHS on supply in different specialties (p.8).

Not surprisingly, it concluded that '... no single method has yet achieved widespread acceptance' (p.3).

A few years later a report from the Public Accounts Committee[4] came to similar conclusions:

> All methodologies for determining nursing manpower (sic) requirements have shortcomings. But we consider there is merit in the development of a more limited range of methods which the DHSS and the NHS could commend to health authorities. We find it surprising that this has not already been done (para.42).

The lack of an agreed method reflected the difficulty of the task but also a lack of basic information. The Department was, at the time, imposing a ceiling on nursing staff numbers but the Committee found that 'DHSS do not have the information ... to say whether there are too many or too few nurses employed in the NHS' (para.42).

As we shall see later, changes have taken place since this report was written, which introduced new organisations – the Education and Training Consortia – with responsibility for training nurses and other professionals in association with employing NHS trusts. These consortia, however, do not have at their disposal the information the Public Accounts Committee was expecting the Department to have available more than ten years ago. As noted in Chapter 5, information on staff turnover and shortages is often poor, at both local and national level and, where information exists, it is rarely well analysed: more fundamentally, there is very little research evidence bearing on the central question of how many nurses the NHS should employ, given its current and expected workload and the changes that are taking place in the way that care, particularly in hospitals, is provided.

The same is true of the medical workforce. In its 1980 report,[5] the Medical Manpower Steering Group identified a series of factors which made its task very difficult – in particular, the general uncertainty as to the future level of spending on the NHS and the nature of the services it would be delivering in the future, the potential for substitution between medical and other staff, and the risks inherent in making a massive investment in human capital of a particular kind against such an uncertain background. The report concludes:

> *Imprecision and uncertainty are inevitable in making projections about the future – indeed, any calculations of this kind which purported to be precise would be bound to be suspect. We cannot know what resources will be available to the NHS over the next 20 years or how those resources will be spent or what changes will have taken place in the demand for services and the pattern of health care delivery* (p.2).

Despite its clear identification of the spurious nature of apparently precise calculations, the report went on to conclude that '… a reasonable case can be made for either of the projections of 1.0% and 1.7% per annum' (p.33).

Given the report's own analysis, it is hard to see how such figures could inspire any confidence. The difference between them is so small, given the wide margin of uncertainty that the report itself identified.

The third report of its successor, the Medical Workforce Standing Advisory Committee[6] published towards the end of 1997 recognised the same difficulties but without being able to tackle them any better:

*32. The rate of change in the NHS has been rapid throughout the 1990s. It is extremely unlikely that anyone in, say 1975, could have anticipated the present organisational and management structure of the NHS nor many of the medical advances witnessed over the last twenty years. The further one looks into the future, the greater the extent of uncertainty. Change is likely to continue over our projection period. Uncertainty therefore plays a significant role in our thinking and in framing our recommendations (p.23).*

They go on to point out, as their predecessors had done, that they were having to work with imperfect methods and imperfect information:

*Given that the health and healthcare environment is continually changing, further consideration should be given to the likely effects on the demand for doctors of policy changes, demography, working patterns (including skill substitution) and economic factors, with a view to continuing to refine the approach and analysis in the future (p.44).*

As these extracts covering some 20 years indicate, virtually no progress has been made in estimating the numbers of doctors to be trained in terms of the 'needs of the Service'. The Advisory Committee, like its predecessor, identified with great clarity the difficulties it faced, but went on to recommend a sizeable increase in the number of doctors in training.

Unfortunately, the task is becoming more difficult. Changes in technology, demography, general clinical knowledge and the organisation of care delivery lead to or require changes in skills, new forms of training and reinvestment in new knowledge which the very notion of a profession undermines – a point we return to in Chapter 11. The 1997 Committee, however, also had to take into account changes in career patterns, which made their task even more difficult than their predecessors'. In the past, the vast majority of those trained in medical skills have remained in the profession most of their life. The old career patterns are increasingly under threat, as those entering the medical profession now see their commitment to it in a different light to their predecessors.

The changes in doctors' views of their careers noted in Chapter 2 mean that it is no longer possible to assume automatically that the vast majority of those trained will practise full-time for a 'full' working life. Moreover, the international context in which the British medical labour market works is also changing. In the past, the NHS relied heavily on doctors from the New Commonwealth staying in this country for some years after basic training.

That pattern is less common now. On the other hand, the integration of the UK and the European market is growing while changes in other countries such as the USA and South Africa have meant that doctors from other countries are more footloose than they used to be. One-third of doctors practising in the UK are now trained overseas.

These developments mean that the medical labour market is becoming more like a normal labour market with large numbers of entrants and leavers at any one point of time, the rate of both being influenced by a large range of economic, financial and social factors. The potential greater volatility which market-type behaviour tends to produce implies a need for more sophisticated understanding of how those trained to be doctors are likely to respond to the new environment. In general however monitoring of the medical workforce remains poor. As a recent analysis[7] of the human resources in the NHS requires points out:

> It would seem a self evident truth that any organisation training nearly 5000 people a year, and (including Scotland and Northern Ireland) employing nearly 100,000 highly trained specialists, would have a sophisticated mechanism in process for monitoring the careers of these vital personnel, for predicting future needs and possible excesses or shortfalls, and for deciding numbers of new trainees ... Needless to say, the NHS has almost no such mechanisms in place (pp.106–07).

The authors go on to add that ' data from general practice are so poor that primary care cannot be discussed here'.

The Specialist Workforce Advisory Group, in its 1995/96 report[8] made similar comments:

> We have [also] experienced difficulty identifying the correct baseline establishment for the various specialties, i.e. the current number of higher specialist trainees on which any expansion will build. Conflicting information was available from three sources (the census, the deans' database, and Royal College figures), and reconciling these has proved to be a major task (p.4).

Their conclusion, predictably enough, was that '... better information is needed for the future ...' (p.4).

These complaints echo those of the Pay Review Bodies, noted in Chapter 5, about the quality and quantity of the information available to them.

While information remains poor, the underlying issues identified by the Medical Manpower Steering Group 20 years ago are still to be addressed in a fundamental way. The first of these is specialisation. Part of the difficulty the Group and its successors have faced stems from the changing content of medical training, in particular the rapid development of specialisation. This trend, mirrored in other disciplines, is a natural reaction to the growth of clinical knowledge and it appears as an obvious route to the provision of better patient care. The issue, from the workforce planning point of view, is that the larger the number of specialties, the more difficult the forecasting task becomes since the 'need' for more and more sub-divisions of the workforce has to be forecast, against a highly uncertain background.

More fundamentally, whether greater specialisation is desirable remains to be established. In general, the case for more and more specialisation has largely been taken for granted. As we noted in Chapter 6, the Royal College of Physicians has recognised that the relative merits of generalists and specialists had not been systematically assessed. Neither has the need for a postgraduate retraining facility – enabling specialists to retrain in other disciplines – been seriously discussed.

Furthermore, any 'hard' boundary between the different skills that health care requires imposes costs on the Service as a whole by restricting the scope for re-deployment in the face of changing needs for care. On the basis of a review of the published evidence, *The Future NHS Workforce,*[9] a report commissioned by the Institute of Health Services Management, concluded:

> *A growing body of work on re-profiling and patient-focused care demonstrates the significant areas of overlap between different occupations. These overlaps are both horizontal (between different occupations on the same level) and vertical (between professionals and support workers). Research for patient-focused projects found that the problems attributable to the fragmented workforce are:*
>
> - *problems in the provision of cross-cover*
> - *inflexibilities in responding to peaks and troughs in workload*
> - *lack of clarity of accountability*
> - *increased delays and confusion for patients*

- *wasted time as staff wait for completion of work by other occupations*
- *increased time spent in co-ordination and meetings* (p.77).

In other words, even if there were benefits from further specialisation, there could also be substantial costs, including poor-quality care. But, as we noted in Chapter 6, the push towards specialisation continues, regardless of the consequences for the health service as a whole or indeed for the quality of care offered to patients.

The 'costs' of specialisation and the difficulties of forecasting future numbers are compounded by the maintenance of 'hard' boundaries between and within professions which makes movement between them rare once training is complete. Furthermore, the potential for substitution – particularly of medical skills by those trained in other disciplines – was identified as a central issue 20 years ago.

Recognising the essential riskiness of the way medical training needs were being defined had important implications for the way medical staff were trained. The Steering Group argued for example that:

> ... *we consider that the increasing inflexibility of medical training and career structure should be counteracted wherever possible by developments such as the promotion of the hospital practitioner grade, and further experimentation with a different mix of staff groups together with better evaluation of the results of such experiments, and by resisting the recognition of new small specialties in, for example, pathology and psychiatry which increase the rigidities of medical training programmes* (p.5).

These suggestions have been generally ignored.

The role of nurse practitioners in the community and specialised nurses within hospitals are examples of where boundaries are being broken down in the day-to-day deployment of staff. But while such developments open the way for new forms of service delivery, they do not represent a fundamental change in the way that roles and professions are defined and training organised.

That would require, according to *The Future NHS Workforce*:

- unbundling what professions actually do and what if any are the inherent differences in their respective knowledge bases. The ultimate aim would be

the 'health care professional' (i.e. that professional boundaries should disappear)
- devising new forms of training to make it easier to change career path or to allow late entry
- creating new forms of career, straddling hospital/community and even management
- developing multi-professional education and training
- removing statutory barriers that currently determine which professions can prescribe or provide care, e.g. in general practice.

Our own analysis suggests that the way that professionals are currently trained, with their distinct if overlapping bundles of knowledge, has led to a lack of training in issues which run across boundaries or bear on the Service as a whole, and the skills required to ensure that whole systems of care are appropriately designed, implemented and monitored. These include the broad service issues set out in Chapters 6 and 7 as well as the changes in the external environment set out in Chapter 2.

The content of medical training and clinical training generally has not responded fast enough to changes in the NHS environment, internal and external. It has remained dominated by the individual clinical intervention: the issues raised by the management and planning of service delivery are generally not a feature of undergraduate or postgraduate training. Furthermore, despite the imbalance of doctors in some specialties such as obstetrics and gynaecology, the Postgraduate Colleges and the General Medical Council have not made it easy for doctors to retrain in different specialties.

While there have been attempts to forecast the number of doctors and nurses required, the same has not been true for managers and other disciplines the NHS requires. Since the first Griffiths report, the needs of managers for training has been accepted but, despite the increasingly prominent role of managers (from whatever disciplinary background) within the NHS, there is no parallel Committee to that for the medical workforce charged with the task of determining how many managers are needed and with what skills. In fact, despite the Service becoming more complex and challenging, government policy over the last few years has been to reduce the number of managers through blanket management cost reduction targets.

We have noted already persistent gaps in the knowledge and understanding required for some of the central tasks the NHS must discharge. Some such as purchasing skills – a long-standing area of weakness as we showed in Chapter 5 – are specific and there are established training and professional organisations dealing with them. But many are less specific, lying at the intersection between clinical knowledge and the wider organisation of the Service, in areas such as the management of emergency admissions or the provision of whole systems of care such as those envisaged in national service frameworks.

Furthermore, much of the training that has been on offer to managers, or clinicians in management roles, has been directed at only a part of the spectrum of issues with which managers must grapple. Issues such as change management and organisational development, have been given more attention but there has been much less emphasis on the wide range of skills which are required to understand in analytic and quantitative terms the issues that managers face, such as the changes in the environment within which the NHS works, as well as changes in the way that services are provided, areas where both managerial and clinical skills are required. The scale of the Service requirement for people to cope with such issues has never been estimated, in large part because the need for it has not been clearly recognised.

## Recent developments

During the 1990s, attempts have been made to create more effective links between service needs and those responsible for training the workforce. The NHS and Community Care Act 1990 gave the responsibility for workforce planning for non-medical professions to regional health authorities.

Following the Functions and Manpower Review and the subsequent demise of regional health authorities, the responsibility for planning the non-medical workforce was transferred to new organisations known as Education and Training Consortia, operating at sub-regional level and Regional Education and Development Groups at regional level. Although the Regional Offices of the NHS Executive took the lead in developing plans for purchasing training places, they did so on an interim basis only. The new arrangements are intended to off-load responsibility for estimating future workforce requirements away from the Centre.

The Education and Training Consortia represent NHS employers and providers such as health authorities and NHS trusts rather than the professions themselves – although they are required to have professional input to their decisions – and may be expected to place greater weight on the skills that in practice appear important in service provision rather than on those deemed to be important by the professions. It is too soon to be sure how they will work, but they clearly embody the potential for significant change in the content of training. For example, the previous Government supported the role of National Vocational Qualifications for skills which can be used in the provision of health care as supplements or alternatives to professional qualifications in order to encourage new roles and job flexibility.

Moreover, at a general level, the need for greater flexibility has been acknowledged. The *Education and Training Planning Guidance*,[10] issued by the NHS Executive in June 1996 states that:

> *The NHS Executive recognises the need for better integration of medical and non-medical workforce planning. The moves currently underway to achieve greater multi-disciplinary team working, together with the blurring of traditional roles and responsibilities, requires a more integrated approach to planning medical and non-medical education and training. In drawing up workforce plans, there needs to be a clear view of how services will need to be developed across both the primary and secondary care sectors. This will provide consortia and other relevant bodies, with the strategic framework in which to make their decisions. Similarly, ways of integrating medical and non-medical workforce planning and practice should feature highly on consortia and Regional Education and Development Groups agendas.*

This general statement is clearly pointing in the right direction. But apart from a central programme of work on the nursing labour force, it was not backed by substantive analysis of the issues which it encouraged Consortia and Regional Offices to take on, nor by any clear central view as to how services will develop in future – a view which, as previous chapters have shown, is likely to prove hard to develop.

Furthermore, it is hard to understand why, against this policy background, a separate line of advice on the training of doctors continues in operation – the Standing Advisory Committee on the Medical Workforce – and a separate planning framework exists for primary care as outlined in a subsequent circular:[11]

> *It is recognised that there is a need for more local flexibility in the provision of family doctor services. In this context it will be increasingly important that Health Authorities in understanding the health needs of their populations,*

*understand the actual and expected demands for General Medical Services and the consequent implications for the workforce. In particular, health authorities will need to consider the appropriate balance of services between secondary and primary care, and the spread of provision – including GPs – required to achieve an equitable distribution of services* (Annex A).

The circular does not specify how the required understanding of the 'appropriate balance' between secondary and primary care is to be obtained. As we noted in Chapter 6, how that balance should be struck remains contentious, in large part because much of the evidence, on which informed judgement might be based, is missing. Thus both these circulars reflect the point made at the start of the chapter – that the Centre can see what ought to be done but does not have the capacity to specify how it should be done.

The failure to integrate the planning of human resources with other developments was acknowledged by the NHS Director of Human Resources when giving evidence to the Health Committee[12] in 1998: 'We need a stronger alignment between policy development and assessing the workforce implications' (p.xiii).

We noted in Chapter 5 the Secretary of State's admission that the data held by the Centre was poor. In May 1999 it published *Modernising Health and Social Services: developing the workforce*,[13] which acknowledged: 'The quality and type of workforce information ... needs to be improved ...' (p.6), and indicated:

> **15.** *workforce information will also be the basis for quality assuring the performance targets set out in Working Together. The information collected will need to be expanded to enable the creation of consistent data sets that can inform local benchmarking and the performance framework for NHS organisations* (p.6).

Thus, while the general need for better information has been explicitly acknowledged, there clearly remains a long way to go before it is available. Nevertheless, *Working Together: securing a quality workforce for the NHS*,[14] published in 1998, required all local employers to have an annual workforce plan in place by April 2000, as well as training and development plans for the majority of health professional staff.

The Health Committee itself made a number of recommendations bearing on the weaknesses identified in this chapter. In particular, it urged 'improved interaction between the medical and non-medical planning bodies' and a 'national strategy for workforce planning'. The Committee did not however systematically address the definition of professional roles and the links between investing in human resources and future patterns of service delivery.

In its reply to the Health Committee report,[15] the Government acknowledged that the present arrangements were unsatisfactory, in remarkably candid terms:

> The Committee is right to acknowledge the notoriously problematic nature of workforce planning in an organisation of the size and complexity of the NHS and where the lead times for professional education and training are so long (p.4).

After indicating a number of recently introduced improvements, it went on to acknowledge that 'fundamental improvements to workforce planning are required' (p.4).

To this end, the Government committed itself to a major review but what its scope is to be, was not clear at the time this book went to press.

## Conclusion

As the Government response to the Health Committee notes, there are already signs, such as the creation of Education and Training Consortia, that the NHS is beginning to make effective links between the needs of service provision and planning for the number and kind of staff it requires. The terms of reference for national service frameworks also imply the need to link training to service development.

There are also signs, including the new skill combinations being tried out within the Primary Care Act 1997 pilots and national measures, such as the proper recognition of the role of nurse prescribing, that the need to think across professional boundaries is being effectively recognised, in practice and in principle. But current arrangements continue to treat medical staffing separately. In the light of the recognition of the potential for substitution or changes in skills mix in both primary care, as the Primary Care Act 1997 pilots indicate, and in secondary care, as the British Medical Association and the Royal Colleges have recognised, this remains completely anomalous. The Government response accepts that.

But even though the Government has promised a major review, improvement will not be easy. *Modernising Health and Social Services: developing the workforce,*[16] issued in May 1999, acknowledges that: 'Workforce plans and training strategies that are fully linked into service and business plans will take time to develop' (para.12).

Confirmation of this came from the 1999 pay round. In its evidence to the Doctors and Dentists Pay Review Body, the Government requested that the pay award should be designed to ensure that the NHS had available the staff required to ensure that the Government's targets for the Service were met. But, as the Review Body pointed out in its 1999 report:[17]

> ... *in the absence of a direct link between output targets and manpower requirements, in particular a lack of detailed information about the numbers of doctors and dentists required to deliver the outputs, their workload assumptions, and future changes to work practice, it is difficult to draw conclusions which would significantly influence our recommendations* (p.16).

Unsurprisingly, it adds: 'We hope that the evidence might be developed in ways which are more helpful to us in future' (p.16).

In part this is a matter of getting processes right. But it also a matter of the basis on which the processes work. As with system and service design, information and understanding is limited: in large measure the current divisions of responsibility actively discourage certain kinds of research – for example, projects which span the range of issues discussed in this and the previous two chapters. Particularly important are the links between the development of professional skills and current service patterns. As noted in Chapter 6, changes in medical education have had, and are having, major impacts on what are considered viable hospital configurations. But these impacts have not been allowed for in making these changes – not even when they are actively promoted by the Government. The links are largely unexplored in research terms despite their critical importance to the way that care is provided.

One major obstacle in the way of improvement is the wide range of interests involved, many of which lie in the field of education rather than the NHS. A recent report from North Thames, a region which has been particularly active in respect of workforce issues, identifies some 60 organisations or categories of organisation involved with workforce issues. Furthermore, the situation appears to be getting worse. According to a study by the Office for Public Management:[18]

> *One clear area for policy makers to address is the accreditation and standards jungle – both for clinical practice and education. More and more statutory, professional, voluntary and private sector bodies are getting involved in forms of standard setting and/or accreditation. These are proving increasingly complex and costly to handle at planning and service provision levels. Whilst the Department of Health does not have overall control in this area, it does have the ability to engage each of the key parties to establish how their respective approaches can be meshed and simplified (p.35).*

The jungle to which the report refers arises because responsibilities are partial, and the way they are discharged in one area has implications for others. Some roles are national, some local, some professional, some administrative. It is scarcely surprising that the Health Committee found a failure at the Centre to tackle properly the relationship between human resources and the wider framework within which they work.

The need to do so has now been recognised. But whatever new machinery is put in place, progress will be slow since much of the groundwork, in terms of information and understanding is missing. In the light of the Government's response to the Health Committee report, which suggests that it does not intend to plug the gaps in basic information on the workforce that the Pay Review Bodies and others have identified, our suggestions are focused on broader issues.

First, a realistic assessment should be made of the scope for long-term workforce planning. Any such assessment should comprise a consideration of how the boundaries between the professions can be eased for individuals, the extent to which specialisation should be pursued both within and between professions, and the scope for movement between areas of specialisation in mid-career. If, as we expect, any such assessment concluded that firm forecasts of the numbers and skills of the workforce could not be made far in advance, then the implications for the content of its education and the form it takes should be systematically drawn. In particular, the less confidence can be placed in forecasts of the future, the greater the emphasis should be on retaining and promoting flexibility. The agenda set out in *The Future NHS Workforce* on pp.169–170 above remains to be fundamentally tackled.

Second, while the kind of administrative integration of the separate planning mechanisms that now exist should be helpful, the need for which has at last been accepted by the Government, a more fundamental requirement is that the NHS should have available to it the requisite knowledge and expertise to effectively make the links between the various elements that need to be combined. There is undoubtedly scope, as the Government has recognised with the new R&D programme on human resources, for more research into workforce issues. But if the links between these and the issues considered in the previous chapters are to be made, it will require fundamental questions such as the benefits and the costs of specialisation and the definition of professional roles to be tackled. Furthermore, the link will have to be made between planning for more professional staff and the resources available, not simply by asking, as have successive workforce planning committees, 'can we afford more?' but by considering precisely how the Service will benefit from more staff of particular kinds. We cited in Chapter 6 some recent evidence on the link between numbers of doctors and nurses and service outcomes. But such evidence is as yet very limited. Yet it is evidence of this sort which is required to underpin the case for investing further in the NHS's human resources.

Third, more emphasis should be put on the management roles stemming from the need to design and deliver whole systems of care. These roles require skills that may be found or developed in people from different professional backgrounds, some of which are poorly represented in the Service at the moment such as statistical analysis and simulation and other quantitative techniques as well as the more specific skills such as purchasing which have regularly been shown to be in short supply.

Finally, the issues covered in this chapter and the two previous ones require a wide-ranging approach synthesising a vast range of information and research findings, from the physical layout of hospital wards to the latest information technologies, and a vast range of disciplines from building technologies through to fundamental medical research. Within particular services, some of the required synthesis may be done – or at least commenced – through the development of national service frameworks. But, as we noted in Chapter 6, while their development will in time remedy a long-standing weakness in the NHS, there is as yet no sign that the implications of the forces reviewed in Chapter 2 making for change in the broader health care delivery system will be fully taken into account. The National Bed Study represents one part of this, but what is needed is a broader and continuing process, which combines all the elements discussed in this and the two previous chapters. Such a process should include – as well as systematic analysis of specific issues – the use of imagination and speculation about how changes in the NHS's external and internal environment might lead to new and as yet unthought of forms of service delivery. In *Healthcare Futures*,[19] Morton Warner and colleagues have attempted this task for nurses. Many of their specific findings, as well as their overall approach, are equally relevant to the Service as a whole. We return to this theme in Chapter 11.

## References

1. House of Commons Social Services Committee. *Medical Education.* London: HMSO, 1981.
2. Long AF and Mercer G. *Manpower Planning and the National Health Service.* London: Gower, 1981.
3. DHSS Operational Research Service. *Nurse Manpower Planning: approaches and techniques.* London: HMSO 1983.
4. House of Commons Public Accounts Committee. *Control of Nursing Manpower.* London: HMSO, 1986.
5. Medical Manpower Steering Group. *Report.* London: HMSO, 1980.
6. Department of Health. *Planning the Medical Workforce – Medical Workforce Standing Advisory Committee: Third Report.* London: HMSO, 1997.
7. Kitson A, McManus C and Pringle M. A research base for professional staffing of health services. In: Peckham M, editor. *The scientific basis of health services.* London: BMJ Publishing, 1996.
8. Specialist Workforce Advisory Group *Annual Report for 1995/96.* Leeds: Department of Health, 1996.
9. Health Services Management Unit. *The future NHS workforce.* Manchester: IHSM, 1996.
10. NHS Executive. *Education and training planning guidance* (EL (96) 46).
11. NHS Executive. *Workforce Planning for General Medical Services* (EL (96) 69).
12. House of Commons – Health Committee. *NHS Staffing Requirements.* London: Stationery Office 1999.
13. Department of Health. *Modernising Health and Social Services: developing the workforce.* London: Department of Health, 1999.
14. Department of Health. *Working Together in Securing a Quality Workforce for the NHS.* London: Department of Health, 1998.
15. Department of Health. *NHS Staffing Requirements: response to Staffing Requirements.* London: Stationery Office, 1999.
16. See n.13.
17. *Review Body on Doctors' and Dentists' Remuneration 28th report.* Cm. 4243. London: Stationery Office, 1999.
18. Office for Public Management. *The Workforce Project.* London: Department of Health, 1997.
19. Warner W *et al. Healthcare Futures 2010.* Pontypridd: Welsh Institute for Health and Social Care, 1998.

# Chapter 9

# Managing demand

If sustaining the NHS into the future will require a more acceptable balance between supply and demand, then controlling the supply of NHS resources, or raising the efficiency with which resources are used, is unlikely to be effective in itself. Attempts must be made to manage demand better.

The term *demand* is used in this chapter to mean any claim upon NHS resources for care, whether by patients or professionals. Managing demand implies not only curtailing the use of services that are ineffective, in clinical and cost terms, but also stimulating demand for services known to be cost-effective but underused.

Government policy since 1948 has been not to manage, but crudely to limit, use of NHS services by controlling the overall supply of resources available, for example by setting a ceiling to NHS expenditure in a global budget. Control within that ceiling was largely left to the medical profession, which was seen as being in a better position than the Government to discriminate between appropriate and inappropriate demands for care. That this policy has failed to control pressures on the NHS budget adequately is not surprising. Driven by the latest technologies, the medical profession has pushed against the ceiling of the global budget since it was imposed in 1951. From their vantage point, the profession can only believe that the NHS is underfunded; doctors have had little reason to manage their own demands on NHS resources, and limited training and support to do so.

At the same time, government policies have actually encouraged an increase in activity in the NHS. Furthermore, that increase, as we noted in Chapter 2, has been used as a measure of success in managing the Service. The notion that a lower level of NHS activity – such as fewer hospital admissions, out-patient visits or GP consultations – might actually be a legitimate measure of success because people may be healthy, or knowledgeable, enough not to require NHS care, has never taken root in government policy.

Instead, the NHS has been constantly urged to do more with the resources at its disposal. On the one hand, this policy has been successful – more patients are being treated now than ever before. But, on the other, the emphasis on more activity led to demands for more treatments, as greater access to services has prompted higher expectations by the public and NHS staff. The result has contributed to over-stretched staff, low morale and increased staff sickness rates, budget deficits, longer waiting lists, services gradually slipping off the NHS menu, such as long-term care, community paediatric nursing, and infertility treatment. These recurrent problems are portrayed so vividly in the media that it appears as if the NHS is in terminal decline, and that the 'gap' between supply and demand grows ever wider.

Is there an alternative to this seemingly inevitable path? In this chapter, the determinants of demand for NHS care will be explored more fully, and some options for managing demand better in future examined.

## What is demand?

Demand is not necessarily the same as need for care, and neither necessarily results in utilisation of care. It is over 20 years since Julian Tudor Hart[1] wrote about the concept of the 'clinical iceberg', suggesting that patients who demand care only represent the tip of the iceberg of need as illustrated in the Figure 9.1 below:

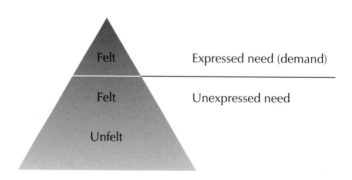

**Figure 9.1:** The clinical iceberg of disease

The iceberg analogy implies that there is more unexpressed than expressed need by patients. 'Need' in the population may not come to the attention of those providing care in the NHS unless patients actually express their need as demand. That demand in turn may not result in service use – if there are barriers to accessing care, which deter service users.

Figure 9.2 (below) is often used to illustrate the differences between need, demand and use.

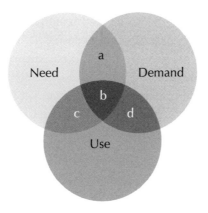

**Figure 9.2:** Need, demand and use

Area (a) illustrates the case where care is needed and demanded but not provided by the NHS, for example care that may no longer be available on the NHS such as cosmetic surgery. Area (b) indicates that care can be needed, demanded and utilised, for example patients undergoing effective elective surgery. Area (c) indicates that care can be needed and utilised but not necessarily demanded, for example routine immunisation or population screening for cervical cancer which people must be actively encouraged to use (and some do not). Area (d) indicates that care can be demanded and provided but not needed, for example antibiotic treatment of viral infection.

A crucial question raised by the second diagram is who defines whether care is actually needed or not? Typically, 'need' for care is defined by health care professionals, usually members of the medical profession, rather than patients. Furthermore, the type of care provided to patients is almost always decided on the basis of professionally defined, or 'normative', definitions of need.

Figures 9.1 and 9.2 suggest that there are two key decision points that have crucial influence on the use of NHS resources:

1. The point at which a *patient* with a perceived need actually expresses this as a demand for care in the NHS
2. The point at which an NHS *professional* decides whether the needs of the patient and the type of care, if any, merit a response by the NHS.

These two types of demands resulting in the use of NHS care, those made by patients and those made by professionals on behalf of their patients, are interrelated. Demands by patients (called here 'patient-led' demands) typically result in service utilisation, for example self-referral to a consultation in general practice or to an accident and emergency (A&E) department. Most other forms of NHS care generally cannot be used by patients directly without reference to a professional, although patients can obviously influence the type of treatment received. Demands by medical, or other NHS professionals (called here 'professional-led' demands), result in all other forms of care being utilised such as prescription drugs, out-patient consultations and admission to in-patient care. Both broad types of demands are increasing.

**Table 9.1:** Trends in NHS use

| **Estimated number of GP consultations, UK (millions)** | |
| --- | --- |
| 1985 | 238 |
| 1996 | 294 |

| **Total attendance at out-patients, UK (per 1000 population)** | |
| --- | --- |
| 1986/87 | 1096 |
| 1996/97 | 1155 |

| **Finished consultant episodes (in-patients and day cases), Great Britain (per 1000 population)** | |
| --- | --- |
| 1986/87 | 101 |
| 1996/97 | 172 |

**Source:** Office of Health Economics. *Compendium of Health Statistics* 11th edition. 1999.

Virtually all forms of patient-led demands have increased since the foundation of the NHS: consultations with general practitioners have risen for all ages but especially in elderly people, and for conditions classified by GPs as 'minor'. As shown in Chapter 2, the best available assessment of overall population health – from the General Household Survey – indicates that levels of morbidity in the UK have risen very slowly over time[2] – nowhere near the same scale as the rise in NHS utilisation. Furthermore, demands for non-NHS health care services are also increasing, e.g. over-the-counter drugs, alternative therapies and social care. Professional-led demands are also growing: referrals to out-patients, prescriptions and hospital admissions show uninterrupted growth.

Both patient-led and professional-led demands are significantly influenced not only by the changing external environment – as argued in Chapter 2 – but also by the way that the NHS itself is organised and financed. For example, in the early 1990s, the Government devoted extra resources specifically to reduce waiting times for elective surgery, and at the same time the NHS efficiency index was introduced to encourage the Service to increase its productivity. The result of both initiatives helped to contribute to a 30 per cent increase in hospital in-patient activity between 1991 and 1996. This could be termed 'Service-led' demand.

The figures for increasing utilisation shown above sit awkwardly alongside evidence that many crude indicators show a concurrent improvement in the health of the population. Crude death rates for males and females are still falling, infant and pre-natal mortality rates are declining, and life expectancy is slowly increasing. There has also been progress towards achieving some of the health targets set out in the previous Government's health strategy, *The Health of the Nation*, for example a reduction in mortality rates from stroke and coronary heart disease, and the Labour Government's recent White Paper, *Saving Lives*, promotes efforts to help continue these favourable trends.

If demands are rising and if the prevalence of ill health – the size of the iceberg in Figure 9.1 – does not appear to be changing as much, then the implication is that either the threshold between patient unexpressed need and expressed need (demand) is dropping (patients with disease are more likely to feel a need and express it as a demand for NHS care), or that clinical thresholds for treatment are dropping, or both.

Why could this be? We argued in Chapter 2 that demands on NHS care are rising for a number of reasons relating to changes not only in the external environment – such as social structure, the media, the increasing availability of treatments, increasing expectations, the impact on professional behaviour of complaints and litigation by patients – but also the internal NHS environment, i.e. how the Service itself is organised and financed.

Many of the forces in the external environment pushing up demand are obviously beyond the direct control of the Service. However, how the NHS itself responds to these forces *can* be managed, although any attempt to do so appropriately will need to take the complexity of these forces into consideration. Furthermore, the incentives that exist within the NHS internal environment for patients, professionals and providers *can* be controlled directly.

In the next section, a number of policies that might be used to better manage demand and use of services will be explored. These are divided into those directed at patients, at professionals and at the Service itself.

## Routes to managing demand better

### Patient-led demand

The obvious way to reduce, or even curtail, patient-led demand is by reducing access to the NHS. One way is simply not to fund a service on the NHS. As we pointed out in Chapter 3, such decisions have been taken at national level in respect of some elements of eye and dental services, while locally other treatments such as *in vitro* fertilisation, cosmetic surgery, wisdom teeth extraction, and drug therapies such as Beta-Interferon have been withdrawn in whole or part. This has meant in effect that the NHS has effectively imposed a 100 per cent user charge on these services.

Another way is to impose a partial user charge – for example to introduce a fee to see a GP, or hotel charges for hospital stays. Other ways are to reduce physical access to services that patients can use directly, such as the GP surgery or A&E department, by reducing opening hours, increasing the distance to facilities, or ensuring that there are long queues for care.

But while these methods have been shown to be effective in reducing utilisation, they are blunt instruments, because they indiscriminately reduce appropriate and inappropriate patient-led demand. Barriers to access put the onus on the patient to decide whether or not his or her condition is significant enough to be worth paying a user charge to seek treatment, rather than a health care professional who is likely to have greater knowledge about the illness. Patients who delay seeking care as a result may be at risk of substantial avoidable morbidity, which may incidentally also be more costly for the NHS to treat in the long run.

So, while creating access barriers directly to deter patients is effective, it may not be the most appropriate way forward, and fortunately up until today has also not been politically acceptable either. A better option would be to maintain or even improve patient access to the NHS, but at the same time pursue initiatives that seek to route patients towards the most cost-effective source of care – whether inside or outside the NHS. Such sources could include self-care, or care from more cost-effective providers than GPs or the A&E department, which are normally the patient's first point of contact with the NHS.

Five initiatives along these lines are outlined below:

1. improving the quality of information about illness and treatment in the public domain
2. providing telephone advice
3. increasing access to medication
4. providing more accessible face-to-face support and advice about the management of illness
5. better routing to non-NHS providers of care.

### 1. Improving the quality of information about illness and treatment in the public domain

Until recently, very little information has been directly available to the public from 'official' NHS sources about, for example, the self-management of common conditions, the use of over-the-counter medication, or the risks and benefits of new treatments. This information can serve to uncover hitherto unrecognised needs, or encourage greater self-care, which could potentially substitute for NHS care. In the *Priorities and Planning Guidance 1996–97*, the NHS Executive agreed to produce and disseminate information for users – for example by identifying and facilitating the production of effectiveness information in a form helpful to individual patients, and strengthening the Health Information Service – a telephone information service – and to evaluate the impact of both. The *NHS Handbook of Self-Care* was published in 1997, while *Saving Lives* set out plans for NHS *Direct* On-line which will provide an interactive self-care guide and accredited information about hundreds of diseases and self-help groups on the Internet.

The *NHS Handbook of Self-Care* and NHS *Direct* On-line are a helpful start. More effective relations with the media, particularly correcting misleading information about the benefits of new treatments or about health scares is also required. At the moment, the bulk of information on health and health services comes from the private or voluntary sector, for example in magazines, on television, or on the Internet, and its quality is poorly controlled. For example, a recent study[3] published in the *British Medical Journal* showed that the quality of advice on the Internet for the treatment of high temperatures in children was inadequate. The NHS could be proactive and capitalise on its name, and reputation, as being an authoritative source of information which is subject to the best available quality control, for example by the Royal Colleges, or the new Commission for Health Improvement and National Institute of Clinical Excellence.

## 2. Providing telephone advice

Telephone advice lines can offer several levels of advice, for example: general advice on specific illnesses, or the risks and benefits of new treatments or lifestyles – a service which could be run nationally; or more specific advice to individual patients – a service which would best be linked to local services such as primary care. Other countries such as France and Denmark provide telephone advice extensively, and in the USA up to one-third of all ambulatory care contacts occur over the telephone and are initiated by patients. The Labour Government has introduced a new service – NHS *Direct*, a 24-hour nurse-led advice line on health matters, which will cover the UK population by the end of 2000.

This source of advice has the potential to substitute for other forms of NHS care, such as that provided in general practice or A&E departments. But it could equally well swell patient-led demand, especially if needs are uncovered or if NHS *Direct* reduces the threshold at which patients seek formal health care. Evidence from the UK and USA is inconclusive in this respect. The impact on demand depends crucially on the advice given, for example whether or not the advisers can instil confidence in patients to encourage self-care where appropriate, or whether cases are simply referred on, after minimal advice, to their local NHS facility. Early findings[4] suggest that a considerable proportion of those approaching NHS *Direct* do switch to lower intensity forms of care as a result. But there is no information as yet available on the consequences of those decisions.

## 3. Increasing access to medication

The previous Government introduced the Deregulation of Medicines Act in 1988, which expanded the range of medicines that could be bought over-the-counter without a prescription. Sales are rising and evidence suggests that patients opt to buy over-the-counter drugs for reasons of cost and convenience. But little information was available from the NHS to the public to support the decision to self-care, or to point patients towards the most appropriate medication. Also, as with telephone advice lines, it is not clear whether or not the public are making an appropriate choice to self-care, whether the treatment option chosen was appropriate, or whether it has substituted for NHS care, or added to it. Nor is it clear that demands on the NHS drugs budget are reduced as a result. For example a study by Baines and Whynes[5] recently showed that GPs tend to prescribe drugs which are available over-the-counter to patients who are exempt from prescription charges and who account for 85 per cent of prescriptions.

## 4. *Providing more accessible face-to-face support and advice about the management of illness*

Regardless of the availability and quality of advice via the telephone or other public sources such as the Internet, it is likely that substantial demand will remain for prompt face-to-face contact with a health care professional. In Chapter 2, it was argued that social fragmentation and loose family ties are resulting in a reduction of those lay sources of advice, which provide reassurance and give confidence to individuals in dealing with illness and which in the past may have reduced reliance on the NHS, particularly for treatment of minor conditions.

At present the main, and most direct, source of face-to-face help and advice for patients in the NHS is through the general practitioner and the A&E department. But there are more cost-effective alternatives, for example using nurse practitioners instead of the GP in general practices, or using nurses or pharmacists to offer advice in other more convenient locations, such as in high street retail outlets. Currently the significant knowledge of pharmacists about the treatment of common conditions is underused despite their lengthy training. This is recognised by the Department of Health, which has made some effort to encourage a greater advisory role for pharmacists. However, since no payment is on offer (unlike in other countries such as Australia), the enthusiasm of pharmacists for this role has been muted. New primary care 'walk-in' centres, offering extended opening hours, are now being piloted. While the form that these will take is unclear, the cost-effectiveness of such options compared to simply extending opening hours for normal existing primary care services will need to be carefully evaluated. The Primary Care Act 1997 allows the funding and piloting of better access to primary care through further initiatives along these lines. However, again a big question mark remains over their ultimate impact on the overall demand on NHS resources.

## 5. *Better routing to non-NHS providers of care*

Finally, better and more accessible information, possibly through an expanded form of NHS *Direct*, could help to route patient-led demand more appropriately to non-NHS providers of care, for example to local authority social services, and alternative therapies available privately, and relatively cheaply, for example osteopathy. Information given by telephone or by the Internet, could also be expanded to include advice about services available from non-NHS providers. This would require much closer liaison between the NHS and other organisations such as local authorities and bodies responsible for accrediting non-NHS providers.

*Overall*

Each of the options discussed above would have to be carefully designed so that even if access to the NHS for patients is enhanced, that does not lead to unrealistic expectations of what the Service can provide and inappropriately reduced thresholds for demanding care. It will be crucial not only to give scrupulously accurate information to the public, but also to present it in a balanced way: on the one hand, the information should not encourage inappropriate demands on the Service by the 'worried well', or on the other encourage inappropriate self-care. Quite where the balance lies will depend upon the extent to which the Government, or the bodies advising it such as the Royal Colleges, are willing to tolerate risk on the public's behalf, which in turn may be influenced by concerns about litigation. To get it right will require much closer working between those currently involved in reviewing evidence of best practice (such as the NHS Centre for the Reviews and Dissemination) and developing clinical guidelines, as well as those involved in reviewing sentinel adverse events as indicators of clinical performance such as the National Confidential Enquiry into Peri-operative Deaths. The new National Institute for Clinical Excellence could be an obvious focus for these twin activities.

## Professional-led demand

Many of the suggestions made above have the distinct potential to encourage patients to seek to make more use of the NHS rather than less. If these initiatives are taken, it will be important to structure incentives for professionals and for the Service as a whole so that only appropriate (patient-led) demands are met by the NHS, and the rest routed elsewhere. In turn this will require much greater knowledge of the impact of specific incentives on clinical behaviour.

A variety of factors currently influences the volume of professional-led demands:

- the doctor's role as agent for the patient
- the effectiveness of treatment and acceptability to the patient
- the potential for the doctor to gain professional kudos
- the availability of new treatments/new technologies
- the expectations of patients and their families
- the principle of clinical freedom.

Doctors are naturally oriented to maximising benefits for individual patients, rather than the population as a whole. Up until now, they have been largely reluctant to accept the need to consider the costs (including opportunity costs) of treatment of individual patients when making clinical decisions. But even now, precious little information on the effects of different treatments is available to practising doctors, especially not in a form that is relevant to decision-making in practice.

Professionals are also naturally oriented to achieving recognition for their work from their peers. In medicine, kudos is more obviously conferred on those pushing at the frontiers of specialist care in hospitals, for example in trying out and evaluating new (often high technology) treatments on patients who may not have been treatable in the past (such as premature infants). While new technologies are available, there has been every incentive to use them. Professional prizes glitter less obviously for the generalist, such as the geriatrician or general practitioner, for whom the emphasis of practice is to provide low intensity services at, or near, the patient's home and to keep patients out of hospital. Similarly, there is less obvious peer recognition for doctors who are not only good clinicians, but are also good managers and take an interest in the wider Service rather than clinical practice.

The expectations of patients also influence clinical practice. A frequent complaint by the medical profession is that patients are at once more demanding of the latest clinical innovation and more likely to question professional advice. In turn these pressures, plus the increasing level of litigation in the NHS, may serve to decrease the clinical threshold of professional-led demand.

The large amount of clinical freedom enjoyed by the medical profession has resulted in wide variations in both the thresholds and rates of treatment but little systematic scrutiny of these differences and attempts to reduce them. There has always been some effort to identify gross errors in clinical practice, through the activities of the General Medical Council and the National Committee of Enquiry into Peri-operative Deaths. There has also been some effort to increase scrutiny of clinical practice, for example through clinical audit, through the development and use of guidelines, and through the work of the Audit Commission, and the Royal Colleges. But these have mostly been professionally driven and oriented towards improving quality rather than managing patient-led and professional-led demand. The effect of these efforts has been hard to detect; successive Governments have, until recently, refrained from attempting to influence clinical practice more directly.

Overall, therefore, the drivers of professional-led demand have almost all tended to act to increase utilisation in the Service. Any attempt to manage demand or use must tackle these existing incentives, and possibly introduce new ones to counter the tendency to lever up demands, where appropriate. Such incentives may range from the mild – for example providing an environment to promote more informed decision-making – to the severe – sanctions for not following rules, as Figure 9.3 indicates:

**MILD**

- providing clinical decision-makers with better information on costs and effects of treatment, in a user-friendly format

- training and ongoing support to use this information in clinical practice

- providing better information about the local availability of alternative, more cost-effective sources of care

- rewarding professionals, individually or in teams, for practising good quality, evidence-based and cost-effective medicine

- introducing explicit guidelines linked to information about effectiveness of treatments

- making information on clinical performance, particularly for individual clinicians, readily available to the public

- introducing financial incentives to reward clinicians for providing cost-effective clinical practice (for example using through capitated devolved budgets, such as in GP fundholding), and to use sanctions against those who do not

- introducing mandatory monitoring of clinical practice by third party organisations (such as the Commission for Health Improvement) using techniques such as utilisation review or physician profiling. Combine with rewards and sanctions

- introducing nationally defined clinical criteria for the treatment of specific conditions – for example coronary artery bypass surgery – with sanctions for non-adherence.

**SEVERE**

**Figure 9.3:** Potential measures to manage professional-led demand

Many of these initiatives are already in operation in the NHS. For example, more information is now available to doctors on the effectiveness of treatment, through the work of the Centre for Reviews and Dissemination and the Cochrane Centre, while institutions such as the Centre for Evidence-Based Medicine in Oxford have supported the process of putting evidence-based medicine into practice.

The principle of giving doctors resources to manage, to encourage greater consideration of costs, is illustrated by the resource management initiative, introduced in hospitals in the late 1980s, and GP fundholding, which gave incentives to GPs to scrutinise the clinical care provided in hospitals and in their own practices. These incentives remain in a weaker form in primary care groups.

Up until now, most of these initiatives have been driven by the Government, and taken up largely voluntarily by the medical profession. The White Paper *The New NHS* shifts the Service somewhat towards the lower part of the list in Figure 9.3, by proposing that scrutiny of clinical performance should not only be conducted by the professions, but also by the NHS itself, particularly through the Commission for Health Improvement. Chief executives of NHS trusts will now be accountable for the clinical performance in their institutions to the NHS Executive, just as members of the medical profession are to the General Medical Council. These moves will create a much stronger central grip upon clinical performance than ever before. This is part of an international trend for non-professional bodies, particularly payers of care, to scrutinise clinical behaviour more and try to influence it with rewards and sanctions. But so far, successive UK Governments have shied away from more top-down prescriptive and punitive approaches, represented in the options at the lower end of the list, partly because they may be costly, bureaucratic and politically difficult to implement and partly because of the reluctance to challenge clinical freedom so directly.

But much more could be done to create an environment more conducive to better decision-making. Large swathes of the medical profession still do not practise evidence-based medicine, let alone consider costs in their decision-making. Huge variations in clinical practice still exist. Much more could be done to train and support clinicians at undergraduate and postgraduate level, the latter possibly in continuing professional development. To help, the professional reward system – for example the passing of exams, revalidation, promotion, or achievement of a merit award – could be much more explicitly linked to demonstration of cost-effective clinical practice and continuous self-audit. This would require a new and much closer working relationship between the Royal Colleges and the NHS, and a vastly increased commitment by the professions to be responsible for the wider Service.

Similarly, a number of measures could be taken to support the medical profession in the face of increasing expectations of patients. One option might be for the NHS to provide better, more timely and more accessible information to doctors about the risks and benefits of treatment, particularly where this contradicts messages in the popular media. The uncontrolled escalation of information in the media and on the Internet makes it difficult for doctors to make sense of the claims made about specific treatments. Information about NHS treatments is currently available to doctors from a large number of sources and the volume of information is increasing. Furthermore, such information often does not have any obvious reference to that which the public may have obtained through the media.

The NHS could respond in various ways. First, on-line information about the risks and benefits of treatments could be made available in one source to NHS professionals, and advice from experts on which patients are best considered for treatment. This could be done via the NHS *Net* when it is fully operational, possibly in conjunction with the new National Institute for Clinical Excellence, the National Electronic Library for Health and the Commission for Health Improvement, and regularly updated. The NHS could be much more active in scanning the media for stories about particular treatments, making sure that currently known information was made available centrally, and promptly, to NHS professionals about the treatments, again possibly through the NHS *Net*. Where information in the press is misleading, the NHS press and communications function could take a more proactive role by providing appropriate briefings.

A second related option might be to involve patients far more in decisions about their own treatment, by providing much more information about the risks as well as benefits. This may well be encouraged anyway in response to increasingly litigious behaviour by the public. Pioneering work by Ware and colleagues in the USA,[6] showed that patients who were given more information about the risks and benefits of prostatectomy through the medium of interactive videos, were more risk averse than their doctors and tended to choose non-surgical treatment. Such work is at an early stage in the UK, through, for example, the Patient Partnership Initiative. It is of course possible that involving patients more in clinical decision-making could result in higher demands upon the service. Too often inadequate information is available to both patient and doctor about the risks involved and the benefits of treatments, which may lead to false optimism particularly if doctors have an in-built bias towards trying out new treatments.

Shared decision-making shows promise with regard to surgery, where there are obvious risks to treatment. However, it is not clear how shared decision-making would work in general practice, for example in relation to the decision to refer the patient to a specialist, or to prescribe drugs. Much more research is needed into the tools that would equip general practice to cope with inappropriate demands for treatment. Better routing to alternative sources of care/advice may be an answer, for example through telephone advice as outlined above.

As well as providing more accessible information to support clinical decision-making, some extra incentives may be used to nudge clinicians to use it. Despite seven years of fundholding, the impact on clinical practice and professional-led demand is far from clear, largely because, as we discuss further in Chapter 11, evaluative research in this area was not particularly encouraged or funded. Evaluating the impact of incentives inherent in managing a capitated budget, for example in the new primary care groups, on demand, the use of information on costs and effects of treatments, and peer review of clinical practice should be an urgent priority of the NHS R&D programme.

The tools listed above in Figure 9.3 all push the medical profession to a greater or lesser degree in this direction. For lasting change, it will be crucial to create an environment of trust and responsiveness in which continuous review of practice is seen to become an integral part of medicine, rather than an environment of threat and sanction in which clinical practice is seen to be under the thumb of the State. So far the UK is in the early stages of using some of these tools, although *The New NHS* signals that the new Government is more impatient than its predecessor with huge variations in clinical practice, and favours greater external scrutiny of clinical practice through the process, yet to be fully worked out, of clinical governance set out in *A First Class Service*. So far, more draconian measures of control, such as the utilisation review practised within US managed care organisations, have not been adopted, although information to the public on the clinical performance of providers was published in 1999.[7] If the softer measures do not work, then we believe that both of these options are more likely to be used in future.

### Service-led demand

As noted above, both patient- and professional-led demands are significantly influenced by the organisation and financing of the NHS itself. But successive Governments have failed to grasp the need to manage demand or to allow for the impact of NHS policies on demand. For example, when deciding upon the requirements for human resources in the NHS, particularly the number of doctors required, scant attention is paid to the demands they may generate on the Service. With this gap in thinking and analysis, it is little wonder that the Service is under stress as a result of the supply–demand imbalance.

As a result, the Service has resorted to deterring use of services apparently regardless of need, by removing whole services such as cosmetic surgery and *in vitro* fertilisation from the NHS and imposing restrictions on the use of new drugs. Both, as argued in Chapters 1 and 10, have added to public unease about the fairness of access to care on the NHS, and whether the Service is coping.

Much more could be done to obviate the need for further unsystematic reductions in access, in particular:

1. more and better analysis of what is driving up demand, in particular the effect of new policies
2. better design of incentives in the NHS, particularly for providers
3. a tighter grip on the use of new technologies
4. more external scrutiny of clinical performance, particularly of the threshold which, when crossed, leads to professional-led demands.

### 1. More and better analysis

One way of ensuring that the impact of service change on the demand for NHS care is taken into account would be to introduce a 'demand audit' of the likely effect on utilisation of, at the very least, all new policies. In the design stage, potential effects could be identified to inform later evaluation, and policies altered if their impact is likely to conflict with others already implemented – as was the case with the drive towards a primary care-led NHS and the NHS efficiency index. Also, there should be mandatory evaluation of utilisation after implementation of national policies. This should be a key strand of the NHS R&D programme, but much more importantly, routine real-time monitoring of the impact of policies on patient- and professional-led demand should be performed by the NHS itself at Regional Office and health authority level and in primary care groups. While this sort of activity does go on in pockets, there is little co-ordination across the NHS. The result has been large gaps in understanding of some very basic dynamics, for example the rise in emergency admissions or the persistence of waiting lists. Similarly, the knock-on effect on the NHS of changing the availability of new or alternative sources of care paid for, or subsidised by, the public purse is rarely estimated. For example, the effect of reducing the availability of social care, of encouraging private health insurance for elderly people through tax breaks (scrapped by the current Government), of removing certain services off the NHS, or making a wider range of over-the-counter medicines available, all remain unknown.

## 2. Better design of incentives

There is an urgent need to structure incentives better, in order to encourage appropriate provision by professionals, and encourage better co-ordination across providers. As noted above, most of the incentives for hospitals are to increase in-patient throughput rather than provide more cost-effective forms of care, for example in the community. The interests of hospitals in this sense often run against those of the primary care purchasers who may wish to reduce hospital utilisation by their patients where possible. If incentives for both GPs and specialists in hospitals were better aligned, this might encourage hospital clinicians to work with GPs, particularly GP purchasers, to route patients to most cost-effective forms of care, and possibly using a reduction in hospital admissions as a measure of success. *The New NHS* made a start by implying that local purchasers, be they primary care groups or health authorities, could enter into flexible arrangements with NHS trusts about the care offered and how it was purchased. The door is left open for vertical integration between hospital and general practice, through for example disease management, and it is not difficult to see that in principle hospitals could be reimbursed for a variety of measures of performance, including reducing avoidable admissions, or providing effective outreach care for patients with chronic disease. Similarly, primary care groups will be responsible for budgets for hospital, community health, and primary care, and the possibility of primary care groups merging in one organisation with local community trust as the new primary care trusts provide new budgetary incentives to offer seamless care and reduce demands for hospital care.

Similarly, better alignment of incentives between the NHS and other forms of care such as social care is desperately needed. Stress on local authority budgets for social care and NHS budgets has resulted in cost shifting between both sectors. Hospitals are stretched because a lack of social support at home, particularly for the frail, and this both increases the risk of admission and delays discharge. General practitioner services are stretched for similar reasons. Care provided by social services and the NHS is not well integrated because of long-standing budgetary boundaries, and cultural, professional, and institutional differences between staff.

Initiatives within the NHS alone are unlikely to improve working between agencies to route patients better to the most appropriate sources of care. Recent attempts such as joint commissioning of services between health and local authorities have overall had only marginal effect. New developments involving local authorities in developing health improvement plans, and developing the Health Action Zones, encourage integration and begin to blur the budgetary boundary between health and social care. But these do not go far enough to tackle seriously the huge 'Berlin Wall' which has existed between health and social care since 1948. The proposals set out in *Modernising Social Services* for pooled budgets – where health and social services put a proportion of their funds into a mutually accessible joint budget, lead commissioning – where one authority transfers funds to the other who will then take responsibility for purchasing both health and social care – and integrated provision – where one organisation provides both health and social care – should reduce the size of the 'Wall' considerably.

### 3. A tighter grip on the use of new technologies

Many believe that the single biggest driver of higher expenditure in health care systems is the increasing availability of new technologies. But the NHS is not powerless to control their introduction – there is plenty of evidence to suggest that the speed with which a new technology is adopted is influenced by the national policy framework and the constraints and incentives it embodies. The elements of such a framework include: spotting new technologies; obtaining evidence of costs and effects; giving guidance to purchasers and providers; and creating incentives for appropriate use.

Methods of spotting new technologies in the UK were strengthened in 1992 when a Standing Group on Health Technology was established by the Department of Health. Through the NHS R&D programme, research is commissioned to evaluate cost effectiveness, results are disseminated and recommendations made to purchasers and providers. But a significant number of new treatments can diffuse into the NHS before they are spotted or properly evaluated. For example, new drugs have to be licensed for use in the UK, but the licensing process does not yet require manufacturers to provide evidence of effectiveness or costs relative to other drugs on the market, only that the drug is not harmful. There are even fewer controls over the introduction and practice of new surgical techniques and devices.

Even with better information on costs and effectiveness, health authority purchasers have shown themselves to have limited influence in the face of the interests of providers to use new technologies. Even this limited influence may weaken if management costs are further reduced, and purchasing is devolved further to primary care groups. Furthermore, without regional health authorities, no part of the NHS has a strong grip on shaping and planning access to services at a regional level, and inadequate controls may result in excessive duplication of expensive technologies within an area.

To promote more rational diffusion of technologies, new approaches could be tried which include a combination of targeting providers with information on costs and effects, rather than purchasers, and structuring incentives for the medical profession to encourage appropriate use. For example in a recent study of the introduction of three new technologies in the UK, Rosen and Mays[8] suggest that a useful model to promote rational diffusion could be to use in-hospital committees to review existing research on cost effectiveness – published, or unpublished from other local hospitals – and conduct in-house research to support clinical decision-making. As discussed earlier, the NHS *Net* could also be used as an up-to-date source of information for providers in this way, underpinned by evidence reviewed by the National Institute for Clinical Excellence and available through the National Electronic Library for Health. Other computerised sources of summarised information on the costs and effects of treatments targeted at clinicians are already in use, for example the PRODIGY system to aid prescribing in general practice. These could be combined with the shaping of incentives for professionals, described earlier in this chapter, to take more account of evidence on costs and effects, and to audit their own performance and that of their peers.

## 4. More external scrutiny of clinical performance

If increasing information and incentives for the profession to review and modify professional-led demand fail to have much effect, then there will be more strenuous efforts by the State, as payer, to monitor and influence clinical performance. This is a trend seen throughout OECD countries, most notably the USA. As noted above, external scrutiny of clinical performance has already begun, with the expansion of the activities of the Audit Commission into health care in 1989, and the formation of the Commission for Health Improvement in 1999.

But while *The New NHS* announced that specifications of how a range of services are to be provided will be drawn up in national service frameworks, so far the Government has largely refrained from being very prescriptive about specifying the clinical thresholds of care to be provided, even in the face of large variations in care. For example, the symptoms and signs in patients that are appropriate to 'justify' specific operations, such as coronary artery bypass grafting, have not been spelt out at a national level, although some health authority purchasers, NHS trusts and general practices have taken this step. Making criteria explicit in this way could mean that professional thresholds of care vary less throughout the NHS, and fewer treatments are offered to those who are, for example, less sick. Access would be essentially reduced for this group of patients in a more explicit and systematic way with regard to need, rather than curtailing access to whole services for groups of patients regardless of need. The result, as we argue in Chapter 10, could be a more equitable distribution of the resources the NHS has available to it. But the Government is a long way from this approach, concentrating more on creating a more conducive environment for more consistent clinical decision-making (the measures in the upper half of Figure 9.3).

## Conclusion

The need to manage demand for health care, the methods that could be used to do it, and the key role of doctors in this process, have not been well appreciated in the UK. There has been no serious published analysis at a national level (at least in England) of why utilisation appears to be rising, and no visible attempt to forecast future demands upon the Service. The NHS has been subject to a global cap on expenditure, and thus had to restrict crudely overall use of the Service. At the same time, Government attempts to increase efficiency in the NHS have probably stoked up demand and utilisation, both frequently used as measures of Government success in handling the Service. The medical profession has had little or no reason seriously to scrutinise, or manage, demand.

That this policy has been inadequate to respond to the powerful forces that are increasing pressure on the NHS budget is not surprising. While most of these forces are part of wider change in society which it is impossible for the NHS to hold back, what can be controlled is how the NHS responds to them. A response could be made at several levels, trying to influence patient-led demands, professional behaviour and NHS 'service' behaviour.

A number of ways of influencing patients directly was examined in this chapter. Blunt methods such as removing services from the NHS or increasing user charges were rejected because they deter appropriate as well as inappropriate demand. Instead it was argued that it may be better to pursue initiatives that might increase access of patients to the NHS but which also route patients to more cost-effective and appropriate sources of care within or outside the NHS. Those that encourage safe self-care seemed particularly promising.

Our first recommendation therefore is that much more action should be taken to increase the availability of simple and accurate information to the public. Some steps have already been taken by the current Government, for example NHS *Direct*, but others have not, for example ranging from greater availability of over-the-counter medication to more information on the latest health scare or on the latest new technology, and how to stay well.

Such initiatives have the potential to increase demands on the NHS. However, to sustain itself we believe that the NHS has no choice but to meet the public appetite for prompt and relevant information about health and health care. Both the content of information and how it is presented to the public will be crucial. In turn this will depend upon how far the Government, or the professional bodies that advise it, are willing to allow the public to carry the risk of self-care. Currently the NHS has an uneven policy towards risk, for example there are strict controls on the registration of doctors and, to an extent, medicines available over-the-counter, but far fewer on the quality of care doctors provide after qualifying.

If patient-led demands are inflated by greater availability of information, then it will be all the more important for the Government to act to create an environment within the NHS such that only appropriate demands are met. This will require much closer scrutiny of what we have defined as professional-led and Service-led demands, and creating a more conducive environment for routing demand appropriately.

Our second recommendation is that professional behaviour bearing on service utilisation must be systematically scrutinised. Professional peer review through clinical audit, development and use of clinical guidelines and protocols, and the practice of evidence-based medicine is slowly increasing. But huge variations in professional-led demand still exist. To help encourage better informed and more consistent clinical decision-making, the Government could take a number of steps. These range from developing much more accessible forms of information on costs and effects, which are relevant to practical clinical decision-making, to introducing incentives to encourage doctors to use the information. Early and significant steps have been taken in this direction with the formation of the Commission for Health Improvement, the National Institute for Clinical Excellence and national service frameworks. The incentives range from those that give greater reward to professionals for self-audit and cost-effective practice, to those that reward doctors financially for managing a budget effectively or which encourage greater peer review of clinical practice, and those that require the medical profession to act in a particular way or risk being sanctioned. So far the Government has proposed methods to encourage more cost-effective practice, through providing more information and through the use of incentives such as allowing doctors to manage capitated budgets (as in the case of primary care groups). Monitoring and stiff sanctions have appropriately been off the agenda, so far.

Inadequate professional peer review of clinical performance is likely to lead to greater scrutiny of clinical practice by the State or a third-party organisation such as the Audit Commission or the new Commission for Health Improvement. This could eventually lead to detailed specifications to the medical profession of the clinical criteria that will justify a professional-led demand to be met by the Service. However, in the shorter term we believe that the Government should hold back from such draconian measures and concentrate on encouraging an environment more conducive to peer review and evidence-based practice (the points at the top rather than the bottom of Figure 9.3).

Third, we suggest that a mandatory 'demand' audit should be performed on all new policies, starting with the introduction of PCGs and NHS *Direct*, and this should be a major strand of the NHS R&D programme. At a national level, far too little is known about the effects on demand of national policies, such as requirements to increase productivity, increase staff numbers, reduce waiting times for elective care, changes to methods of reimbursing hospitals and changing provider configuration. It is likely that many of these initiatives have pushed up demand, and been in conflict with other policies such as encouraging a shift from secondary to primary care. More careful thinking is required when policies are designed as to their incentives, and how far they are aligned with those in other major initiatives within or outside of the NHS, such as in social care. Better 'real time' monitoring of demand in relation to new policies is also required in the Service itself.

Finally, how control of the diffusion of new technologies in the NHS is managed needs more careful consideration. Up until now responsibility for this has been largely in the hands of purchasers, who have had little influence over providers. Even this influence may weaken if purchasing devolves to primary care groups. Giving greater support to providers – in the form of better information and stronger incentives to use it – may be a more fruitful way forward. The National Institute for Clinical Excellence should provide at least the first of these.

Of the three types of demand – patient-led, professional-led and Service-led – the Government has most capacity to influence Service-led and then professional-led demands. This is where most effort should be focused in the short-term. But in the medium term, the nettle of managing patient-led demand will have to be grasped.

## References

1. Tudor Hart J. *The inverse care law.* No. 7626 (27 February 1971), pp. 405–12.
2. Dunnell K. Are we healthier? *Population Trends* 1995; 85: 12–18.
3. Impicciatore P, Chiara P, Casella N and Bonati M. Reliability of health information to the public on the world-wide web: systematic survey of advice on managing fever in children at home. *BMJ* 1997; 314: 1975.
4. Munro J *et al. Evaluation of NHS Direct first wave sites: first interim report to the Department of Health.* Sheffield: University of Sheffield – School of Health and Related Research – Medical Care Research Unit, 1998.
5. Whynes D and Baines D. Income based incentives in UK general practice. *Health Policy* 1998; 43: 15–31.
6. Kasper JK *et al.* Developing shared decision making programmes to improve the quality of care. *Journal of Quality Improvement, Quality Review Bulletin* 1992; 18: 183–86.
7. NHS Executive/Department of Health. *Quality and Performance in the NHS high level performance indicators and clinical indicators.* London: Department of Health, 1999.
8. Rosen R and Mays N. The impact of the UK NHS purchaser–provider split on the 'rational' introduction of new technologies. *Health Policy* 1998; 43: 103–23.

# Chapter 10

# Sharing the cake

In a *national* health service, as we suggested in Chapter 3, it would seem reasonable that everyone, in all parts of the country, should have access to more or less the same range and quality of service and hence that two people with similar clinical conditions but living in different areas should be treated in similar ways. If there are differences, these should arise because of differences in personal circumstances which might make one form of treatment more appropriate or acceptable to one person and another form more appropriate to the other, not differences in the availability of financial or human resources in different parts of the country.

But while it appears reasonable that, in a national health service, each part of the country should have available to it the same level of resources relative to need, after allowing for differences in costs of service provision, that goes only a little way towards bringing about a situation within which any two people with similar conditions do in fact receive similar treatment. Unlike, for example, social security, both health care provision and the health care needs of individuals are very diverse. Consequently, the allocation of health resources cannot be reduced to a series of rules and formulae such as govern the distribution of income support, which would allow the type of treatment for each user to be determined in a more or less routine matter in the way that an entitlement to benefit is calculated.

But if this extreme of codification is not attainable, that leaves open two questions. First, on what basis should resources be allocated to broad groups of individuals such as mentally ill people, cancer sufferers and so on? And second, within such groups, how should decisions be made as between individuals 'competing' for the same resources? In other words, how to handle the inevitable gap between what people might want and what can be provided.

As we outline in the first part of this chapter, the NHS has been slow to address this issue directly. Indeed, most Governments have been reluctant to admit that the issue arose at all and, where it was recognised, have always preferred to refer to 'setting priorities' rather than 'rationing' – the term we use below. In the absence of a central lead, the question of 'who gets what' has been answered implicitly, largely at local level, and largely through the exercise of clinical discretion. But as we argued in the first section of this book, the context within which the NHS now works makes that approach less tenable than it was 50 years ago. The greater visibility of instances of care being withheld or new forms of care being introduced selectively means that the question has to be answered more explicitly than in the past.

But while the environment within which the NHS works makes that inevitable, to attempt to answer the question of how best to ration NHS resources raises a number of tensions between different views of what the role of the Centre should be and precisely how the broad objectives within which the NHS works should be interpreted. In other words, how the overall resource cake is shared depends on the answers to a series of further questions about the nature of a national health service, such as precisely what the scope for local discretion should be and what considerations are relevant to choosing between people and between services. We discuss these in the second part of the chapter and then draw out some general conclusions and suggestions for a way forward.

## The development of rationing

For nearly all the life of the NHS, the implications of an effectively constrained budget – that choices have to be made as to how those resources are used as to who should get care, what level of care should be available and precisely what range of services should be on offer – have been resolutely ignored by the Centre.

*Consciously and explicitly* choosing who received NHS benefits was simply not a public issue during the early decades of the NHS. No public discussion, or government document, gives any indication that minds were specifically focused on principled ways of distributing the benefits. It seems curious now, when any instance of an NHS 'failure' or 'cut' is termed *rationing*, that the word itself was not used until the mid-1960s and not regularly until the 1980s. Nevertheless rationing was pervasive, often hidden under the notion of clinical freedom.

The lack of public debate in the early years of the NHS might be put down to the fact, that the NHS was still something of a novelty and its 'consumers' were simply pleased to be offered free health care of high quality. Clinicians for their part were glad to be relieved of the concerns of financial insecurity and were confident in their ability to manage the pressures from what was then a largely undemanding public. There were financial pressures of course, even in the early days, but they derived from a Service that was enjoying new social obligations, and not one which yet had to struggle with the notion of withholding treatment. Enoch Powell's reflections on being Minister for Health in the early 1960s are now widely acknowledged as highly prescient on many current issues in health care, and rationing is no exception. He noted[1] that:

> ... *the public are encouraged to believe that rationing in medical care was banished by the NHS, and that the very idea of rationing being applied to medical care is immoral and repugnant* (p.38).

He went on to assert:

> ... *that the worst kind of rationing is that which is unacknowledged; for it is the essence of a good rationing system to be intelligible and consciously accepted. This is not possible where its very existence has to be repudiated* (p.38).

Rationing continued to be repudiated at least as far as public policy-making and official reports were concerned. Instead, concern about the distribution of resources focused initially on the vast differences in physical and human resources in different parts of the country. We consider next how this issue was approached and then the impact of this process. We go on to look at some of the issues that must be resolved if the NHS is to distribute its resources more fairly.

## Equitable distribution of resources

In 1948, the NHS took over health services that varied markedly in quality and availability. In some parts of the country the hospital service was scarcely developed: in others, such as London and the other big cities, there were massive concentrations of both physical capital and professionals. The more poorly served areas were often those in which population was growing: those well served, in which population was declining. The 1962 Hospital Plan was designed to ensure that such gross disparities were removed by ensuring that people in all parts of the country did have reasonable access to a district general hospital.

Later, the so-called 'Crossman formula', which operated from 1970 to 1975, was devised to promote a fairer distribution of financial resources between different parts of the country although the measures used were widely criticised at the time.[2] But it was only in 1976, with the publication of the Resource Allocation Working Party report,[3] that systematic attempts were made to equalise, relative to need, the revenue resources available across the country for hospital and community health services.

The formula derived then has been changed several times in the intervening period, but the broad objectives of the process have proved largely uncontroversial. Indeed the changes made consequent on the NHS and Community Care Act 1990, which reduced the level of discretion enjoyed by regional health authorities over how resources were allocated to health authorities, meant that the objective was pursued more rigorously than ever before, at least as far as revenue resources for hospital and community health services were concerned.

The situation in primary care was different when the NHS was established. The national Medical Practices Committee was charged with ensuring the availability of general practice services in all parts of the country. Its main lever of control was to prevent new practices being established where there were already judged to be enough. But it could not compel practitioners to move to areas judged to have too few. Money, however, followed general practitioners and hence their decisions determined where financial resources went, not the other way. Areas that remained less well served did not get extra cash to use, for example, on more nurses by way of compensation.

The first steps were taken in the 1970s towards the development of a national policy for the distribution of resources between broad groups of the population through the creation of a so-called 'programme budget'. This identified the resources that each group received and provided the basis for recommendations from the Centre as to their future growth rates. Then, as now, the concern was to shift resources away from the acute hospital and towards neglected groups such as mentally ill and elderly people. These were termed 'priority' groups to highlight and help to counter their evident neglect.

Subsequently, the Royal Commission on the NHS devoted a whole chapter to 'Priorities' in which a commitment to elderly mentally ill and handicapped people was supported and encouraged. But the Centre did not follow through to ensure that resources were shifted according to national guidelines. The programme budget still exists, but as a retrospective reflection of what has happened as a result of local and national decisions rather than as a guide to what ought to happen prospectively. The same group of services continued to attract the priority label throughout the 1980s and into the 1990s when some NHS community trusts adopted the word in their title.

The practical impact of 'priority' status is very hard to discern. It certainly did not lead to a central prescription as to exactly what form of services should be provided and how individuals should be judged to be eligible for them. Even when a specific element for mental health services was introduced into the formula for distributing finance for hospital and community health services, no link to services on the ground was made by, for example, creating a specific grant only to be used for mental health care on the basis of the element in the formula.

There have been and remain some exceptions to this broad pattern. First, in a few areas, the Centre has taken initiatives designed to influence the availability of particular services and by implication ensure all parts of the country enjoyed a reasonable level of service. In some exceptional instances such as the national response to AIDS, when it appeared to have the potential to become a mass epidemic, funds were allocated centrally to ensure a proper level of local provision. In the field of preventive care, screening and monitoring programmes for children, women and older people have been developed on a national basis, and, by being entrenched in the GP contract, a clear, if not entirely effective, incentive was created for national coverage to be attained, particularly for children.

Second, as noted above, the process for determining the allocation of resources to general practice has been quite different, and has demonstrably failed to produce an equitable result. The Medical Practices Committee has been successful in closing popular areas to new practices and in this way steering GPs to the less popular. But this process has fallen far short of direction. In effect, successive Governments have accepted that the nature of the NHS's relationship with general practitioners meant that it could not be directive, thus ruling out 'perfect' territorial equity for primary care services. The result has been noticeable differences in the volume of medical resources available in different parts of the country which, even with combined primary and secondary budgets, will take a considerable time to even out.[4]

Third, the allocation of capital resources has always proved difficult largely because of the complexities involved in measuring the quality and quantity of the capital stock in different areas. This is, however, essentially a technical matter. The introduction of the private finance initiative posed a different issue. In effect, the way that the policy was introduced under the Conservatives meant that access to capital would be determined by factors totally unrelated to the aim of territorial equity such as the interests of the private sector and the ability of local teams to put successful bids together. The Labour Government has attempted to correct the worst effects of the previous 'free for all' system by introducing a centrally run capital prioritisation process. But, as noted in Chapter 5, that can only operate on the schemes submitted to it, that is, it cannot make good any shortfall of schemes coming forward. In effect, given its hope that private finance will produce more cost-effective schemes, the Government has accepted the risk of some inequity as the price of presumed greater efficiency.

Fourth, the Centre has introduced a number of special funds in recent years, such as the mental health challenge fund and monies to ease winter pressures, which have been used to encourage innovation and prevent local crises. The Comprehensive Spending Review went further by setting aside £5 billion for the so-called 'Modernisation Fund' over three years. In practice, this means that the Centre can impose its view of where additional resources should go, both in terms of the services that should attract them and the purchasers who should get them, and thus bypass the established systems of resource allocation. For example, the primary care 'walk-in' centres mentioned in the previous chapter will be funded from this source and they will not, initially at least, form a national network.

## Impact

With the exceptions noted, the way that financial resources have been allocated to regional health authorities and then to health authorities left the question of 'who gets what?' ultimately to them or to the providers themselves to resolve. In the case of primary care, the decision as to the use to which the budget for general medical services was put was also firmly in the hands of GPs themselves. Whether equity in provision or access between different parts of the country was in fact achieved by the various measures set out above, despite it being a fundamental objective of the NHS since its foundation, has never been systematically monitored by the Centre. Similarly, whether the criteria used locally by individual clinicians to allocate resources contravened the values, implicit in national legislation, of racial or gender equality has never been systematically tested.

Such a strategy worked remarkably well for the first 40 years or so of the NHS in the sense that there was no sustained public outcry over the inevitable differences in provision, even though those working within the Service or, close to it by virtue of their academic activities, were well aware of the wide variations in what was on offer and how it was provided in different parts of the country.

But the cracks started to show in the 1990s, partly as a result of changes within the external environment, as outlined in the first part of this book, but also because of changes within the NHS itself. One of the under-estimated consequences of the 1991 NHS reforms has been the impact of health authorities' responsibility to purchase care for *specific populations* (or lists of patients in the case of GP fundholders) and to specify the range and volume of services they should benefit from. This contrasts quite sharply with the situation prior to 1991 under which a patient requiring secondary care could, in principle, be referred by a GP to any consultant he or she wished, irrespective of the location and cost. The place of residence of an individual patient was not intended to have a decisive effect on the nature of treatment received, though of course it would have an influence, with proximity of hospitals always a relevant consideration in referral decisions. Those providing services, such as hospital consultants, would determine the nature of treatment delivered as well as its timing, regardless of the particular health authority in which the patient lived.

The rhetoric of the NHS and Community Care Act 1990 emphasised the scope for local choice that the newly created health authority purchasers enjoyed: in effect the intention was to move the seat of discretion from providers/professionals to more broadly based purchaser organisations. It was recognised at the time of their creation that this would have the effect of making the implicit processes of determining who got what explicit, and in due course that occurred. As we noted in Section 1, cash-strapped authorities started to take a hard look at the bundle of services they were purchasing and many decided that some services should be excluded from the NHS bundle.

The outcome has been the development of *overt* geographical variations in availability. Couples seeking fertility treatment might be aware of close neighbours receiving care on the NHS, when they were denied it. Two patients in the same cancer ward might discover they are on different drug regimens because one lives in an area where the health authority has decided that a new drug is worth purchasing and the other does not.

Such variations between identifiable individuals could be defended as the legitimate working of a local NHS following local priorities, or as the result of legitimate differences of judgement about what is the most cost-effective treatment. However, such judgements are now no longer just those of individual consultants, but of corporate bodies – health authorities and primary care groups. The perception, therefore, is that these decisions are 'managerial' and 'arbitrary' rather than clinically based on need. Furthermore, they are specifically related to a geographical place of residence, something that the on-looking public view as entirely irrelevant to clinical need. We noted in Chapter 2 that the process of identifying apparent inequities is driven by the media, which thrives on stories of denied health care. An increasingly well educated and informed public are now becoming exposed to such incidents and are starting to question the basis and legitimacy of such decisions. The introduction of primary care groups may, despite the clinical involvement in decision-making that they will entail, make the situation worse. Because of their smaller size the risk of anomalous differences in the availability of services will rise.

Some of these incidents have focused on particular cases such as 'Jennifer's Ear' – which belonged to a child waiting for an operation to insert grommets – at the time of the 1992 election and 'Child B' – a child with leukaemia refused experimental treatment on the NHS – in 1996. Others, such as decisions by some health authorities not to fund *in vitro* fertilisation, raised the issue of where the boundary of the NHS was and who should determine it. Still more concern variations in availability of particular drugs such as Beta Interferon and the drugs to treat cancer, which gave rise to the phrase 'rationing by postcode' a phrase that encapsulated the apparent arbitrariness of what the NHS was, and was not, providing.

At the service level, as we also noted in Chapter 2, similar issues arose over the availability of dentistry and long-term care, both of which have partially slipped out of the NHS. The latter is a particularly striking example of changes being made surreptitiously without public debate. Grass roots anxieties expressed, for example, through the charity Age Concern failed to make the issue a national one: the turning point was the Leeds case[5] referred to in Chapter 3 which stemmed from an individual complaint to the Health Service Commissioner. The case led to recognition by the Centre that guidelines were required for the provision of continuing care within the NHS. But these left the precise rules for local determination, even though the potential for inequity was vast since differences of local interpretation have potentially massive financial consequences for the individuals concerned – the difference between free care provided by the NHS and an annual bill of £20,000 or more for care provided by the private sector or local authority. The 1999 Coughlan case[6] served to emphasise, at a high cost in terms of legal bills, the failure of the guidelines to produce a fair result.

Local discretion has also largely determined access to elective care. The waiting list is perhaps the most visible sign of the NHS having to curb access to care; its rationing role has been recognised at least since the Royal Commission in the 1970s. Over the years, successive governments have tried to eliminate or at least drastically cut back the numbers waiting for elective hospital treatment. But no government-inspired attempt has been made to ensure that access times were similar in different parts of the country or in line with any explicit set of principles as to who, or what kind of cases should have priority. There is one exception to this: the two-week target set for access to a consultant for women who might have breast cancer.

The number of people quoted as waiting for elective treatment is a national total. That total is the sum of several thousand individual lists, each of which is determined by the relevant hospital consultant using his or her discretion. So despite the fact that the Conservative Government introduced national targets for access to elective care, it did not attempt to ensure equality of waiting times for people with the same clinical condition and the same degree of urgency in different parts of the country, nor indeed to measure what the differences in waiting time were for these patients.

Labour made it a priority to introduce common waiting lists for GP fundholders, who held a budget for elective care, and non-fundholders, so as to avoid a situation in which fundholders' patients could 'jump the queue'. But, despite adopting a very active centrally directed policy designed to cut numbers recorded as waiting, it also has done nothing to tackle the implicit inequities arising from differences in waiting times for similar procedures between areas, nor to ensure that patients with different conditions are treated in the 'right' order, and still less to ensure that their need for treatment is spotted at the same stage in the development of their illness. The majority of clinicians do not, as a matter of routine, apply any formal tests of health status to those waiting for treatment and even if they tried there is very little systematic and reliable information available to them as to the clinical, personal and economic costs incurred by those waiting to be treated.[7] In these circumstances, differing levels of access are bound to occur even within the same health authority area.

In some parts of the country attempts have been made by clinicians to devise ways of prioritising patients in terms of relevant characteristics such as the degree of pain they are in or the stage of their disease. So far central support for these initiatives has been very limited. The Centre has not, with the exception of breast cancer, attempted to specify any method of prioritisation or of treatment thresholds.

The new Government has, however, taken a significant step in relation to service provision. The plans announced in *The New NHS* and *A First Class Service* for eliminating poor practice in clinical and economic terms, by setting national service frameworks and standardising the existing range of clinical guidelines, should in time lead to greater uniformity of service standards. So too should the performance assessment framework, which includes a set of measures designed to identify whether service levels are roughly similar in different parts of the country. In these ways, differences in access that reflect different degrees of availability should eventually be reduced.

## Unresolved tensions

Although these developments promise to move the NHS in the direction of greater uniformity, any attempt to go very far down this path highlights a number of fundamental tensions between different views as to what a national health service should comprise and how choices between different users ought to be taken.

### No shared consensus over objectives

The new visibility, and different mechanisms for making many of the choices that have always taken place, has revealed an absence of a clear, shared understanding of the role of the NHS, of the objectives it is intended to pursue and of the appropriate criteria for discriminating between those who make a claim on its resources. Even amongst those who acknowledge that rationing is inevitable and that it will persist, regardless of increased funding, there is no consensus about the principles on which those choices should be made. For example, is the NHS about producing maximum gains in health or relieving suffering? Or, as the recent emphasis on health inequalities would suggest, about raising the health status of those whose health is poorest at the possible expense of reducing services to others?

In those countries where the rationing issue has been explicitly addressed – The Netherlands,[8] New Zealand,[9] the US State of Oregon and the

Scandinavian countries[10] – there has in every case been a government-sponsored committee tasked with analysing the issues and making recommendations, usually set up by the minister or health department but independent of both. As a consequence, public debate has not been hindered by ministers of health contradicting logic and the evidence of ordinary people's experience that access to NHS resources is in fact rationed, as it has always been.

This is not to say that progress has been rapid, or even that any 'solution' is possible. Of the countries named, most have developed some set of criteria, or 'values', which are designed to establish the principles by which choices should be made. These principles reflect what is believed to be the motivations behind having a public health care system in the first place. The Netherlands emphasises 'necessity, effectiveness and efficiency' as well as 'individual responsibility'. New Zealand also promotes concepts of effectiveness and efficiency. Sweden favours an emphasis of 'dignity, equity and respect'. Norway refers to 'severity of disease' and effectiveness. All make some reference to the fundamental importance of health care.

There has been no such Commission in the UK. However, in the annual *Priorities and Planning Guidance* the NHS Executive has for several years set out three broad criteria by which the NHS should be judged: equity, efficiency and responsiveness. While laudable, the trouble with these concepts, like those mentioned above, is their essential blandness. Most, if not all, people agree that the Service should be efficient, that only treatments that are necessary and which work should be provided, that we should have respect for human dignity, that equity and fairness are important, and that responsiveness to the individual is valuable. They are all 'first-order' principles, so-called because they do command general agreement.

But this consensus contrasts with the fact that we may disagree strongly about precisely how we are to attain equity, responsiveness and efficiency or any other of these values. Is responsiveness about responding to every demand made by patients or to demands made on patients' behalf by health professionals? Is fairness about minimising inequalities in health status, or maximising the good, i.e. the health gain, that can be achieved? Does efficiency relate to minimising waste or to maximising health gain?

On top of these disagreements, there is no accepted way of measuring the relative importance of each of the elements. So, we might agree that the NHS is legitimately pursuing objectives that aim to provide as much health care as possible while also 'rescuing' those most in need but who can benefit little, improving the health status of disadvantaged groups, restricting 'inappropriate' interventions, controlling national expenditure and providing reassurance and security. These reflect many of the values articulated above and it is hard to disagree violently with any of them. But clearly the more emphasis is given to health gain for the whole community, the more this is likely to militate against rescuing at high cost all those who are extremely sick but for whom little can be done to change their health status. The more we wish to improve the health status and access to health care of disadvantaged groups, the less we will be able to meet demands from others. The objectives have to be traded off one against the other, even where we may agree about the validity.[11] Making these trade-offs is perhaps best regarded as impossible except through the unfathomable, implicit, processes of individual judgement.

This conclusion is based on the arguments of Calabresi and Bobbitt.[12] They argue that societies adopt and then discard a particular set of values as the consequences of following them become clear. They then adopt a new set, and the process continues, with conflicting values and objectives taken up almost 'in rotation'. In the context of the NHS, where decisions are taken by a large number of individuals every day, this means that a life-saving decision with a small probability of success may be taken one day, whilst the next a decision may be made to devote resources only where they will have maximum effect. The trade-off does not remain constant, but shifts in an endless attempt to escape the 'tragic' consequences of actions. The harsh reality of the world, which involves death and suffering for some at all times cannot be avoided, but we can *act as though* it is possible to avoid them, or at least so that a particular form of consequence does not become the norm. For if this 'rotation of values' ceased, then particular classes of person may well appear to be publicly and visibly less 'eligible'. That such a process has evolved may support one overriding objective of the NHS, that of reassurance and security. But if so, it sets limits on the scope for reducing choices as to how health care resources should be allocated to a single calculus.

The annual NHS *Priorities Planning Guidance* manages to side-step these complexities. It contains a large number of objectives that imply a commitment to use resources in particular ways, but the balance between them is left to local discretion. Thus, choices appear to be being made by the Centre, but *only* at the level of appearance since the Centre has no way of guaranteeing that resources will be committed to its priorities.

That might change: the development of national service frameworks could lead in the direction of earmarked budgets – mirroring the pattern of specific grants which the Centre used extensively to influence the spending priorities of local government. But although such a move is administratively feasible, it would not itself resolve the tensions set out here. Indeed, it could serve to highlight them – if, for example, resources had to be denied to 'needy' patients with one form of illness because they were 'ring-fenced' for patients with another.

## Conclusion

Since the foundation of the NHS, there has been substantial progress in making the allocation of resources to different parts of the country more equitable for hospital and community health services, but less for family health services and for capital.

As far as variations in the availability and quality of services are concerned, measures set out in *The New NHS* such as national service frameworks and the establishment of the National Institute for Clinical Excellence will, albeit gradually, push the Service towards a more uniform pattern of provision.

But at the level of the individual much less progress has been made. Successive Governments have been reluctant to admit that beneficial health care should ever be withheld and hence to become directly involved in determining 'who gets what'.

The benefit of this approach is that responsibility for rationing between individuals lies with clinicians and is implicit. But the danger of continuing in this way could be that it will only breed mistrust amongst the population at large about the NHS as a whole, uneasy that they will be denied care, arbitrarily, when they need it. Given the media attention the resulting 'hard cases' can attract, there is really no alternative but to admit that choices have to be made and to ensure that the reasons for this are widely understood.

The admission that resources are finite and that the answers to the questions posed by this chapter must be tackled directly, must principally come from the Centre. No significant progress can be made in establishing a fairer or more democratic means of choosing between claimants on health services whilst the Centre hinders progress by refusing to acknowledge the true nature of the issue. A broad framework to help hard-pressed health authorities would be a useful start.

But even if this step *were* taken the dilemmas set out above would still remain. As we argued in Chapter 3, until we are clear what a *national* health service should be, the way in which scarcity should be managed cannot be determined. As the previous discussion has shown, the tension between diversity and uniformity can be recast as tension between the Centre and the local NHS as to where decisions about 'sharing the cake' should be made. The media pressures described above push decisions upward, but not only is the Centre currently unprepared to make them but, in the absence of agreed criteria and a calculus of benefit, it could not make anything other than broad-brush recommendations. As we have argued above, the case-by-case basis through which access to financial support is determined within the rules governing social security is not a practical mechanism for health care. No centralised system of rules can ever hope to be sufficiently flexible and sophisticated to accommodate all circumstances.

We have argued that any attempt to specify which treatment is appropriate for which patient in any individual circumstance is doomed to failure because of the specificity of the decision and the variation in individual circumstances. Because of the heterogeneity of patients, clinicians will always and necessarily be the ultimate arbiters of the individual decision. In order to sustain public confidence, and to accommodate conflicting and continually shifting objectives for a national health service, it is necessary to respect a host of criteria or guidelines that may be deployed by the clinical professions in individual cases. But if the Centre cannot provide a precise calculus, how can progress be made towards a 'fairer' NHS?

If it is accepted that perfect uniformity cannot or should not be striven for, the question is, what kind of broad framework can the Centre reasonably provide? A 'fair' financial framework is essential. As the present Government has recognised, the basis for allocating revenue resources to different geographical parts of the NHS must be kept under review, so as to allow new factors to be taken into account or new data sources to be exploited. As part of this process, the implications of using specially allocated funds, e.g. to Health Action Zones or waiting list reductions, and use of the private finance initiative for equity in distributing capital funds need to be taken into account. Finally, as the Government has also accepted, more effective measures to improve access to general medical and general dental services in areas that are currently under-served are required.

But once such broad matters are dealt with, in which areas and on what terms, does the Centre stand aside and allow local choice as to what is available, the way that services are provided and the volume and standard which are purchased, the thresholds at which care is offered and the nature of the evidence used to support particular choices? These issues can only be resolved as part of broader discussion of the role of the Centre and the local NHS. That clarity will be hard to achieve, a point we return to in Section 3 of this book. However, even without clarity as to how their respective roles are defined, there are areas where progress could be made.

First, criteria can be identified which are clearly and unambiguously *not* appropriate, such as the income of the patient or their ethnic origin, or their clinical 'interest' to the physician. The General Medical Council's guidance to doctors, *Good Medical Practice*,[13] states that:

> **12.** *You must not allow your views about a patient's lifestyle, culture, beliefs, race, colour, sex, sexuality, age, social status, or perceived economic worth to prejudice the treatment you give or arrange* (p.5).

These may seem uncontentious. Age Concern has, however, pointed to variations in access based on age in relation to cardiac rehabilitation[14] which are hard to justify in terms of ability to benefit. Furthermore, the research evidence is itself 'ageist' since most has been conducted with younger people. In other words, biases can be buried deep within established custom and practice – and if no-one tries to find out whether elderly people can benefit from particular treatments, then they will almost inevitably not receive them.

The commitment to unacceptable sources of variation in access to services could, therefore, be made more explicit and effective. Any steps in this direction could be accompanied by measures within the performance assessment framework which might identify where access for particular groups appeared to be poor. As it stands, the high level performance indicator set[15] contains no measure bearing on access for particular groups. An alternative approach would be to embody criteria of this kind in the audit process by extending the remit of the Audit Commission to cover equity in respect of access to services, particularly for those where there were prima facie grounds for believing that unacceptable variations existed.

But are these all the considerations that *should* be taken into account? The guidance states:

**33.** *You should always seek to give priority to the investigation and treatment of patients solely on the basis of clinical need* (p.9).

While that may seem appropriate guidance for clinicians, it flies in the face of the reality of day-to-day implicit rationing.

However, the former Chief Medical Officer, Sir Kenneth Calman, has argued[16] that the Hippocratic oath should be reformulated to take into account the medical profession's responsibilities towards the whole community not just the individual patient. His suggested modification reads:

> I will recognise that the decisions I make will have consequences for the patient, for the community and resources (p.223).

That formulation still leaves the precise balance between competing considerations to be resolved, but it does have the substantial merit of recognising the situation in which clinicians actually practise as well as the needs of the Service at large.

Second, within the existing bundle, more can be done to even out geographical variations in access. In the case of elective care, the Government's current emphasis on reducing the total number of patients waiting is completely misplaced. Equity of access requires a focus on the factors that determine how people are accepted for treatment, particularly the thresholds at which they are offered treatment and the effectiveness of the Service in identifying their needs.

The desirability of agreed thresholds for access to elective care has been recognised in a series of official reports. Little has happened as a result but the limited evidence available suggests variations for common conditions are considerable. A report by the National Audit Office[17] on cataract surgery in Scotland found, in line with academic research, that there were considerable differences in the extent to which people receiving surgery had lost their sight, even though there was reasonable agreement among hospital-based clinicians as to appropriate indications for the degree of sight loss that should trigger surgical intervention. The differences arose largely because of variations in the ability of GPs to identify need for treatment and that in turn reflected their training and their relationships with hospital-based consultants. The wide variations in access identified in the study could not be defended on any grounds.

Thresholds for some other conditions may be harder to derive, but, as the British Medical Association itself has recently argued,[18] some move in this direction is required, if the Government is to be shifted from its preoccupation with numbers waiting. In New Zealand this approach has been taken much further: access thresholds have been defined for a wide range of conditions: those not attaining them are in effect being denied part of their health 'cake' – until their condition changes. The result has been an approach to waiting lists that is open and hence subject to debate and improvement, and which, moreover, reduces the risk inherent in the present Government's policies of the less urgent taking precedence over the more urgent.

Some sources of variation in access lie outside the NHS itself. The factors underlying poor take-up of preventive care include personal as well as social, economic and ethnic elements, which are hard to disentangle. As Goddard and Smith[19] have shown, there is evidence suggesting that access does differ as between different groups, but as they point out, the evidence is often hard to interpret precisely because so many factors bear on how people decide to use the services that are available, so even where differences are identified, what measures should be taken is far from clear. The way ahead therefore is to focus on services such as cancer care where poor or delayed access, typically before patients reach the hospital for diagnosis, is of critical importance to final outcomes. To do this, however, requires much more information than is currently available on the actual delays people experience in obtaining care and on the nature of the obstacles that hinder them. The Government has begun to target cancer waiting times for out-patient consultation, but it has so far not tackled the access issue more broadly.

Third, changes to the bundle of services that the NHS comprises should be made explicitly. In A *Service with Ambitions*, the Conservative Government stated that no clinically effective treatment would be ruled out, effectively leaving decisions as to who to treat (and how) to clinical discretion – a discretion that was not even limited by a central statement as to the criteria that might or might not be relevant to such decisions. Furthermore, the Government did not attempt to define what bundle of services the NHS should comprise.

Although international and UK experience suggests little scope for cutting back on the current bundle of services, changes to the bundle do occur. In the cases of dentistry and long-term care cited in Chapter 3, the bundle was reduced without public debate. Not only was that unfair to individual users, as cases brought to the Health Service Commissioner have revealed, but as we have argued already, the gaps in coverage that emerged in dentistry and the apparent denial of NHS care to those needing continuing care have served to undermine the NHS itself. It has seemed to be backing out of service obligations which the public at large thought it had entered into. What this suggests is that the Centre has to be explicit about the process of reducing the bundle: any other course risks, as did these changes, undermining general confidence in the NHS. Experience in other countries suggests any attempt to do so would have been unsuccessful, and possibly unpopular. But the risks of not doing so are greater unpopularity in the longer-term.

The same is true of additions, particularly new drugs or surgical procedures. The introduction of an explicit process of health technology assessment under the Conservatives has worked to reduce variations in availability. The proposals made in Chapter 9 for stronger central control of the introduction of all new technologies, resisting their introduction except on experimental grounds, until some kind of national clinical consensus has been established on their cost-effectiveness, will promote uniformity. The National Institute for Clinical Excellence will move the Service in this direction but there are limits to its role. The statement by the Secretary of State – of a kind the Institute may be expected to make in future – on Viagra,[20] which provided a clarification of the conditions it should be used to treat, should reduce local variation. But it also comprised judgements about the scope of the NHS, which are properly political in nature and not suitable for technical resolution alone. Similarly, judgements about the health/social care divide are political as much as they are technical.

Similar issues are raised by the development of the public health agenda, which involves forms of intervention that fall outside the usual bounds of the NHS. Should these, like health care, be free? And if fitness training is 'in' why is some nursing 'out'? The introduction of Healthy Living Centres funded by the National Lottery is almost bound to lead to differences in the availability of services that are explicitly promoted as being 'good for health'.

These issues could be handled by a standing version of the Committees other countries have used to define the boundaries of their national health services. Such a Committee might aim to devise general principles, based on extensive public consultation and debate, and make recommendations on specific issues which would be subject to a final political decision.

Alternatively, such differences as do arise could be defended either in terms of local experiment or local choice. Either way, the Centre should prepare the ground by explaining and, if necessary, justifying such variations in principle. The same holds for variations arising from local experiments in service delivery of the kind we argued in Chapters 6 and 7 were desirable. It will be particularly important to do this for those services, such as those covered by national service frameworks, where the Centre is closely involved but where a single 'best' system of care cannot be confidently determined.

Finally, the Centre should encourage debate around criteria and objectives, including 'acceptable variation'. The statement on the availability of Viagra is the nearest that this or any other Government has come to making a clear decision to restrict access on grounds of cost. The media reaction suggested that there was general recognition of the need to make decisions of this kind. On this basis, the Government could well move on to tackle in public the range of issues discussed in this chapter, taking lessons from New Zealand and The Netherlands, two countries that have attempted this.

## References

1. Powell E. *Medicine and Politics: 1975 and after.* London: Pitman, 1976.
2. Beech R *et al.* Spatial Equity in the NHS: the death and rebirth of RAWP. In: Harrison A, editor. *Health care UK 1990.* Hermitage: Policy Journals, 1990.
3. Report of the Resource Allocation Working Party. *Sharing Resources for Health.* London: HMSO, 1976.
4. Maynard A and Bloor K. Regulating the Pharmaceutical Industry. *BMJ* 1997; 315: 200–01.
5. Health Service Commissioner. *Failure to provide long-term NHS care for a brain-damaged patient. (Leeds case). Second Report for Session 1993–94.* London: HMSO, 1994.
6. Case reference: QBCOF99/10110/CM54. See also *Ex parte Coughlan:* follow-up action (HSC 1999/180).
7. Tudor Edwards R. Points for Pain: waiting list priority systems. *BMJ* 1999; 318: 412–14.
8. Ministry of Health Welfare and Cultural Affairs. *Choices in Health Care.* Rijswijk, 1992.
9. National Advisory Committee on Core Health and Disability Support Services. *Second Report.* Wellington, 1993.
10. Ministry of Health and Social Affairs. *No Easy Choices – the difficult priorities on health care.* Stockholm, 1995.
    The Royal Ministry of Health and Social Welfare. *Retningdlinjer for prioritering innen Norsk helesetjeneste.* Oslo: NOU, 1987.

11. New B. *A Good-enough Service*. London: King's Fund Publishing, 1999.

12. Calabresi G and Bobbitt P. *Tragic Choices: the conflicts society confronts in the allocation of tragically scarce resources*. WW Norton, 1978.

13. General Medical Council. *Good Medical Practice*. London: GMC, 1998.

14. Whelan J. *Equal access to cardiac rehabilitation: age discrimination in the NHS: cardiac rehabilitation services*. London: Age Concern England, 1998.

15. Department of Health – NHS Executive. *Quality and performance in the NHS: high level performance indicators*. London: Department of Health, 1999.

16. Calman K. *The potential for health: how to improve the nation's health*. Oxford: Oxford University Press, 1998.

17. National Audit Office. *Cataract Surgery in Scotland*. London: HMSO, 1997.

18. British Medical Association. *The Waiting List Problem*. London: BMA, 1998.

19. Goddard M and Smith P. *Equity of Access to Health Care*. York: University of York, 1998.

20. Department of Health. PN 1999/0274.

# Chapter 11

# Ensuring the knowledge base

Few would dispute that the NHS is a knowledge-based service. It employs more professionals than any other sector of the economy. Outside the Service, there is a massive investment in this country and world-wide in research directed to improve clinical care, both publicly and privately funded, and a large range of other activities designed to disseminate what has been discovered or established.

Despite the critical importance of knowledge and intelligence, our earlier analysis has brought out a general and persistent failure to provide the NHS with information about, or understanding of, a wide range of issues which are central to the effective running of the Service. Earlier chapters have identified shortfalls in knowledge at national and local level, both of very basic information about 'what is going on' and of some of the most fundamental features of the Service and its clientele which bear on the way that the Service is managed. They also identified a wide range of technical issues, many of which had been recognised since the early days of the NHS but which had not been tackled systematically.

As we have already argued, the need for information and understanding in these areas is growing rather than declining. The development of the central management agenda discussed in the following chapter implies an increased need for the knowledge and intelligence required to guide the Service in whatever are the chosen directions. Some of this need is for clinical information of a kind which is in short supply, for example that bearing on the best way to organise those services which need to be closely linked if they are to be effective in the production of better outcomes for patients. Other needed information concerns the behaviour of individuals and organisations and, in particular, their response to central initiatives as well as the wider environment discussed in Chapter 2. As the next chapter brings out, in many of these areas, the central and local management of the NHS has to proceed in ignorance of precisely these factors.

The central question addressed by this chapter is how far current policies on the development and dissemination of knowledge and intelligence are appropriate to the tasks that the NHS faces now and in the future. We begin by considering the attempts made in recent years to develop an explicit policy towards knowledge and intelligence for the NHS. We argue that although recent changes have undoubtedly moved the Service in the right direction, they have not gone far enough, while other changes have been in the wrong direction. We, therefore, conclude with a series of suggestions for improvement.

## How policy on producing and disseminating knowledge has developed

### Clinical and biomedical dominance

There is no comprehensive source of information on the pattern of spending on health related research including both the derivation of new knowledge and its dissemination. However it is clear enough that the bulk of spending on research takes place in the private sector and most of that within the pharmaceutical industry (see Table 11.1). Nearly all of the latter is aimed at providing new and better forms of treatment rather than the needs of the Service as we have identified them in earlier chapters.

**Table 11. 1:** Spending on R&D in health and health care 1996 by source

|  | £ million |
| --- | --- |
| Private sector | 1852 |
| Medical Research Council | 278 |
| Department of Health | 63 |
| NHS | 408 |

**Source:** Department of Trade and Industry – Office of Science and Technology. *Science, Engineering and Technology Statistics 1998.* Cm. 4006. London: HMSO, 1998.

The private contribution would be all the greater if spending in other countries were included. New drugs and other new medical technologies are internationally traded commodities: new forms of treatment, although not traded, also travel in the sense that a procedure invested in one country can be adopted in another. In contrast, service and organisational knowledge specific to a particular country is less 'tradeable'.

The current pattern of spending reflects the view that has underpinned the development of health care provision world-wide during the 20th century: that improvements come largely from the 'appliance of science'. That belief has justified not only the vast investments in research in both public and private sectors but also the content of the training of the professionals who provide health care. That, as we saw in Chapter 8, is geared overwhelmingly to clinical care, to the relative neglect of other disciplines, even where these bear directly on the efficient and effective application of clinical resources.

In large measure, the NHS has gone along with the view that the bulk of research spending should be devoted to clinical issues or the underlying science. Central government has supported clinical research since the foundation of the Medical Research Committee – later the Medical Research Council – in 1913, but despite this early example, the NHS has had no systematic policy towards the generation of the knowledge required to *run* the Service for most of its life.

The Ministry of Health had a small budget for non-clinical research into the provision of health care services in the 1950s, but as recently as 1977/78 the sum available for this purpose was some £13 million, a tiny amount relative to the costs of the Service as a whole and to the sums being spent on research within the private sector. The Royal Commission on the NHS[1] devoted only a few paragraphs to research but nevertheless concluded that:

> *Biomedical and clinical research were … adequately catered for by the existing agencies, particularly the Medical Research Council. We considered, however, that [non-clinical] health services research needed to be developed* (para.22.63).

But there was no significant response to this observation. A Health Services Research programme was developed by the Centre during the 1980s but Sir Kenneth Stow, a one-time permanent secretary at the DHSS, has remarked[2] that:

> *I know of no strategic issue with which Ministers were concerned during my time as Permanent Secretary which was illuminated by the Health Services Research programme* (p.32).

The failure to tackle such issues stemmed in large part because the Centre was not organised to do so. Research outside the Service was beyond its control. Research within the Service came largely within the field of clinical discretion, or of commercial influence through contracts between parts of the NHS and private sector pharmaceutical companies.

Until recently, this situation went unchallenged. The Centre lacked both the will to control, and the means of controlling, or even influencing the level and deployment of resources devoted to the search for new knowledge related to health care. That was as true of the public as the private sector and even of research carried out within the NHS's own hospitals. The clinical research community within the NHS, as well as that outside it in universities or other research centres, was effectively autonomous or subject to the diverse criteria imposed by funding agencies such as the Medical Research Council, charities, or the private sector.

This situation was effectively challenged for the first time in 1988 in a House of Lords report, *Priorities in Medical Research*[3] from a sub-committee of the Science and Technology Select Committee. Evidence submitted to it identified a large number of weaknesses in the way that health-related research was supported in the universities and elsewhere and major gaps, where significant clinical needs attracted no attention, particularly chronic conditions, primary care and health promotion, as well as the planning and management of health services. It also showed that there was little research into the way the NHS actually worked, and that there were no means of ensuring that the research that was carried out met the needs of the Service.

The Sub-Committee found that '... there appears to be no coherent means of setting [research] priorities' (para.3.15), and went on to remark that: 'The lead from the Department of Health and Social Security is weak' (p.3.15).

In the light of this, echoing the Royal Commission, it concluded that:

> *Public health research and operational research have been inadequately supported. It is especially serious that so large an organisation as the NHS devotes so small a part of its budget to seeking how to improve its own operations. Since public health and operational research will repay investment, spending should be markedly increased* (para.4.12–14).

The Committee was also dismayed to find, in the words of the DHSS evidence, that the main aim of its research programme was to 'provide guidance to Ministers', rather than help the Service directly. The Committee went on to recommend that a National Health Research Authority should be created which would, among other things:

- *identify on behalf of the NHS, and in consultation with medical research interests, both public and private, those areas of research which should be given priority on the basis of service need;*
- *ensure, in conjunction with the Medical Research Council, an adequate research capability for the needs of the NHS in clinical, public health and operational research;*
- *ensure that the results of research are efficiently disseminated and implemented within the NHS;*
- *promote the evaluation of existing clinical practice and undertake technology assessment of both new and current procedures;*
- *promote systematic clinical audit (the evaluation of the appropriateness of treatment in specific cases);*
- *oversee the provision of statistical information for the NHS, in co-operation with the Office of Population Censuses and Surveys (para.4.6).*

The report recommended that the Authority should be organisationally separate from the central department but nevertheless would be an 'integral part of the NHS.' That recommendation was not followed to the letter but its main thrust was accepted. Michael Peckham was appointed as the first Director of Research & Development in 1991.

## A national R&D strategy

In the words of *Research for Health*,[4] Professor Peckham's first report:

> *The NHS R&D Programme was created in 1991. It is a new departure; the first attempt by any country to establish a coherent R&D infrastructure to support the promotion of health and the provision of health care. The programme is intended to correct existing deficiencies in knowledge and provide a basis for improvements in the approach taken to health care by managers, health care professionals and the users of health services. The potential gains in terms of efficiency and improved quality of care are large (p.8).*

The creation of an explicit R&D strategy for the NHS was only a first step towards the goal of ensuring that the resources devoted to research were in line with service needs. In itself it did not bear on the bulk of the research carried out by the NHS or within NHS establishments. The scale of the resources involved in the wider NHS was, at the time the strategy was formulated, unknown, as was its content.

In 1993, a Task Force under Professor Antony Culyer was established to examine the basis on which research, by and within, the NHS was funded. The immediate stimulus to its establishment was the fear that NHS trusts carrying out research would be handicapped within the internal market that the 1991 Act promised to create. Previous funding mechanisms had allowed for the costs associated with research but only in a broad brush manner, so that NHS trusts carrying out high levels of research could not be confident they would not be at a disadvantage in respect of the price of their clinical services in what was then expected to be a competitive environment.

More significant in the present context is that the funding arrangements did not allow for any degree of central control over the content of what was done. The Culyer Task Force proposed a new explicit funding mechanism, which would in principle allow some control over the content of research and where it was carried out. The Task Force was not itself able to establish the scale of research within the NHS, nor the scale of the funding it absorbed. But acceptance of the Culyer proposals led to the first ever attempt to identify the number, scale and content of research within the NHS. It identified expenditure of some £400 million consisting of several thousand projects, the bulk of them taking place in a small number of institutions, mainly teaching hospitals.

The range of its recommendations are too wide to consider here but their very number and scope indicate that the task of modifying the way in which the NHS generates knowledge itself or supports the generation of knowledge by others is a demanding one. Not surprisingly, therefore, the process of implementing the Culyer recommendations is still under way and, by mid-1999, the shift in the volume of funds from one use to another that could be attributed to the new regime was still modest. The time when the whole of the effort that the NHS devotes to R&D can be judged to be in line with service priorities – assuming that they are correctly identified – is some way off. But at least the process had begun.

The impact of the NHS R&D programme is already clear in some of the areas we have argued have been neglected. Programmes of work have been developed in new areas such as the Primary–Secondary Care Interface and most recently, Service Delivery, Organisation and Management and Human Resources. However, the bulk of NHS R&D spending remains focused on particular clinical areas rather than the larger questions of how these areas relate to each other and to the range of issues we have identified earlier in this book.

Furthermore, it is noticeable that very few studies have been funded either on the more 'political' government policies or with a national rather than local flavour even though there has been a centrally managed Policy Research programme in operation since the establishment of the R&D programme. For example, the internal market reforms, the effects of devolution of purchasing, the effects of the NHS efficiency index, waiting time policies and the impact of reducing the number of acute beds have attracted virtually no centrally funded research monies. By 1995, of the projects funded within the Policy Research programme under the theme 'generic matters of organisation and delivery', only one focused directly on the impact of the 1991 NHS reforms. None evaluated the impact of NHS trusts or other forms of purchasing/commissioning. Subsequently, the Department funded a programme of work on the effects of different models of purchasing and commissioning of which the bulk went on the evaluation of total purchasing pilot sites, and Primary Care Act pilots. More recently, monitoring programmes have been set up for primary care groups, booked admissions from the waiting list, Health Action Zones and other policies introduced by the Labour Government.

## Reductions in analytic capacity

The NHS R&D programme is of course only one means by which the needs of the NHS for research and intelligence are met. The Centre has always had some research and analytic capacity of its own such as the Economics and Operational Research Division of the DoH as well as an extensive system for collecting data about what the NHS is doing. In the past, much of what is now done at the Centre was in fact carried out by regional health authorities which had statistical and analytical teams of their own which analysed changes in demand, bed use and other managerial and operational matters.

Both the Royal Commission and Sir Roy Griffiths, in his report on management arrangements within the NHS,[5] had argued for a stronger regional administrative tier because the management task facing the central department was too large. The regional health authorities, as they were at the beginning of the 1990s, were substantial bodies in terms of both powers and expertise. But regional capacity to monitor the Service and inform the Centre has been steadily reduced, as regional health authorities became Regional Offices of the NHS Executive. At the same time, there has been a slimming-down of the Centre's professional and analytic staff. This transformation has also meant that crucial areas of expertise have been lost such as informal knowledge based on long experience of how the NHS actually works and institutional memory.

The need for analytic support was, in fact, recognised in the *Review of Functions and Responsibilities in the New NHS*[6] carried out in the wake of the 1991 Act, which stated that:

> The NHS needs to have access to high quality analytical support in statistics, operational research and other disciplines. Most analysis will be done by purchasers and providers who are the main users of the results (p.29).

In practice, what local analytical capacity existed has been squeezed by successive cuts in so-called 'management spending'. One result of the extensive changes within regions and the Centre has been a reduction in the flow of useful analysis and information downwards to the Service as a whole as well as the other way round. At the same time, the gap has not been filled within the Service. NHS trusts and health authorities, as a result of cuts in management costs, have little internal analytic capacity and within general practice there is virtually no capacity for such work. Within this overall trend, a few exceptions can be identified such as the projects run by former Anglia and Oxford Regional Office of the NHS Executive on Emergency and Intermediate Care,[7] both of which have been successful at bringing together a wide range of material and assisting the Service as a whole in using it.

Nevertheless, the wider NHS contributes a vast amount of information to the Centre, as part of its reporting on performance together with routine statistical returns. As far as the upward flow of information is concerned, this primarily concerns finance, the *Patient's Charter*, hospital activity, staffing and bed capacity and there is a separate stream to the Prescription Pricing Authority which monitors prescribing activity.

This upward flow of information is critical to a number of central functions but it is highly selective. Historically it failed to cover key areas such as clinical quality and the patient's experience. The new NHS performance assessment framework, comprising a range of indicators including clinical as well as economic and financial performance, was explicitly designed to provide a more balanced picture of the NHS. Similarly, the National Survey of Patients and Users begins to fill a long-standing gap.

These recent developments only serve to highlight the main point of this section: that for 50 years of its life, both research and intelligence gathering in the NHS has been skewed away from most of the areas that we have identified as being critical to the key tasks facing the Service. Although they plug some of the gaps, they represent only a modest contribution towards understanding how the Service works and the influences upon it. Proper interpretation of the indicators will itself require understanding, based on the informal knowledge referred to above, of what may lie beneath them – of the complex processes that can give rise to legitimate differences between apparently similar parts of the health service – nor can such indicators shed much light on the impact of particular policy instruments on the way the NHS works. That requires substantial additional research and analytic capacity.

Furthermore, very little use appears to be made of the information flowing upwards to inform policy-making at local or national level. For example, apart from the regular series of statistical bulletins using Hospital Episode Statistics, which contain only national summaries, there has been no published analysis covering the country as a whole by the Centre (or indeed any one else) of the hospital activity data now being collected – at least in England. One exception is a computer programme called PRODIGY which does exploit the vast NHS database on prescribing to support local clinicians.

## External bodies

While the internal analytic capacity of the NHS itself has been reduced, the capacity of external bodies to monitor the NHS has increased substantially during the 1990s. Prior to 1990, the performance of the NHS was monitored by the Health Advisory Service, the Mental Health Act Commission, the Health Service Commissioner, responding to the complaints of individuals, and the National Audit Office. The Health Advisory Service was founded in 1969 and, until it was wound-up and re-launched in 1997 as HAS2000, commented primarily on care for elderly people. The Mental Health Act Commission, established in 1983, monitors general developments in mental health care and inspects the services provided by NHS trusts through site visits.

The Health Service Commissioner (Health Service Ombudsman), established in 1973, investigates complaints by individual patients or their relatives and for that reason is not primarily concerned with the general development or performance of the Service. But from time to time, as with the Leeds case (see p.63) or in respect of the handling of complaints, wider issues emerged from the specific investigations. As noted in the previous chapter, it was the Leeds case that led to the Centre accepting that the role of the NHS in long-term care was not properly defined and issuing guidelines to health and local authorities to try to ensure they were.

The National Audit Office is Parliament's instrument for scrutinising the Executive and its writ therefore runs right across the public sector. As a result, it can devote only limited resources to the NHS. However, it does have the significant advantage of presenting its findings to the Public Accounts Committee, which can compel officials and Ministers to attend and give evidence. The reports the Committee issues receive a formal response from the Government in the form of a Treasury Minute, usually covering a series of reports.

Although the National Audit Office addresses national issues such as the implementation of the *Health of the Nation*, the health strategy introduced by the previous Government, it has had perhaps most impact through its reports on specific failures in accountability, such as the scandals cited in Chapter 10, which led to the development of explicit rules for the corporate governance of the NHS at local level. Reports such as these are essential to the accountability of the Service but not to the effective design or provision of services. The National Audit Office has, however, conducted a series of enquiries into screening programmes, which revealed substantial weaknesses in their management and implementation, and which appear to have had a substantial impact on central management of the programme.

In the 1990s, external scrutiny was strengthened by the arrival on the scene of the Audit Commission and the Clinical Standards Advisory Group. The Audit Commission, originally established to monitor the performance of local government, was given a similar role in relation to the NHS in 1990. It is formally independent of the Department of Health and hence free to choose the subjects it wishes to audit. The Commission's reports have added substantially to publicly available knowledge of the way the NHS works in practice. Its primary focus is service delivery and, through its national level reports and subsequent audits with NHS trusts and health authorities, it aims to help the local NHS to discharge its roles better. Although the remit of the Commission means that it rarely addresses national policies directly, its reports inevitably have implications that go wider than questions of local implementation. In the case of its report on the purchase of specialist services for example, as we noted in Chapter 6, the Commission made a series of recommendations which only the Department of Health could address – and which in fact were subsequently addressed in *The New NHS*. Similarly its report on services for elderly people[8] identified a series of obstacles to change at local level such as the financial system, which only the Centre could remove. In this way it has become an effective critic of the national management of the Service.

The Clinical Standards Advisory Group was established in 1991 to meet the concerns of the medical establishment that the market arrangements introduced by the NHS and Community Care Act 1990 would lower clinical standards. It was not formally independent of the Government but has enjoyed de facto freedom to choose what it investigates and how. Its main contribution was to provide a commentary, based on site studies like those of the Audit Commission, of the way that services are currently being provided. The result was a series of reports that have revealed substantial weaknesses in service delivery and organisation at local level. Each concludes with recommendations as to appropriate management action but unlike the Audit Commission it does not have a body of local auditors in the field to follow them up with further local studies. One report on cleft lip and/or palette services[9] was adopted as a model for Service design, but others, such as that on district elective surgery,[10] had no obvious impact. As noted above, the Group is being wound up, although its role will continue through the Commission for Health Improvement.

We have left the role of Health Committee of the House of Commons until last, as it consists of politicians, albeit supported by professional advisers and in contrast to all the other organisations considered here, can and does address policy issues directly. It can call on Ministers to give evidence as well as experts or indeed the general public. Its annual publication on public expenditure contains vast amounts of information on the allocation of resources within health and social services and its subject area reports also succeed in providing information and analysis of what has been happening within them. Furthermore, and this is true of the Public Accounts Committee as well, its reports receive a formal response from the Government. We noted in Chapter 8 its recent report on workforce planning succeeded in opening up a neglected area and eliciting an admission from the Government that the existing arrangements were unsatisfactory.

Over and above these official bodies there is a vast range of professional organisations providing information or analysis on the NHS, such as the Royal Colleges for clinical staff and the Institute of Health Services Management for managers, as well as others including charitable trusts such as the Wellcome Foundation, the King's Fund and the Nuffield Institute.

In some areas, 'non-official' bodies play a leading role, or have done at times in their history, in plugging gaps left by the official bodies. In the case of clinical care for example, the Cancer Research Campaign is a major source of finance for university-based research: the Medical Research Council's evidence to the House of Lords Committee noted that 'medical oncology as a speciality has developed almost entirely through the support of the cancer charities'. As other evidence to the House of Lords Committee indicated, disease-based charities are most effective where there is strong public concern: they are less effective in other fields. As a result many gaps are not plugged.

In other areas, charitable organisations have been effective in making up for failures on the part of the Centre. In the early days of the NHS, the Nuffield Provincial Hospitals Trust (as it was then called) supported a series of studies into management techniques and service issues – particularly the design of hospitals – which it perceived as being neglected by the Department of Health. This contribution was matched by the King's Fund in the 1980s with its initiatives in the then neglected field of health care management as well as its contributions through, for example, *Independent Living Options* promoting new concepts of how support should be offered to disabled people which the NHS – and social services – had not been responsive to. At other points in this book we have drawn heavily on others such as the Institute of Health Services Management/University of Manchester report, *The Future NHS Workforce*, as well as a number of reports on clinical services from the Royal Colleges.

These examples can only be illustrative of the major contribution of both official and other bodies but there is no doubt that taken together they provide a vast amount of information and analysis which the Centre, the Service itself and the general public can use. Valuable though this is, however, what they can achieve is necessarily circumscribed. Each body, both official and non-official, has its role defined by its own financing and reporting requirements. The charitable bodies – the Wellcome Trust apart – have modest resources at their disposal. The official bodies have more, but they are subject to other limitations. The Audit Commission, for example, is bound by nature of the funding to devote most of its resources to topics which it can 'sell' as local audits to NHS trusts and health authorities. The National Audit Office, like the Clinical Standards Advisory Group, lacks a substantial presence in the local NHS and is bound, by its terms of reference, not to challenge directly government policies of the day.

Only the Health Committee among official bodies is in a position to challenge central policy itself. Independent bodies can and do challenge current policy and at times make substantial contributions to knowledge and intelligence about the Service as well as to policy debate. None can commission regular statistical surveys or long-term research. Individually and collectively, they cannot fill the whole range of gaps we have identified, particularly those bearing of the workings of the health care system and the needs of those who manage it.

## Fundamental weaknesses

The picture sketched out in the previous section is a vast and complicated one to which we have not had space enough to do full justice. But it provides sufficient basis to identify several fundamental weaknesses in current arrangements.

### Inadequate focus on service delivery and organisation

The research supported by the NHS is now more relevant to the needs of the Service than it once was and the potential exists, given the machinery now in place, for it to be steered further in this direction. But most investment in the creation of knowledge remains heavily focused on clinical practice. The bulk of private and public money is devoted to clinical issues, either the basic science underlying advances in clinical medicine or the development of new products or the practice of medicine itself. The bulk of the NHS R&D programme has been in this area, including much of the Department's own Policy Research programme.

The continuing emphasis on clinical issues in research priorities means that the issues identified in earlier chapters as critical to the running of the Service remain neglected. This neglect is not simply a matter of lack of resources: rather, it stems from a persistent failure to acknowledge the implications of the central and the local management role, in particular, the vast range of areas where clinical and other issues interrelate and can only be tackled by combining skills and disciplines. In other words, the needs of the NHS as a system of health care delivery have been neglected.

The present Government has defined a series of central roles, such as the creation of national service frameworks, which imply the need for knowledge of whole care systems of the kind that the current balance of research tends not to supply. In these and other areas, a need for better central intelligence and understanding than currently exists is required. *The New NHS* acknowledges the need for change, as follows:

> ... *A new programme of work on service delivery and organisation will look at how care is organised. It will provide research-based evidence about how services can be improved to increase the quality of patient care. In addition the NHS Executive will take a systematic approach to scanning the horizon for emerging clinical innovations* (p.57).

This points in the right direction, but it embodies no sense of the nature of the changes required or the scale of what is needed. However, the terms of reference of the national service frameworks under development require that they identify gaps in knowledge and hence research needs. It remains to be seen how quickly and on what scale the R&D programme will respond but the frameworks should in time help to move the balance of research spending in the right direction, for the services and topics they cover.

## Neglect of the private sector

A second weakness is that the NHS R&D programme has not been based on a proper appreciation of the role of the private sector. The key factor for the private sector is realisable profit potential and the scope for ensuring effective property rights in the results of research. This set of incentives has proved to be effective in encouraging a rapid growth of knowledge bearing on a wide range of clinical interventions of primary interest to the pharmaceutical industry. The regulation of the British pharmaceutical industry has been explicitly aimed at promoting further research and development of this kind.

As we noted in Chapter 5, the Health Committee suggested that the Department of Health should take a more active interest in the content of the research carried out by the pharmaceutical industry, a suggestion that the Government did not adopt. However, 'active interest', even if it were shown, is unlikely to be effective in promoting investigation of treatments that avoid the need for pharmaceutical interventions, nor the use of natural products that are cheap and readily available or where the markets are likely to be small.

There is currently no systematic mechanism for identifying and plugging such gaps by appropriate public action. The Advisory Council on Science and Technology published in 1993 A *Report on Medical Research and Health*,[11] identified a number of areas where links between the needs of the NHS and the private sector were poor and made a series of recommendations designed both to remove generic obstacles such as confusion over property rights as well as to encourage specific initiatives within for example the Department of Trade and Industry's research programme. There has been some response; for example, a research programme on ageing within the LINK initiative (a co-operative programme run by the Department of Trade and Industry consisting of a large number of distinct topic areas largely of interest to business) but no substantial effort to redress the weaknesses identified. As a result, there is a deep-rooted bias within the current pattern of research activity towards areas where profits can be realised rather than health benefits created. The two may coincide, but are not identical. There may be areas, such as the development of 'me-too' drugs which offer little additional therapeutic value over existing ones but which are profitable to the private sector though not to the NHS. There are areas that the private sector is not likely to find profitable, but which may be very valuable to the NHS, such as the development of cheaper alternatives to existing drugs, or where the market is too small – so-called 'orphan drugs'.

## Neglect of users and the public

The shortfalls also lie in a third area, that of users and the public at large. Earlier chapters have pointed to the increasing importance of the user's role. In part the role turns on the user's perception of his or her own needs and personal response to different possible courses of treatment. But it may extend beyond that, as discussed in Chapter 9, to self-treatment, or decision-making as to where and when to seek treatment and also to choose between different forms of treatment. In future, we argued in that chapter, the public will demand more information at the point of use, as well as before it.

The main emphasis of existing policy represents an attempt to improve on a model of delivering health care which is slowly being undermined in part by its own success and in part by wider developments in society. This model is based on professional expertise. As the Merrison Committee[12] pointed out:

> The essential character of a profession is that the members of it have specialised knowledge and skills which the public will wish to use (p.3).

This traditional, indeed medieval, concept of the profession is being undermined by development in the volume of knowledge which now exceeds the abilities of the individual professional to master it, the pace at which new knowledge appears and old certainties are undermined and the ability of information technology to make available professional knowledge either from other professionals or from data banks. In other words, it is becoming harder for individual professionals to master all the relevant knowledge and easier for non-professionals to gain access to it. Given the massive level of spending devoted to clinical research and the related sciences, it can only become harder still. The implications of this are very considerable. As Weed[13] has argued, only a portion of medical knowledge is ever loaded into the minds of professionals and of that only a fraction is retained. Much of what is retained becomes obsolete. He goes on to say that:

> Even with the limited knowledge that it retains, a doctor's unaided mind cannot reliably integrate that knowledge with the infinite variety of data about patients in order to identify and systematically assess all diagnostic or treatment options based on each patient's unique characteristics and needs (p.232).

If this is right, it should lead to a new approach to investing in knowledge both in terms of research and in terms of investment in people. The result would be a modification of the very notion of professionalism. As Eve and Hodgkin[14] have argued:

> In an increasingly complex world it is quite clear that some people will continue to exercise discretion or initiative on behalf of others. We believe that in order to do this well the definition of a professional task should be amended to one where:
>
> > 'one person exercises discretion or initiative with another in a situation of complexity ensuring so far as possible that all necessary information, together with any financial incentives and constraints which the professional may be under, are transparent to the patient or client' (p.84).

The rapid growth in clinical knowledge has been recognised through the introduction of continuing professional development as well as attempts to improve the availability of existing knowledge to practising clinicians. But welcome though these are they do not address the implications of two other developments, the growing desire of individuals to play a larger role in determining the type of treatment they receive as well as its nature, the ability to gain access to such information through the Internet and other sources together with changes in medical and information technology which expand the scope for self-care discussed in Chapter 9. As a recent review of the implications of the human genome put it:[15]

> *Unavoidably, in the face of all these choices, the individual's own role as manager of his or her health will become more prominent. The increasing impact of the Internet will allow patients much more rapid information retrieval, after suspicions are raised or a firm diagnosis is made, than medical caretakers can ever hope to keep up with. This is both a threat and an opportunity. The opportunity is the ability of the Internet to generate and spread an unprecedented amount of information in an easily accessible fashion. The threat is its current lack of quality control. It is essential that medical professionals rapidly adapt to this new format of communication* (p.9).

As we noted in that Chapter, the NHS has begun to respond in a number of ways, e.g. through a self-care guide and NHS On-line. These initiatives may well have a significant impact on how people use the services available to them. As Chapters 2 and 9 brought out, the Service needs to understand better how the broad forces shaping the NHS's external environment influence the way that the Service is regarded and used. The present Government's commitment to a responsive Service, admirable in itself, risks adding to the pressures it faces rather than reducing them. The NHS must, therefore, aim to understand the market it serves and the factors that influence it. There is no easy way to do this, but at the moment the Service lacks even simple descriptive information about patterns of use and patient preferences.

But the impact of changing roles of professionals and users may go further. Experience with NHS *Direct* may lead to changes in the minds both of professionals and the public at large as to how existing knowledge should be deployed and how services should be designed. To respond will require a major re-orientation of the NHS's knowledge base and the way it delivers care. What that means in terms of specific R&D programmes is hard to identify but at minimum it will require a much more rigorous approach to piloting, both to developing the schemes to be piloted and to their evaluation, than has been evident hitherto. This may in turn require greater reliance on organisations that have the capacity to deploy considerable resources rapidly so as to obtain results that can be used for further service development, building on the initial results.

We also argued that the public is a critical part of the NHS environment, as the ultimate financier of the NHS. What information it gets about the NHS as a service, whether directly or indirectly, will determine the extent of its support for the objectives the NHS is designed to promote and the particular means employed by the Government of the day to further them. How these needs should be addressed has attracted only occasional attention and virtually no resources. As we argued in Chapter 10, the public needs to be engaged with the strategic choices which the Service faces in the way it uses resources, be these restrictions on the use of drugs, changes in hospital configuration or priorities on waiting lists. Here, the requirement is explanation and the achievement of greater shared understanding of the issues involved and the choices facing the Service. We return to this in Chapter 13.

## Inadequate assimilation

The NHS has not available to it any systematic means of assimilating the potentially vast amount of knowledge and intelligence relevant to its work. Vast strides have been made through the Cochrane Centre, the NHS Centre for Reviews and Dissemination at the University of York, and the formation of the National Institute for Clinical Excellence in assimilating the evidence world-wide bearing on the provision of clinical care. In contrast, little or no progress has been made in assimilating change in the external environment or in bringing together knowledge and intelligence from different disciplines and fields of study.

As Stow[16] puts it:

> *Health care, including of course, care for ill-health, is so vast and complex a subject that those engaged in giving it are increasingly very specialised indeed. They are also, in general, highly motivated and committed to their special discipline, skill, or subject. Taking a broad view is not their normal approach. Each and every specialism or discipline generates a lobby among those who practice it, commonly supported by those who benefit or hope to benefit from their services* (p.7).

He points out that in the Department itself the blinkers were also worn, 'in order to make progress down difficult paths'. But one result has been that, as noted in earlier chapters, some issues are scarcely addressed at all, such as the future pattern of hospital provision or the links between human resources and service delivery, and some areas such as the labour market within which the

NHS works are poorly illumined by existing data. Although project work is as applicable in these fields as in others, they also demand a complementary approach, which involves bringing together findings and data from many sources and assessing their significance.

In many of these areas, clear conclusions on the basis of well-conducted research may not be achievable. The merits of different forms of purchasing for clinical services, for example, are hard to establish when the policy framework within which purchasing takes places changes rapidly, as it has done during the 1990s. Decisions must inevitably be made on imperfect information, at both clinical and national level. In these circumstances, what is required may be what Gordon MacLachlan[17] termed an 'intelligence' approach, covering a broad field and drawing on as wide a range of data, knowledge and practical experience as possible.

It may also require a quite different approach to research than that which is currently embodied within the R&D programme. New methodologies are required to provide rapid input to the policy process by, for example, field studies carried out within tight timescales into current issues facing the Service such as winter pressures, or by exploiting NHS *Net* when it is fully operational to take soundings throughout the Service, for example from patients or particular staff groups such as clinical staff or managers.

## Conclusion

The NHS R&D programme and the associated programmes are moving the NHS in the right direction as far as the delivery of particular clinical interventions is concerned. But as we have shown, there does not appear to be a strategy covering the full range of knowledge and intelligence that the central management of the NHS and its constituent parts requires.

Against this background, several changes are required:

First, the priorities of the R&D programme need to be further pushed towards operational, organisational and policy issues. A start has been made in this process through, for example, the new NHS R&D service delivery and organisation and the human resources programmes, but change is painfully slow. In part that can be attributed to a continuing shortfall of relevant research skills and funding in these areas, but unless a major emphasis is placed on this area of work, that shortfall will never be made good. A long-term, continuing investment is required. Research into the effects of organisational and staffing factors on the outcome of care should be a priority – as we noted in Chapter 8, work in this area at the level of the hospital or a system of care is extremely limited.

Second, the significance of the development of the role of the user combined with developments in information technology requires fundamental assessment. The proposals for NHS *Direct* On-line and the expert patient – as set out in *Saving Lives* – represent part of what is required. But the process of re-thinking professional roles has also scarcely begun. More effort is needed to understand the way the public and the Service interact. The People's Panel and the NHS National Survey of Patients' Views represent only a start. A more systematic and thorough approach is required combining elements of other existing surveys, such as the General Household Survey and the British Social Attitudes Survey, to provide a more comprehensive assessment of how the public views the Service overall and particular parts of it.

Third, the areas we have covered in this chapter, along with the development of the human capital of the Service needs to be considered as a whole. The field of responsibility of the Director of NHS R&D is too narrow, and there is no other official with a major commitment to knowledge and intelligence across the whole field. A new locus – inside or outside the Service – should be created which spans the full range of knowledge and intelligence bearing on the NHS. Because the range of knowledge that thinking about and planning health care delivery requires is so vast, for any one organisation to encompass it would be doomed to failure. It might, therefore, be more productive to create a small organisation which, aided by modern technology, would be at the centre of a series of interlocking and frequently changing networks, each of which would bring together disparate and diverse groups of people.

Fourth, the design and implementation of all major new policies should be based on a proper understanding of the impact of previous policies. They should be accompanied by a defined monitoring and evaluation programme and, as we argued in Chapters 6 and 7, implementation of proposals for service development should proceed on a pilot basis accompanied by monitoring and evaluation. If existing evaluation methods produce results too slowly, then new methodologies should be developed to produce quick but usable findings combining qualitative data and more effective and rapid analysis of routine statistics. The same capacity is required to respond to other urgent needs for information, be it nurse shortage or winter crises.

Fifth, the implications of our analysis for the education and training of all health professionals needs to be assessed. As we argued in Chapter 8, analytic and other management skills need to be strengthened across the board, before and after professional qualifications are acquired.

These proposals only make sense, however, if the needs of the NHS for knowledge and intelligence are properly recognised. The first prerequisite is that the Service as a whole and the medical profession in particular should more fully recognise the need to manage and take responsibility for systems of health care delivery rather than individual clinical interventions. The second is that those responsible for national policy formulation and implementation also acknowledge the complexity of the system they are aiming to influence. The first will be hard to realise, the second perhaps impossible.

### References

1. Merrison, Sir Alex (chair). *Report of the Royal Commission on the National Health Service.* Cmnd. 7615. London: HMSO, 1979.
2. Stow, Sir Kenneth. *On Caring for The National Health.* London: The Rock Carling Fellowship 1988 and Nuffield Provincial Hospitals Trust, 1989.
3. House of Lords – Select Committee on Science and Technology. *Priorities in Medical Research.* London: HMSO, 1988.
4. Department of Health. *Research for Health: a research and development strategy for the NHS.* London: Department of Health – R&D Division, 1991.
5. Griffiths R. *NHS management inquiry* ('The Griffiths report'). London: DHSS, 1983.
6. Department of Health. *Managing the New NHS: functions and responsibilities in the new NHS.* London: NHS Executive, 1994.
7. NHS Executive Anglia and Oxford Region. *Opportunities in emergency health care: summary report from the Anglia and Oxford emergency health care project.* London: Arena Communications and Design, 1995.
   NHS Executive Anglia and Oxford Region. *Opportunities in intermediate care: summary report from the Anglia and Oxford intermediate care project.* Milton Keynes: NHS Executive Anglia & Oxford, 1997.
8. Audit Commission. *Coming of Age: improving care services for older people 1997.* London: HMSO, 1997.
9. Clinical Standards Advisory Group. *Cleft Lip and/or Palate: Report of a CSAG Committee.* London: Stationery Office, 1998.
10. Clinical Standards Advisory Group. *District elective surgery: access to and availability of services.* London: HMSO, 1996.
11. Cabinet Office Advisory Council on Science and Technology. *A Report on Medical Research and Health.* London: HMSO, 1993.

12. Merrison A (chair). *Report of the Committee of Inquiry into the Regulation of the Medical Profession*. London: HMSO, 1975.

13. Weed LJ. New Connections between Medical Knowledge and Patient Care. *BMJ* 1997; 315: 231–35.

14. Eve R and Hodgkin P. Professionalism and Medicine. In: Broadbent J, Dietrich M and Roberts R, editors. *The End of the Professions?* London: Routledge, 1997.

15. van Ommen GJB, Bakker E and den Dunnen JT. The human genome project and the future of diagnostics, treatment, and prevention. *Lancet* 1999; 354 (supp. I): ss.5–10.

16. See n.2 above.

17. McLachlan G. *What Price Quality? The NHS in Review*. London: The Nuffield Provincial Hospitals Trust, 1990.

# Chapter 12

# Managing the Service

In Chapter 1 we argued that the growing complexity of policy-making was one of the four main factors compelling a re-think of the nature of the NHS. The earlier chapters in Section 2 have put flesh on that argument by showing, in the different fields each has considered, the range of considerations relevant to policy-making and hence the range of knowledge and intelligence required for good decision-making.

However, the perception that health care policy-making is highly and possibly uniquely complex is not new. In the words of a former Permanent Secretary of the Department of Health, Kenneth Stow:[1]

> *The national system of health care is extraordinarily complex. Few fields of scientific endeavour are irrelevant to it ... Its administration and development invoke the most profound issue of morality, philosophy and social responsibility ... I know a few individuals who have managed to acquire – usually over a life-time – an informed understanding of it ... Yet there is no field of endeavour that ... has greater need of a breadth of vision (p.3).*

Since Stow identified the central importance of complexity more than a decade ago, the task facing policy-makers in dealing with it has grown more difficult, not solely because the policy environment in which it operates has become more demanding, but also because the ambitions of policy-makers have expanded. Whereas in the 1970s, the Centre made some very tentative attempts to influence the broad allocation of resources between competing uses, in the 1980s and even more the 1990s, the Centre has actively sought, through a wide range of initiatives, to influence the way each organisation and clinician in the Service works.

As policy-making has become more ambitious in its aims, trying to move the NHS in specific directions and to promote specific objectives, the question arises as to whether or not the management capacity exists to ensure that the desired effects are in fact achieved. That capacity requires an ability, primarily at the Centre, to develop policies that take account of the complexity of the NHS and the environment within which it works.

This complexity can be described, as Stow does in the quotation above, in terms of: the range of disciplines and fields of knowledge, such as epidemiology, biotechnology, economics and so on, which bear on the provision of health care; or the range of pressures, such as new medical technology, which creates and shapes the way that care is provided; or the multitude of factors, economic, social and personal, which contribute to the level of ill health experienced by the population; or political factors bearing on the possibilities for reform. The sheer breadth of the knowledge and intelligence in each of the fields, which bears on the efficient working of a health care delivery system and which must be integrated across the divides of disciplines and subject areas, is daunting in itself.

From the viewpoint of the present chapter, however, the key attribute of complexity is that 'everything connects'. Such 'inter-connectedness' requires a capacity, as yet to be clearly demonstrated in the NHS, for seeing the links between what are still largely distinct policy areas. The consequences of failing to do so are that issues such as the appropriate degree of clinical specialisation are ignored even when identified by expert and distinguished committees because to tackle them properly requires not only contributions from different disciplines but also a full appreciation of the links between the structure of the hospital system and the composition and training of its workforce. As we noted in Chapter 8, the present Government has explicitly acknowledged this failure to link service and workforce planning.

When such 'connectedness' is ignored, then policies introduced in one area may have unexpected and unintended consequences in others. In the case of hospitals, the changes in postgraduate medical education, known as the Calman reforms, were one of the precipitating factors in the restructuring of hospital services in recent years. But that impact appears not to have been anticipated or allowed for.

In Stow's words:[2]

> It is not possible to demand or enforce change in any one area of this vast array of institutions and processes without affecting other areas, some or all, in some degree (p.39).

Stow drew the further conclusion that:

> It is beyond question not possible to 'manage' the whole of this in any real sense from one central point of authority (p.39).

If these conclusions were right in the 1980s, they are even more compelling in the late 1990s, when the management agenda arising from central initiatives is even broader than it was then, an agenda which implementation of the policies set out in *The New NHS* seems set to expand further. The question we consider in this chapter is whether the NHS has the capacity to cope with it.

We begin by tracing recent development in the organisation of the NHS and in the role – in England – of the Department of Health (and its predecessor the Department of Health and Social Security) and subsequently the NHS Executive. We then go on to consider the implications of policies since the NHS and Community Care Act 1990 and their consequences for the central management role, and then put forward some suggestions for improvement.

## The growing central role

The earlier chapters have brought out that the NHS has never been run as a national service to a common and explicit set of rules as to what and how services should be provided. With a few major exceptions, such as the 1962 Hospital Plan for England and Wales, the extent of effective devolution to the professionals actually providing the service was substantial. Even in the case of hospitals, the 1962 Plan proved in practice to be compatible with a great diversity of provision in the light of local circumstances and local judgements. Other roles, particularly those concerned with the training of professionals, have been left until recently almost entirely in the hands of other organisations, for example the Royal Colleges and the universities.

This limited central role reflected, among other factors, a recognition that in a service as large as the NHS, central direction had to be selective in its focus. The key question therefore has always been: on what basis should that selectivity be exercised? Even in the period before 1981, when there were few national policy targets, getting the balance of responsibilities right between the Centre and the local NHS proved difficult. The Royal Commission on the NHS,[3] reporting at the end of the 1970s, concluded that:

> *The DHSS (Department of Health and Social Security) has tended to give too much guidance to the NHS both on strategic issues and matters of detail. Too often national policies have been advocated without critically evaluated local experiment (para.19.22).*

The Commission cited a former minister, David Owen, who argued that:

> *The Department has become bogged down in detailed administration covering day-to-day management that has been sucked in by the parliamentary process. The answerability of Minister to Parliament may have given the semblance of control, but on some major aspects of health care there has been little central direction or control* (para.19.19).

The Commission also suggested that the central role had not been carried out effectively:

> *It seems to us that the fact that the Secretary of State and his officials are answerable for the NHS in detail distorts the relationship between the DHSS and health authorities. It encourages central involvement in matters which would be better left to the authorities. In consequence no clear line is drawn where the Department's involvement ends* (para.19.23).

When the Commission reported, the DHSS had been running what was then called a planning system for the NHS as a whole for some years. The 1977 White Paper, *The Way Forward*, set out a series of broad proposals for service development and illustrative figures to the desirable rate of growth of spending on broad service areas. But the means did not exist to ensure that expenditure did grow at the desired rate. A study for the Royal Commission[4] in the late 1970s found that:

> *Most respondents in most, but not all, areas and districts did not feel that planning had got off the ground or had a meaningful impact on operations … At the moment plans coming to the (authority) are not very realistic; they require breaking down into costed items and strategies, with priorities indicated. There is no sequential thinking or development of alternative strategies. This is partly because the professionals do not give enough attention to finance, the changing economic climate has not been grasped and staff are still acting as if the health service can continue growing* (pp.84–85).

The so-called 'priority services' identified in the White Paper for extra growth continued to attract that name precisely because in practice they did not receive priority relative to general acute services. The central capacity to plan services in detail did not exist nor the ability to implement even broad policy guidelines, still less to assess impact. As a result, the influence of the Centre on local developments was weak and even where there were clear national policies, the Commission identified the limits of the central role in practice:

> It is clear that neither the DHSS and the Welsh Office nor some of the ... health authorities in England and Wales are carrying out their monitoring functions adequately ... (para.19.43).

Although the Minister might have to respond to day-to-day issues arising at the front line of the Service, this role reflected the nature of political accountability for the use of public funds rather than any real ability on his or her part to control events at local level. As a result, Stow[5] argued in the 1980s that:

> This has over the years led to an increasing expectation that the Secretary of State, which means a small group of Ministers and senior officials in the Centre, will 'manage the service' – with only a vague idea of what the words 'manage' and 'service' mean – and, by implication, be responsible for making good any deficiency. For so long as Exchequer funding remains the main or only source of money, that expectation will remain. But it cannot be 'managed' in any meaningful sense of the term at this level (p.70).

In common with other parts of the public sector, the NHS was subject to strict financial and reporting rules, and tight control over capital. But none of these bore directly on services and, as monitoring was poor, the Centre had no sound knowledge of how effective they were. Managers and clinicians might all feel tightly constrained by finance and other rules such as those governing consultant appointments, or terms and conditions of service for staff, but in other respects, particularly service delivery, day-to-day freedom was the norm. So although the NHS could be said to be controlled so that spending limits were not breached and malfeasance was kept in check, it was not actively managed so as to achieve specified objectives.

Perhaps more surprising, accountability against the NHS's fundamental objectives such as equity of access was absent. As noted in Chapter 10, only with the 1976 report of the Resource Allocation Working Party did an explicit and systematic attempt begin to equalise relative to need the resources available for hospital and community services between different parts of the country. Furthermore, while the distribution of finance which followed the report created the potential for equalising access, it did not ensure it and no central monitoring was established to check if it was achieved for particular services or particular population groups.

The same was true for quality of care and efficiency in delivering care. With the exception of areas covered by the Health Advisory Service established in the wake of the Ely Scandal (against the opposition of Department and professions), there was no external or systematic internal check on how well services were provided. The pressures described in Chapter 2 have meant that the NHS has always been conscious of shortage and the need to economise. But like the rest of the public sector, there were few attempts actively to promote efficient practice, before the Conservatives under Mrs Thatcher began their attempt to roll back the frontiers of the state in the 1980s.

Despite its relatively limited role, the Royal Commission found that the Centre was doing too much. It therefore concluded in 1979 that major change was required in the NHS's management arrangements. Its solution was to break up the central task into smaller bits by giving responsibility, including parliamentary accountability, to regional health authorities. This would, in effect, have meant a series of independent regional health services, analogous to the then typical structure of much nationalised industry. The Commission went on to argue that:

> *The division of responsibility between the regional health authorities and the DHSS would need to be worked out, but in broad terms we see the former as accountable for the delivery of service and the latter for national policies and functions* (para.19.42).

In the event, that recommendation was not accepted. The Conservative Government's consultation paper, *Patients First*, accepted the case for the elimination of area health authorities and the creation of district and regional health authorities. It also emphasised the desirability of local choice and local initiative – notions that the Government were promoting at that time in other parts of the public sector, such as local government. In the foreword, the then Secretary of State, Patrick Jenkin told the Service:[6]

> *You have therefore a wider opportunity than your predecessors to plan and develop services in the light of local needs and circumstances.*

But as Klein[7] has noted, 'The era of devolution was not to last long' (p.48).

## The drive for better performance

Previous chapters have identified the host of policies which emerged in the 1980s as the Conservatives took what now look like their first faltering steps to make the NHS a more efficient user of resources: competitive tendering for ancillary services, publication of performance indicators and the introduction of general management in the wake of the Griffiths report. These required a strong Centre to define new roles and procedures, but at the same time they created additional management tasks down the line. Tendering for ancillary services, for example, required local management to define precisely what services were required, in most cases for the first time, and then to implement what were then unfamiliar procedures.

These measures bore primarily on the hospital and community health services, but with the introduction in 1990 of the GP Contract the first steps were taken to defining nationally what the role of general practice should be. As we noted in Chapter 6, for most of the post-war period, general practice had been left to go its own way. The 1990 Contract represented a radical change; for the first time, remuneration was linked to the attainment of centrally determined targets which specified, if only in part, the content of the GP role, chipping away at the GP's status of independent contractor. This imposed a burden both on GPs, who had to account for what they did, and on NHS management at the Centre which not only had to create a supervisory structure but also the task of ensuring that the incentive structures, for example payments related to the level of coverage achieved, were correct.

This task, though not a large one set against the agenda that resulted from the NHS and Community Care Act 1990, illustrates the way the central role has developed. The first additional requirement was that the financial incentives – in this case for preventive health measures – were set appropriately. That required estimation of the way in which GPs would react to them and then subsequently, if the desired level of response was not forthcoming, an adjustment to the original level and structure of payments. In estimating both the desired levels of response and GPs' response to any particular level of incentives, the Centre had to take account of the broader context, for example the obstacles that make high levels of take-up unlikely particularly in some parts of the country. In this way, the Centre began to manage rather than merely administer the primary care system.

The NHS and Community Care Act 1990, however, appeared to reduce the central role. The main thrust of the Act was decentralisation of responsibilities to NHS trusts, health authority purchasers and GP fundholders. The competitive framework apparently created by the purchaser–provider split appeared to promise a self-regulating system containing within it an in-built pressure for improved efficiency. This appeared to offer scope for more effective local management, since NHS trusts would be freed from central control and management, and purchaser pressures, including those from GPs would ensure efficiency. This self-regulating system would, in theory, open the way to reduction of the role of the Centre.

In *Managing the New NHS*, published in 1994,[8] a restructuring of NHS management was announced which was designed as a follow-up to the 1990 reforms. The report concluded that:

> *As the reforms have become bedded down, it has become clear that the central management of the NHS must adapt so that it can better serve the new NHS. A degree of strategic management is needed to ensure accountability but this must be administered with a light touch, respecting the freedoms of both purchasers and providers at local level* (para.5).

The report recognised that:

> *The size, complexity and importance of the NHS are such that its central management must operate through a regional structure* (para.14).

It then went on to propose the abolition of regional health authorities as statutory bodies in their own right and a series of other measures which led to a slimming down, in terms of staff numbers, at both the Centre and at regional level. Regional health authorities became effective outposts of the Centre as NHS Executive Regional Offices and subsequently, as part of the general drive to cut down on management costs, a series of cuts was implemented in both staff numbers and expenditure, as part of the annual efficiency targets set for the NHS.

As we argued in Chapter 11, the net result of these changes was that the NHS was left with a reduced capacity to monitor, understand or plan the system for which it remained responsible even though its responsibilities continued to grow. In the event, the market did not develop in line with the original expectations. Instead, a series of further initiatives added to rather than subtracted from the central role. The hope for a 'light touch' was unrealised.

## Growing central direction

The stream of policy initiatives and directives can be crudely measured in the number of official communications issuing from the Centre (see Table 12.1), about one for each working day in the middle of the 1990s – ignoring the professional letters. The rate of publication somewhat diminished in the subsequent years but fell only slightly below that level: in 1998, 242 Health Service circulars (which combine the separate categories of management letters shown in Table 12.1) were issued.

**Table 12.1:** Management and professional letters sent to the NHS

|  | 1994 | 1995 |
| --- | --- | --- |
| *Management letters* |  |  |
| Executive Letters | 102 | 145 |
| Health Service Guidelines | 56 | 67 |
| Finance Director Letters | 76 | 64 |
| Family Health Services Letters | 67 | 76 |
| *Professional letters from:* |  |  |
| Chief Medical Officer | 13 | 6 |
| Chief Nursing Officer | 17 | 3 |
| Chief Dental Officer | 0 | 6 |
| Chief Pharmacist | 2 | 0 |
| Chief Officer (usually a Senior Medical Officer) | 7 | 5 |
| **Total** | **240** | **272** |

**Source:** Department of Health – NHS Executive. *Seeing the wood, sparing the trees: efficiency scrutiny into the burdens of paperwork in NHS trusts and health authorities.* Leeds: NHS Executive, 1996.

As earlier chapters have brought out, the Centre took a wide range of initiatives which added to the tasks of local managers and which also required substantial work at the Centre: *The Patient's Charter*, the *Health of the Nation*, the NHS R&D programme and its concomitant changes in the finance of research, reductions in junior doctors' hours and changes to medical education, the drive to promote clinical effectiveness, the introduction of a new system of cancer care, a series of measures concerning corporate governance, changes in financial allocations, innovations such as extended GP fundholding and total purchasing, and so on. All these initiatives have added to the management task of people 'down the line', while at the same time absorbing management time at the Centre and creating new requirements for monitoring information to be passed up from the periphery and absorbed by the Centre. Klein's comment on the policy of decentralisation in the early 1980s proved equally relevant in the 1990s.

Against that background, it is scarcely surprising that the Centre could not ensure that its policies were mutually consistent. To give one example, although the responsibility of the same Department, as Gerald Wistow[9] has pointed out, the policies adopted towards health and social care since 1990 were based on incompatible premises: 'Caring for People ... did not take account of the accelerating re-shaping of acute services' (p.23).

The force of Wistow's argument has been demonstrated in the persistent difficulties on the boundary between social and health care and in a succession of advice and exhortation at both 'sides' to collaborate. In effect, localities have been required to paste over the cracks left by failure at the Centre to tackle the boundary issues in a fundamental way. It remains to be seen whether the measures announced in Modernising Social Services will provide a more effective basis for cross-boundary working.

As we argued in Section 2, some 'strategic' issues that only the Centre could tackle well, such as hospital reorganisation or the links between training, research and service delivery, have received inadequate attention on the grounds that they are local issues or the responsibility of others, while the Centre busied itself with other matters. As a consequence, the range of difficult issues surrounding the future of service delivery, discussed in Chapters 6, 7 and 8, and particularly those surrounding the links between service and professional development as a whole, have been relatively neglected.

The policies deriving directly from the NHS and Community Care Act 1990 made the complexity of the NHS greater by creating ever more diversity in the purchasing and provision of care. The creation of more freedom for general practice, be it through fundholding, total purchasing or the framework provided by the Primary Care Act 1997, made the role of the Centre more rather than less demanding. Freedoms can be exploited in inappropriate ways which require monitoring and possibly new regulations to deal with them; a good example in the early days of fundholding was the rules that had to be introduced to stop some GPs paying themselves for services through the device of setting up limited private companies.

The provisions of both Acts allowing diversity and experiment are desirable, as we argued in Chapters 6 and 7. But if the piloting approach is to work it requires better research, monitoring and learning capacity than now exists. The programme for improvement of primary care within London adopted in the wake of the Tomlinson report demonstrates the point. As Mays et al. conclude:[10]

*If evaluation is a concern, then the LIZ experience does not provide a model of how to organise a programme* (p.74).

Their critique reflects on both the style of policy-making and its manner of implementation. The programme was put together quickly, as a matter of political urgency, but even if it had been put together more slowly, it is doubtful whether the appropriate expertise could have been assembled to monitor it adequately. Such monitoring would be inherently difficult because of the range of projects, their overall scale and the changing environment within which they were carried out. But, without it, the merits of what has been a very large investment are hard to demonstrate in any but the most superficial terms.

## The dominant Centre

The upshot of the developments described above is a fundamental change in the nature of the central role from that played in the early days of the NHS. The Centre has become responsible for the performance of the NHS as a whole in a far more demanding way than in 1947. Table 12.2 sets out the main new initiatives that have emerged since the Labour Government came to power in 1997.

**Table 12.2:** Major initiatives since 1997

- establishment of primary care groups
- clinical governance including the National Institute for Clinical Excellence and the Commission for Health Improvement
- national service frameworks
- performance assessment framework
- Health Action Zones
- national waiting list targets
- winter pressures and the Millennium
- *Information for Health* – the information strategy
- human resources strategy
- reform of pay system
- NHS *Direct*

On present trends, the central role seems set for further expansion. *The New NHS* not only set a vast agenda for central and local action, but it also signalled the Government's intention to hold the NHS to account in a more systematic way. As late as the end of the 1980s, there were very few ways in which the NHS as a whole, and individual organisations within it, could be called to account against explicit targets. The financial framework developed for NHS trusts in the first half of the 1990s began the process of introducing such explicit targets. Introduction of the performance assessment framework means that localities will be judged against a wide range of criteria. Failure, as *The New NHS* indicates, will be dealt with by different degrees of central intervention, for example through central 'project management' using a variety of national problem solvers, such as the 'waiting list buster'.

Although *The New NHS* suggests it is attempting to find a 'third way' between central command and control on the one hand and competition on the other, in practice the range of initiatives the Government has launched will require more of the Centre rather than less. At the same time, as we argued in Chapter 2, the external environment will tend to make the central role more difficult. The media spotlight is ever more intense – individual incidents where, for example, patients have to wait for a bed, attract major attention by the national media and require a response by the Centre: the same is true of the availability of new drugs such as Viagra. Incidents such as these tend to overload the Centre by requiring it to firefight but they also lead to the Centre taking a more active role in determining what is provided and how.

Against this background, developments at the Centre and in the local NHS since the passing of the NHS and Community Care Act 1990 have been generally in the wrong direction. The commitment to reducing the resources devoted to 'management' that the new Government inherited from its predecessor remains. Instead of increasing the capacity of the Centre to cope with the complexity of its management task, that capacity has been reduced. At local level, an increasingly ambitious agenda is being presented to a dwindling management and analytic capacity while the mass of central policies discourages local initiative.

The previous Government was deceived by its own rhetoric. The 1990 Act appeared to offer a smaller central role but in fact, we have argued, the opposite occurred. The change did not rest on a serious analysis of what is entailed in managing the NHS in the current environment, what has to be determined centrally and what not, but on a set of mistaken beliefs about what the implications of the 1990 reforms were. The growing role of the Centre was overlooked. So too were the demanding technical tasks that the new style of central management imposed on the Centre itself, as well as on localities.

The present Government runs the risk of deceiving itself in a different way. The policies outlined in *The New NHS* add to the management tasks at both central and local level, but it does not itself indicate how the additional tasks are to be carried out and how the tension between local discretion and central policies is to be resolved. As a result, the Centre cannot be confident that its centrally determined policies will in fact be realised, at acceptable cost.

The waiting list target is a prime example of this. The Conservatives used targeted finance in an attempt to reduce total numbers waiting, and longer waits in particular, but the total continued to rise. Labour came to power with a pledge to reduce the total they inherited but the numbers continued to rise after they came to office. The numbers recorded as waiting for hospital treatment have since fallen in the desired direction, but during 1999 that fall almost came to a halt. Furthermore, the wider implications in terms of clinical priorities, the (opportunity) cost in terms of reductions in other services and equity of access were never allowed for. In fact, the *Priorities and Planning Guidance* issued for 1998/99[11] states that:

> *Work needs to be carried out locally and shared with Regional Offices, to increase understanding of the interplay between emergency admissions, elective care and finance. Health Authorities, GP fundholders and NHS Trusts should look actively into the local balance between these three competing pressures, and analyse in some detail local capabilities to meet them. This work will be supported by the NHS Executive's development of techniques to improve the analysis of these issues* (para.28).

The support proved of limited value, falling far short of helping the local NHS to the full extent of the conflicts they faced. At the same time, the capacity of the local NHS to do work of this kind did not generally exist. This lack of capacity reflects the failure identified in earlier chapters to plan for whole systems of care – in this case the interaction between two such systems, that for elective and that for emergency care.

In other areas, such as NHS *Direct*, the Centre has been able to impose a policy rapidly. It did so by making targeted funds available and by side-stepping existing organisations, effectively managing implementation directly from the Centre. At one level this represents a considerable success but it entails precisely the same risks as waiting list policies. Proof of the merits of NHS *Direct* will not be available for some time – it is being introduced while only initial results are available from the pilot sites. It may be that as NHS *Direct* is more widely known it will do more to encourage service use than the reverse – as we noted in Chapter 9 – and it may be that in order for it to justify its extra cost, other services will have to be reduced or redesigned.

That may be no bad thing, but it will involve quite a different kind of activity for which neither the Centre nor the local NHS is well equipped in terms of data on what users currently do to access care, understanding of user behaviour in choosing between the options available to them and the costs of restructuring local emergency care systems. All that lies further down the line.

## Conclusion

The role of the Centre has become incoherent and inconsistent. The incoherence lies in the growing central role combined with weakened central institutions; the inconsistency in the fact that the range of initiatives have often been in conflict with each other either directly by laying claims to the same resources, or indirectly by pushing the Service in different directions. The requisite knowledge base typically does not exist, locally or nationally, to allow for the interactions between policies, or even to implement individual policies successfully.

More generally, the Centre is intending to extend its grip over the NHS by increasing the role of performance management in relation to centrally determined targets – vertical control – while at the same time urging the local NHS to develop horizontal collaborative relationships both within the NHS and between the NHS and other agencies. But these conflicts are more apparent at local rather than national level where the implications of central policies have actually to be worked out on the ground. In the past, health authorities have struggled to respond to the central initiatives raining down upon them. It remains to be seen whether the new primary care groups will be as willing as health authorities to attempt to implement all the policies initiated by the Centre and, even if they have the will, whether they have the capacity to do so. Against this background, it is arguable that the NHS in its present form is already unmanageable, in the sense that the Centre cannot reliably set out a policy in the secure knowledge that it will be implemented in line with its expectations.

This conclusion suggests that fundamental change is required. Either the Centre must put itself in a position where it can control the NHS closely enough to meet the objectives it sets, or it must recognise the impossibility of this task and reduce the scope of its ambitions.

Is it possible to identify a better balance between central and local responsibilities and powers that would allow more local initiative and reduce the burden on the Centre? This is essentially the same issue raised by each successive examination of the organisation of the NHS. All, including the latest White Paper, have sought to curb the role of the Centre. All have failed to do so. Any new Government is keen to effect change quickly which means the introduction of national policies while the media pressures described in Chapter 2 also encourage national responses when weaknesses are publicly identified. As long as accountability for the Service remains focused on the Secretary of State in Parliament this will continue to be so. But some improvements may be possible even within the existing framework.

Whatever the division between central and local roles, as long as the NHS is a centrally financed service, the central role will continue to be demanding. Our first proposal, therefore, is that the capacity of the Centre to 'understand the whole' needs to be strengthened. In making this recommendation, we are well aware of the risks of claiming too much. The NHS is so complex that for any person or organisation to understand it in its entirety is impossible. But progress can be made in grasping significant parts of the whole and by identifying critical links between those parts. The Government acknowledged in *The New NHS* that the Centre has a responsibility to ensure its policies are mutually consistent.

To state this intention represents a major step forward, but its implementation is no easy matter. The present Government's promotion of the 'whole systems' approach for managing 'winter pressures' and reducing waiting lists represents a move in the right direction, as do the aims of the new information strategy *Information for Health*. In both cases there remains a great deal to be done. The full implications of the 'whole system' approach have yet to be fully worked out, both in organisational terms, as we argued in Chapter 7, and with regard to technique and understanding, as we argued in Chapter 11. The persistent neglect of system issues means that rapid progress will be difficult; we made some suggestions in Chapter 11 designed to increase the NHS's capacity in this area both at local and national level.

Second, any proposed change to the balance between Centre and the local NHS, for example through a new central policy initiative, and any addition to the management responsibilities of the Centre itself, Regional Offices, trusts, health authorities and primary care groups, should be accompanied by an explicit estimate of the management implications of implementing it and the human and other resources required as well as its expected impact. The current commitment to reducing management costs should be assessed in the light of the new commitments the Service is being asked to take on. However, the process of defining national service frameworks is intended to include their human resource implications. Similarly, the public health White Paper, *Saving Lives*, identified the need for a programme of human resource development and research. But it did not go so far as to estimate the resources its proposals required, to many of which other initiatives from the Centre are also laying claims. Estimates of this kind would, of course, be difficult to make and in some cases it would be impossible to produce reliable ones. The implication we would draw is that in these circumstances, central policy initiatives should be piloted, to allow such estimates to be made on a reliable basis.

Third, thought should be given to setting a limit to the range and scale of centrally inspired initiatives put forward in a given period. That would mean, at the least, limiting the number of central priorities defined at any one time. In theory, the annual National Priorities Guidance does this, but its requirements continue to be demanding of local management and they appear to be set without reference to local capacity to implement them. The Guidance published in 1998[12] concludes with a chapter entitled 'How it will work'. Much of it consists of a series of statements about procedures and the expectations of the Centre rather than a practical guide for the local NHS to follow. One approach would be to set a limit to central initiative by bringing together senior health services managers and policy-makers and determining jointly what the Service could realistically take on. A more radical approach would be to define an explicit boundary to the extent of local discretion and the extent of tolerable diversity. As we have argued in Chapters 6 and 7, there is a strong technical case for promoting diversity, particularly in the way that services are provided as well as in the organisational structure of the local NHS. But to allow substantially more local discretion, for example, over the scope of the NHS, would require changes in political accountability. We return to this issue in the final section of the book.

## References

1. Stow K. *On Caring for the National Health.* London: The Rock Carling Fellowship 1988 and Nuffield Provincial Hospitals Trust, 1989.
2. See n.1 above.
3. Merrison, Sir Alex (chair). *Report of the Royal Commission on the National Health Service.* Cmnd. 7615. London: HMSO, 1979.
4. Royal Commission on the National Health Service, Brunel University Department of Government. *The working of the National Health Service: a study for the Royal Commission on the National Health Service by a team from the Department of Government, Brunel University. Research Paper 1.* London: HMSO, 1978.

5.  See n.1 above.

6.  Department of Health and Social Security. *Care in Action*. London: HMSO, 1981.

7.  Klein R. *The New Politics of the NHS*. London: Longman, 1995.

8.  Department of Health. *Managing the New NHS*. London: NHS Executive, 1994.

9.  Wistow G. *Aspirations and Realities: community care at the crossroads*. Leeds: Nuffield Institute for Health, 1994.

10. Mays N, Morley V, Boyle S *et al*. *Evaluating Primary Care Development: A review of evaluation in the London Initiative Zone primary care development programme*. London: King's Fund Publishing, 1997.

11. NHS Executive. *Priorities and Planning Guidance for the NHS: 1998/99*. London: Department of Health, 1997.

12. Department of Health. *Modernising Health and Social Services: National Priorities Guidance 1999/2000–2001/02*. London: Department of Health, 1998.

# Chapter 13

# Making the Service accountable

As the previous chapters of this part of the book have illustrated, many of the knottiest issues with which the NHS must deal have been present from the beginning, but they have been largely dealt with implicitly on the basis of trust: doctors and other clinicians have been trusted to use resources well; administrators and managers have been trusted to behave within a more or less understood set of public sector values and to provide services to a high quality. That trust largely remains, but it is being undermined, in part by specific events, in part by long-term trends.

Specific events include both financial scandals surrounding IT procurement in the former Wessex Regional Health Authority[1] and financial probity within the former Yorkshire Regional Health Authority[2] and the West Midlands Regional Health Authority[3] and by particular and well publicised instances of failures in clinical care such as those in the breast cancer screening services in Devon[4] and Kent[5] or in the Bristol Royal Infirmary.[6]

Long-term trends comprise the broader economic and social pressures described in Chapter 2, which influence the environment in which the NHS works. These have combined, as they have for other services such as education, to raise questions as to whether it is right to let providers provide on their own terms without due regard to the overall Service they contribute to.

As noted in Chapters 2 and 4, the economic environment has also become tougher and the questions asked by the Treasury on behalf of the taxpayers ever more rigorous. Equally, the social environment has become more demanding. Users of the service are less content to accept what they are offered and the terms on which it is offered. As standards of service rise elsewhere, they are looking for a similar response from the NHS.

These developments have important implications for all those who work in or close to the NHS, challenging it in effect to demonstrate that the resources allocated to the NHS are being properly used. The pressure to demonstrate performance has already led to or been used to justify the wide range of measures discussed in Chapter 12, which have turned a largely passive Centre into an active manager of the Service.

While the pressure for the NHS to justify more systematically how it uses public funds has grown, the accountability process that the NHS inherited is largely unchanged. As we have argued in Chapter 12, the Centre is overloaded and cannot, through lack of information and intelligence, confidently direct the performance of the Service at all levels. When it attempts to impose its own priorities, as, for example, with hospital waiting lists, it cannot be confident that it will succeed – in this case, because it has not means of estimating how the NHS and its users will respond to the policies it introduces to enforce them. Even if it does succeed, other priorities might be neglected. Nevertheless, the Secretary of State remains politically accountable for the Service. Failures of service locally, such as have occurred in recent winters, are the focus of national and local press stories, debates in Parliament and hostile TV interviews despite the fact that the Centre has no direct management control over the hospitals or other services concerned. Given the political importance of the NHS to the present Government, the pressure on Ministers is to do more, or appear to do more, rather than less and to claim responsibility for every NHS achievement and to set in train measures to deal with every deficiency.

The first part of this chapter sets out the pressures on the existing system of accountability. In the second part, we briefly set out some alternatives but conclude that none is likely in the medium term to reduce significantly the pressure on the Centre. We conclude, therefore, with some suggestions for more fundamental change for the longer-term.

## A system under strain

It has been recognised since the establishment of the NHS that the administrative and political lines of accounting for the way the NHS functioned did not bear on its real business, the provision of care. Indeed, Aneurin Bevan saw it as a positive virtue of the form of organisation with which the NHS was established that the professionals responsible for clinical care did enjoy such independence. The intervention of Richard Crossman in respect of the scandal at Ely Hospital was a rare exception when the political role made a real impact on the clinical.

To Bevan's mind, the proper basis on which to run a national health service was professionalism, or what might be called 'technocracy'. The public's interest and professional's interest were effectively at one in matters of medicine, so it was thought, as long as the state exercised central control over the finance and ownership of the system. As noted in Chapter 1, the nature of the 'contract' between the State and the medical profession in 1948 meant clinicians were freed from lay 'interference' in matters of medicine, in exchange for hospital doctors giving up their independent contractual status and becoming employees of the State but maintaining their own professional lines of accountability through the General Medical Council and the Royal Colleges. The way they discharged those roles was policed within the profession with occasional litigation in instances where serious failure was alleged.

This gap between political accountability and de facto responsibility for running the Service could be overlooked when the political role was usually limited to issues of organisation and finance and when there was substantial trust in those actually delivering the service to use the resources made available to them well. But as the central role extended in the ways described in Chapter 12, the capacity of the Centre genuinely to account for what was going on in the NHS through the normal political process has looked increasingly over-stretched. As the Centre began to impose itself during the 1980s in terms of particular policies such as competitive tendering or specific levels of cost improvements, the Minister in Parliament became answerable for a wider range of issues and the Service itself for a wider range of performance.

As noted in Chapter 12, the Royal Commission had already recognised the immense pressure on the Centre and proposed that the burden should be dispersed among regional health authorities, which would be individually accountable. This recommendation was not accepted nor, several years later, was another radical solution, the transfer of the NHS to agency status, which the *Functions and Management Review*[7] explicitly ruled out even though many parts of the public sector such as the prison service adopted the agency 'solution' during the 1980s.

Instead, during the 1980s, and through to the present day, the system has remained essentially the same. Indeed, massive changes to the internal management of the NHS, particularly the abolition of regional health authorities, reinforced 'upwards' political and administrative accountability to the NHS Executive. The Regional Offices of the Executive were, and remain, instruments of the Centre, not the independent bodies the Royal Commission hoped to see established.

At the same time, financial scandals led to a much more clearly articulated set of rules of corporate governance, defining both the way that NHS trusts and their boards should behave and how they should account for the resources for which they are responsible. Furthermore, NHS appointments like those in other parts of the public sector came under the scrutiny of the Committee for Public Appointments. The need to introduce a more explicit set of rules can be directly attributed to the attempts to reform the NHS at the beginning of the 1990s. Any increase in delegation risks abuses of the kind that emerged in Wessex, Yorkshire and the West Midlands regions. By creating greater scope for local initiative, e.g. through trusts and fundholding, and explicitly encouraging a more businesslike approach, it permitted behaviour that was not deemed suitable in a public service, which then had to be reined back by the introduction of explicit requirements for behaviour in NHS trusts, particularly at board level.

As a consequence, the requirements of upward administrative accountability placed on the local NHS have expanded during the 1990s. The delegation promised, and to some extent realised, by the 1990 Act led to greater not less reliance on 'corporate governance' – formal rules of accountability for NHS trusts and health authorities set and monitored by the Centre. One exception to this was the change in 1995 when chief executives of NHS trusts became accounting officers for their trusts, which meant that they had themselves to appear before for the Public Accounts Committee where external audit found serious failure. Overall, however, the trend has been the other way.

Very little of this bore directly on clinicians, who remained accountable for their clinical competence only to their professional bodies. Within the NHS, the development of medical and subsequently clinical audit, encouraged by the NHS and Community Care Act 1990, remained a professional preserve. Outside it, the growth in external monitoring organisations such as the Audit Commission and the Clinical Standards Advisory Group meant that for the first time systematic studies became available as to the way that care was provided and to a degree where the quality standard was poor. But the links between their findings to sanctions, professional or otherwise, has been remote. In the case of fundholding, where for the first time clinicians were given budgets for which they were formally accountable, the actual system of accountability introduced for fundholders was weak. While fundholders were effectively held to account on matters of finance, the same was not true for the services bought with those funds. This deficiency might appear all the greater for the new primary care groups unless the new arrangements are managed more firmly.

The situation looks set to change. The proposals initially set out in *The New NHS* and expanded in *A First Class Service* represent a systematic attempt to bring clinical activity within the same framework as that applying to the rest of the NHS through 'clinical governance'. By making chief executives of provider trusts accountable for service quality, the administrative and clinical lines of accountability are to be brought within the same framework. In addition, through systematic publishing of performance data, for example through the performance assessment framework, the setting of national standards through the National Institute for Clinical Excellence and through providing external monitoring of clinical governance procedures via the Commission for Health Improvement, clinical work is to be subject to external and public scrutiny for the first time.

Viewed from one angle, these developments are entirely appropriate for a publicly financed service. The introduction of policies and performance measures bearing on the main activity of the NHS – clinical care – can be seen as a step in the direction of making upward accountability a meaningful process – one in which the upper tiers are in a position to call to account the lower ones for what the Service actually delivers to patients, as well as for broad policy changes. The complementary proposals initially set out in the Comprehensive Spending Review[8] and in the subsequent Treasury White Paper[9] for performance targets to be agreed with the Department of Health – and all other spending departments – are also a natural development of the policies pursued by the Conservatives towards the public sector from the early 1980s onwards.

But while these measures are consistent with the development of the role of the Centre outlined in the previous chapter, they do not deal with the main weaknesses of a system of political and administrative accountability – and soon clinical responsibility – focused upwards to Parliament. The danger with these developments, if they are taken too far, is that they will give the appearance of genuine control, but in fact through unexpected side effects will push the Service in unanticipated directions. That risk is all the greater if heavy sanctions are linked to poor performance as measured by what are necessarily imperfect and partial indicators – as with waiting list policy, as we argued in the previous chapter.

## Other forms of scrutiny

At the moment this risk, for the Service as a whole, is not yet a reality. But even before the Centre assumed the dominant position it now has, its role had been strongly criticised and alternatives sought, designed to link the Service closer to its users and the public at large.

### External monitors

In principle, like the auditors of public companies, the NHS external auditors – for example, the National Audit Office, the Audit Commission, the Clinical Standards Advisory Group and the Health Service Commissioner – reassure the public at large that the 'business' is being effectively run.

Furthermore, the auditors can identify weakness and propose solutions that may not be apparent to NHS management, particularly the 'remote' Centre. However, while external audit supports the Centre in this way, it makes its task more demanding by identifying in a public way failures in performance, which have to be addressed by some form of policy response. In this way, external monitoring both supports and contributes to the growth of the central role, even if many of its findings are intended to be applied locally. In other words, the audit process does not work so as to provide reassurance to the Centre that all is well and hence allow it to relax its grip: rather, it tends to reveal that all is not well. Typically, it reveals serious and often long-standing weaknesses of the kinds we have referred to in earlier chapters such as weaknesses in the way that different elements of a whole system of care actually link together.

When audit reports offer suggestions for improvement, it falls to the Centre to respond itself or to try to ensure that the relevant NHS agencies do. Moreover, although the NHS is undoubtedly much better monitored from the outside than it was 20 years ago, the division of responsibilities between the various different organisations has itself grown up in an unsystematic way. As noted in the previous chapter, their roles overlap and there is currently no means, formal or informal, for bringing together and assessing their findings or, indeed, of making any comparisons of their relative effectiveness. Furthermore, many issues remain un-audited because they do not fit the roles each auditor has been given, particularly issues or topics which run right across large parts of the Service, such as the provision of emergency care as a whole, or the correct balance between general and specialist skills of clinical staff. The Commission for Health Improvement will fill some gaps, but the system as a whole will remain incomplete, and hence cannot even in principle provide sufficient assurance that performance is satisfactory across the board.

### Involving users and public

The hospital governing boards as set up in 1948 had a tenuous link with the local population: patients, or the public, were not seen as competent to assist in making decisions. As Bettinson[10] has put it:

> ... it was natural that for every hospital or group of hospitals there should continue to be a management committee of public worthies, drawn predominantly from 'the establishment'. Among them were captains of industry, members of the professions, men and women from largely middle class families, imbued with a sense of public duty that probably did not extend to active involvement in politics but entailed giving their intelligence and above all their time, to the development of a service for the community (p.73).

The 1974 reorganisation made a two-pronged attempt to address the perceived remoteness of these bodies from local communities. First, the members of new health authorities were to include an appointee from the local government authority, thereby providing the semblance of a democratic link with local people. Although not directly elected, he or she was appointed by locally elected people – a very tenuous link.

The second innovation was the Community Health Council (CHC), established by statute to 'represent the interests in the health service of the public'. This gave the general public a formal channel for making their views heard, although the CHCs had no executive powers, only certain rights to consultation. They were an attempt to balance the centralised accountability of the new health authorities which, leaving aside the local government officer, were accountable only to the political centre.

This period during the 1970s remains more or less the high point of local representation. The health authorities lost their local government representative in 1990 and were slimmed down in an attempt to improve the efficiency (and 'upward' accountability) of their decision-making. The vestiges of local representation were retained in the roles of the non-executive directors but these people were no more closely connected to their community than the original hospital board members. CHCs remain and, though doing much useful work, have never made a significant impact on decision-making as a whole.

More recently, the Major Government of the 1990s published *Local Voices*,[11] which encouraged health authorities to enter into a dialogue with their community so that the local people's voice could be heard. This, again, has had little tangible influence and was perceived by many as little more than window-dressing.

The most recent attempt to link the NHS to localities has been the requirement in 1997 by the new Secretary of State that non-executive members of trust and health authority boards should consist only of local people and that local authority elected representatives should be involved in purchasing authorities. In respect of the former, as they remain central appointments, the link to localities is tenuous.

Alongside these official initiatives, groups perceived to have been marginalised by the decision-making system – such as mentally ill or elderly people – have started to organise more effectively and use their 'voice' to influence the way that services are delivered. The development of patient participation groups dates as far back as the early 1970s; they were then an entirely voluntary attempt, often initiated by clinicians, to obtain improved feedback to providers on the experience by patients of services. Since then their role has developed into provision, advocacy and other services which have allowed them to provide a counter to the professionally dominated service. Local groups of the mental health charity MIND, for example, may be effective in influencing the way that services are provided locally, but their role is essentially informal. They largely work almost entirely outside the formal machinery of the NHS although they may and do express their views on policy development relevant to them at both national and local level.

Although all the developments identified here can be cited as successes in terms of influencing specific decisions such as a hospital closure, the design of a service or protection of the interests of a particular patient, they have remained essentially peripheral, largely outside of the formal organisation of the NHS and insufficiently developed to halt the drift towards a greater central role. They are likely to remain peripheral as long as accountability in the NHS is skewed towards the Centre and Parliament.

The proposals contained in *The New NHS* to monitor, at national level users' experience of the Service are beginning to provide a means of testing whether, in general, the Service meets users' expectations of it. The results may provide some reassurance, or otherwise, of the quality of the Service on offer in terms of user rather than professional perceptions. But, because these will be national monitoring instruments, if poor performance is identified, national action and nationally set targets are likely to result. This is precisely what occurred when, after a campaign in the national press, it was accepted that mixed-sex accommodation had to be eliminated. The National Survey, therefore, is not a new system of accountability: it is more like a process of market research that any private sector company might carry out and, as noted in Chapter 11, highly desirable on those grounds alone.

## Complaints and redress

Over much of the life of the NHS, the systems for dealing with complaints have themselves been the continued subject of complaints. In 1977, the Health Committee delivered a damning critique[12] of the arrangements then in place for hospital services: the Royal Commission sitting at the time found the existing arrangement to be slow and complicated and that there was no system for routine external review of complaints. It concluded that there is 'an undoubted need for a single straightforward complaints procedure'.

This apparently simple objective has proved difficult to achieve. Nearly 20 years later, the Wilson Committee also concluded that existing arrangements for handling complaints were slow and complicated and made a large number of recommendations designed to improve the situation. The principle innovation accepted by the then Government in response to the Wilson report, *Being Heard*,[13] was that there should be a two-stage procedure, the first of which was intended to produce rapid resolution within four weeks.

The new arrangements have not yet fully bedded down but there are signs that, although the first stage procedure, in which attempts are made at informal resolution, has been successful in rapidly dealing with complaints, the second stage of the new procedure, which involves a formal process, is not working as well.

The Royal Commission did not review arrangements for pursuing claims for clinical negligence but these too have long been recognised as being expensive and slow. In 1996, Lord Woolf produced a hard-hitting damning critique in his wider review *Access to Justice*[14] and as a result fundamental changes are being introduced, designed, among other things, to reduce conflict and avoid use of the courts. As a result, the chances of effective redress should increase, or the need for it be reduced, through the introduction of more effective mediation between providers and complainants, as well as a speedier and cheaper legal process.

If these reforms are achieved, the position of the user will be greatly strengthened in ways that do not rely on the Centre. Moreover, it will be further strengthened by the recent extensions of the Health Service Commissioner's role to include clinical matters. It is too early to report on how this new power is working, but it is clear from his latest report[15] that he is making extensive use of his new powers. Overall, it seems that the position of the individual complainant vis-à-vis the NHS has improved in recent years and hence in this sense the Service is more effectively accountable than it once was.

## Open government

The NHS like all forms of government service has been subject to the critique that decisions are taken behind closed doors. Although not part of the formal processes of accountability, public opinion, the media and organised pressure groups together form part of a broader concept of accountability to the public. One way of improving the way this informal system works is to ensure that the public in general has available to it the information on which to assess how well the Service is performing and the power to investigate where it appears not to be.

Making a public service organisation open to external scrutiny by the public at large has long been held to have important possibilities for promoting democratic control, but it has traditionally not been part of the UK's system of accountability. On the contrary, the UK is considered particularly secretive in international terms and this secrecy is increasingly under pressure. More open government has been the proclaimed policy of every British administration since the Wilson Government accepted the findings of the Fulton report on the civil service in 1968. In 1977, the 'Croham Directive' was the first positive attempt to encourage a policy of publishing background material that led to Government policy. The influence of these initiatives has been patchy to say the least. The only significant policy change since 1968 in the UK was a change in the presumption associated with official information: whereas previously the presumption was not to publish, now the presumption was to publish unless there were good reasons to the contrary. However, this shift was accompanied by few formal statements of policy.

The Major Government made some genuine strides to promote more openness. Following the White Paper, the Government published a *Code of Practice on Access to Government Information*,[16] which came into force in April 1994. This code made some significant changes by:

- limiting the grounds for withholding information
- providing for the first time a mechanism for the independent review of refusals of information by officials and ministers (by the Ombudsman)
- introducing the principle that even exempt information may be disclosed if there is an overriding public interest in openness.

In December 1997, the present Government published a White Paper, *Your Right to Know*,[17] which promised to create a legal right to information through a Freedom of Information Bill, which would apply to the National Health Service as well most other parts of the public sector. This, alongside the assertion in *The New NHS* that there will be an end to secrecy *appears* to offer scope for genuine progress.

Whether it will materialise remains to be seen, since the Government's enthusiasm for the required legislation appears to have dimmed. The draft Bill published in May 1999 fell short of the expectations created by the White Paper. But even if access is improved, that will not be enough in itself. A capacity to absorb and interpret the information that does become available is also required. At the moment such capacity is limited: even among the academic community there is little appetite for policy monitoring outside the framework of formally commissioned research, or for the kind of intelligence gathering referred to in the previous chapter. But this deficiency could, as we suggest below, be remedied.

## Communication

The principle of open government is likely to increase the availability of information, but does not address what is perhaps a more significant failure on the part of the NHS positively to explain itself to the public either locally or nationally. In other words, no duty is created to inform and explain. Like open government, such a duty has not been a traditional part of the accountability of public bodies, but in recent years, through, for example, the league tables published as part of the *Citizen's Charter* initiative across government as a whole, it has come into widespread use. The performance assessment framework forms part of this general development.

While the data published in the framework will contribute to the public's capacity to see how the Service is performing, albeit after a great deal of further work and technical development, such data are inherently limited unless they are accompanied by explanation and interpretation. Few indicators can be usefully interpreted in isolation or without further elaboration. For example, the indicators bearing on access to elective care reveal large variations between districts; but whether currently low rates reflect previous high rates and currently high rates previously low it is impossible to say. Nor can the indicators on their own reveal whether or not enough is being spent at the hospital end or whether too few people are being referred and, if referred, too few accepted for treatment.

At local and national level, the NHS has been persistently poor at explaining the reasons why services have to change. In the early 1980s, the need to explain was recognised in, for example, *Health Care and its Costs*.[18] This provided a great deal of information and analysis helpful to an understanding of the Service but publications of this kind are rare.

The Department of Health's annual report and its various statistical bulletins present a great deal of information about the Service, as does the report published annually by the Health Committee as part of its survey of health spending. But useful though these are, what they have to offer by way of explanation of the changes going on within the Service and interpretation of the trends reported in both, is limited. This means, for example, that no one document published by the Centre provides a comprehensive account of change in the hospital system or of the reasons why NHS activity is rising. This is despite the fact that hospital data is widely published – but it appears in separate, generally small-scale publications and there is no overview. As a result, the overall picture of what is happening in the hospital system, even in the areas covered by official statistics, is hard to make out.

Useful though a better annual report might be, a more significant weakness is the lack of any central attempt to explain some of the basic features of the Service which give rise to public controversy, such as the need to control the introduction of new drugs and new technology, as and when issues arise. In these and other areas, such as changes in hospital configuration, it is hard for outsiders to obtain an accurate description of the issues, never mind mount an effective and well-informed critique of it.

Furthermore, the present Government's relentless interest in 'spin' and presentation has made it virtually impossible for anyone to understand what should be straightforward matters, such as the precise increase in resources the NHS is receiving year-by-year from the Treasury and how those resources are allocated. What exactly the £18 billion announced in the Comprehensive Spending Review for the NHS in England meant and how the Modernisation

Fund was to be used was not made clear at the time. Indeed, the introduction of cumulative money totals like the £18 billion has subtly undermined the significance of any Government pronouncement on spending, since it is impossible without detailed examination to determine what mix of price changes and real charges it represents.

As things currently stand, none of these alternative or complementary forms of accountability has been developed effectively enough to modify significantly the nature of accountability within the NHS. Indeed, some, such as more effective external scrutiny, tend to reinforce the trend towards a greater central role. In the case of others, changes are required if they are to be effective as alternative or additional routes by which the NHS can be made accountable. What these changes might be we consider next.

## Conclusion

Given the nature of our conclusions, it may seem that the only route forward is radical change, such as a transfer of responsibility for the NHS to local government – a possibility that received some consideration at the foundation of the NHS. It has been argued ever since that transfer to local government would provide an alternative democratic line of accountability, which would not only reduce the role of the Centre to a manageable one but would also bring those responsible for running the Service genuinely closer to those it served.

But such a transfer would not do the trick. Within social services there already are national rules governing, for examples, charges for residential care, while the proposal contained in the 1998 White Paper *Modernising Social Services*[19] virtually amount to a nationalisation of the services concerned. Pressure groups such as Help the Aged support central direction on the grounds that diversity in such matters as charges for care is inequitable. Furthermore, recent experience in the education sector shows how weak the defences of local government are when the Centre wants to impose itself, for example in respect of the curriculum or the publication of performance indicators. There is no escape, in a unitary state – which each country within the UK is – from the reach of the Centre.

It may be possible to devise a 'local' NHS which is less rigorously 'policed' by the Centre but it could only be implemented if there were greater tolerance of diversity and a relaxation of the equity principle underlying the NHS.

At present, the media pressures described in Chapter 2 are pushing strongly in the direction of uniformity. The changes to London Government and devolution to Scotland and Wales might be the first signs of real diversity developing, but the pressure for devolution in England is not yet strong enough to provide the basis for a fundamental change such as the Regional NHS envisaged by the Royal Commission. We conclude that, within the existing political system as it is in England, and with the NHS financed as it is, there is no clearly satisfactory way forward in terms of new machinery or reporting arrangements. However, a number of changes could be made which would ease the strains on the upward system of accountability or reduce its weaknesses.

First, the current system of external monitoring of the NHS, including the proposals made in *The New NHS*, could be rationalised and developed into a coherent system of external scrutiny. The NHS may be the most scrutinised organisation in the country but, while the various agencies involved all make a valuable contribution, the role of each, as we noted in Chapter 11, is limited by its terms of reference, constitutional position and method of finance. Their separate contributions are never brought together and there are gaps in their coverage. It would be too difficult to combine and merge them: we suggest, therefore, that one is given a broader task than any now has to report on the state of the NHS as a whole, drawing on the full range of material available, and also that one or other is given the powers and is appropriately financed to have a 'sweeper role' allowing it to cover technical matters that fall to none of the others. This might most easily be achieved by giving the Audit Commission sufficient funding for national studies of a kind which need not be 'sold on' to the local NHS.

Second, the Centre, either Department of Health or NHS Executive, backed-up by evidence from routine indicators and commissioned research, should take upon itself a genuine mission to explain, in non-partisan terms the forces making for change in the way that health care is delivered, the changes that are actually taking place and the reasons why policies have been adopted. In Chapter 10, we noted a number of critical areas where such explanations were particularly needed, such as changes to the scope of the Service, the circumstances in which variations in the type of service available were justifiable and the reasons why limits are set on the availability of some new drugs and procedures.

Third, freedom of information must be realised in ways which do not, as such measures have in the past, embody new barriers such as cost or physical access as recent experience with patients' records has shown.[20] It should be complemented by support for one or more institutions or programmes designed to increase the capacity to assess and interpret the information which freedom of information measures reveal. At local level, this might involve provision for local communities engaged in consultation about service change to call on experts to explain and interpret complex official documents, such as those prepared for hospital development or other major services changes. At national level, this might involve support from the Department of Health R&D programme for analysis of existing sources of data.

Fourth, a fundamental review is required of the way the Service interacts with its users. As we argued in Chapters 10 and 11, the relationship between the Service and its users is changing at several levels. But while the Service has started to respond, it has done so in a partial and, with the exception of NHS *Direct*, limited way. As we argue in Chapter 12, it is perhaps this area above all others which requires revolutionary changes. Efforts to improve interactions with users should take at least two main forms:

* better market research, at national and local level, of what the public want from health services, and what they think of the service they receive
* better quality engagement with the public on strategic decisions.

The Government has made a start by introducing the NHS National Patient Survey. But this is too 'national' a view to be of practical relevance to local providers. The national survey should be supplemented by annual local surveys and the results appraised as an integral part of routine performance reviews. Ideally, local reviews would include some questions set nationally, enabling meaningful comparisons between providers to be made, and an encouragement to providers to 'benchmark' their progress against others.

Fifth, new ways of engaging the public in key decisions need to be developed. The NHS Executive, along with the NHS Confederation and the Institute of Health Services Management, published *In the Public Interest*[21] in 1998, which sets out a large number of proposals designed to 'rebuild confidence in the NHS'. Some, such as citizens' juries and deliberative polling, are already familiar even though they are relatively new and most have been tried in some form or other. But what is missing is a systematic approach to public engagement. As this report makes clear, there is no set recipe for ensuring it, so the only practical approach is to experiment. Although much of this must be done locally – by its very nature – the Centre can support it by continuing to develop the National Patients Survey and to commit itself, as we suggested in Chapter 11, to treating the user as a genuine partner to the professional.

The proposals set out above are not designed to hold the NHS to account in the traditional sense, i.e. through a reporting line within a hierarchy. Rather, they are aimed at providing the means to individuals or groups to understand the context within which the NHS works, the factors underlying policy changes and the areas where performance can be regarded as good as well as those where it can not. In private sector terms, it is shareholder rather than managerial accountability that they are designed to improve. Our final group of suggestions goes further, however, as they are designed to make the NHS more accountable to users and the public at large, by taking their views and preferences seriously. How far this can go depends a great deal on professional attitudes and even more on the extent to which the Centre is prepared to limit its ambitions to guide the NHS in what it sees as the right direction. Conversely, the more progress that can be made with these proposals, the stronger the case for a local NHS enjoying substantial independence from the Centre. But as we have already acknowledged, that case is hard to make in the present political environment.

## References

1. House of Commons – Public Accounts Committee. *Wessex Regional Health Authority: management of the regional information systems plan.* London: HMSO, 1993.
2. House of Commons – Public Accounts Committee. *The former Yorkshire Regional Health Authority: the inquiry commissioned by the NHS Chief Executive together with the proceedings of the Committee relating to the report and the minutes of evidence, and appendices.* London: HMSO, 1997.
3. House of Commons – Public Accounts Committee. *West Midlands Regional Health Authority: Regionally Managed Services Organisation.* London: HMSO, 1993.
4. NHS Executive South Thames. *Review of Cervical Screening Services at Kent and Canterbury Hospitals NHS Trust.* London: NHS Executive South Thames, 1997.
5. Calman K and Hine D. *Breast cancer services in Exeter and quality assurance for breast screening: report to the Secretary of State.* Leeds: Department of Health NHS Executive, 1997.
6. Klein R. Regulating the medical profession: doctors and the public interest. In: Harrison A, editor. *Health Care UK 1997/98.* London: King's Fund Publishing, 1998.
7. Department of Health. *Managing the New NHS: functions and responsibilities in the new NHS.* London: NHS Executive, 1994.

8. HM Treasury. *Public services for the future: modernisation, reform, accountability: comprehensive spending review: public service agreements 1999–2002.* London: Stationery Office, 1998.

9. HM Treasury. *Modern Public Services for Britain: Investing in Reform. Comprehensive Spending Review: New Public Spending Plans 1999–2002.* Cm. 4011. London: HMSO, 1998.

10. Bettinson J. Health authority membership and chairmanship. In: Maxwell R, editor. *Public Participation in Health.* London: King Edward's Hospital Fund, 1984.

11. Department of Health. *Local Voices.* London: NHS Management Executive, 1992.

12. House of Commons Committee on the Parliamentary Commissioner for Administration. *Independent Review of Hospital Complaints in the National Health Service.* London: HMSO, 1977.

13. Wilson A (chair). *Being heard: The report of a review committee on NHS complaints procedures.* London: Department of Health, 1994.

14. Woolf HK. *Access to Justice.* London: HMSO 1996.

15. Health Service Commissioner. *Health Service Commissioner for England, Scotland and Wales – Annual Report 1997–98.* London: HMSO, 1998.

16. House of Commons. *Open Government: code of practice on access to Government information.* 2nd edition. London: HMSO, 1997.

17. Parliament of Great Britain. *Your right to know: freedom of information.* London: HMSO, 1997.

18. Department of Health and Social Security. *Health Care and its Costs.* London: HMSO, 1983.

19. Department of Health. *Modernising Social Services.* London: Stationery Office, 1998.

20. Association of Community Health Councils for England and Wales. *Medical records: restricted access, limited use.* London: ACHCEW, 1998.

21. NHS Executive, Institute of Health Services Management, NHS Confederation. *In the Public Interest: Developing a Strategy for Public Participation in the NHS.* London: Department of Health, 1998.

Section 3

# Overview

Chapter 14

# Where the NHS is now

In this chapter we bring the threads of our analysis together. In the first part of the book we set out the challenges and pressures that the NHS faces and the way that it has responded to them. In Chapter 1 we suggested that despite the massive changes that the NHS had been subject to in the 1980s and more particularly the 1990s, the air of crisis had not been dispelled. More fundamentally, we went on to argue that there was a sense in which it could not be: the tension between expectations on the one hand and the actions of a responsible insurer – in the UK's case the NHS and the Treasury – cannot be dispelled. Improvements in efficiency and better clinical performance will never be enough to close the gap between the resources available and the demands users and professionals seek to place upon them. Our review of the external environment in Chapter 2 suggested that there was little reason to believe that the environment will become any less challenging in future than it has been in the past. On the contrary, it will become more so. Thus the sense of pressure and inadequacy can at best only be temporarily dispelled by, for example, an injection of extra funds. Welcome though this would be, what the NHS needs is a sustained increase in resources coupled with significant progress in the areas we have identified in previous chapters as requiring improvement. Only on that basis is the NHS likely to achieve the quality standards to which the Government is trying to propel it.

We went on to point out that the NHS has already shown itself to be flexible and responsive to the pressures upon it. New forms of organisation and new instruments of policy have emerged in recent years. But continuing change in the environment within which the NHS operates means that it will have to continue to adapt. Like other organisations in both the public and the private sector, therefore, the NHS will have to continue to reinvent itself if it is to face the future with confidence. But that reinvention has in the past raised questions about the nature of a national health service and will do so in the future.

While the external environment is changing, the technical tasks the NHS has to deal with remain essentially the same in nature as they have been since its foundation. In the second part of the book we considered a number of policy areas, in all of which we concluded that major technical issues remained to be tackled systematically.

Some of these issues reflect basic and enduring dilemmas to be found within any organisation as large as the NHS. The right balance between local discretion and central control is never going to be determined once and for all nor is the 'right' form of organisation. In these areas, as we argued in Chapter 8, there might be a case for incremental but evaluated change, as well as systematic attempts to learn from the examples of other countries.

Other issues, such as the right balance of skills within the workforce, reflect fundamental uncertainties, which can only be dispelled to a limited extent however much effort is devoted to analysis and forecasting. Here the need is to create genuine flexibility between what are now different professional roles and to redefine those roles. Although such flexibility is creeping in, a root and branch attack on the issues is yet to be carried out. For example, no central body exists to retrain doctors who are in a speciality in which there is a glut, so that they can enter specialties in which there is a shortage.

Yet others, such as finding the best way to purchase supplies, appear fairly well defined technical issues which, over a period of time, should be solvable. In practice, however, they appear not to be – not unless the latest proposals for reform are more successful than their many predecessors. In other areas, such as the future pattern of provision, there can be no once and for all solution, but it would be reasonable to expect that, given its enduring nature, there should be a clear focus in the NHS for dealing with it. But there is no such focus with the requisite scale and expertise.

In Chapters 11 and 12 we argued that gaps such as these stem from the imbalance between professional and other interests. The nature of the implicit NHS constitution determined in the negotiations leading to the 1947 Act has meant that certain kinds of issue and certain kinds of knowledge – particularly non-clinical and managerial knowledge – have been neglected or deemed to be of secondary importance. These gaps have become more and more evident as the NHS has steadily been called to account for its performance as a system of care and as a user of national resources. This 'calling to account', whether it be through more effective external audit or through politically driven measures to improve performance, has revealed an organisation short of many of the skills and the knowledge base required to provide an effective system of health care delivery.

Against this background, it would be easy to present a very gloomy picture of an organisation faced with more problems than it has the ability to solve and attempting to do so within a steadily more open and critical environment. But in nearly all the areas we have surveyed, there are signs that new ways of working, new institutions and new forms of policy-making are emerging which are moving the NHS in what our analysis suggests is the right direction. In the first part of this chapter we set these out. They should be supported by substantial investment, particularly in developing the knowledge base and the human resources they require.

Despite these favourable signs, there remain a number of central issues on which it is hard to identify significant progress and where technical improvement in management technique and the use and availability of data are of only minor assistance. Taken together, these imply there are still significant obstacles to needed change. The last part of the chapter explores some enduring and underlying issues further and the final chapter sketches out some possible ways in which they might be resolved.

## Signs of hope – or why things in some respects are better than they used to be

In this section we briefly set out a number of areas where policies or attitudes have changed over the past few years in ways which we believe point the NHS in the right direction. By identifying them here we are by no means suggesting that change has proceeded far enough; indeed, in most of the areas we discuss much more needs to be done if the gains already made are to be consolidated.

### Style of policy-making

The imposition of the GP contract in 1990 and the subsequent imposition of an untested form of organisation across the rest of the Service in 1991 might have been justified in terms of administering a 'cold sharp shock'. But forcing untried but significant changes across the whole of the NHS is not a model that should be regularly applied. The change might not be the right one or might have unforeseen effects, and furthermore, it risks breeding unnecessary political resistance unless there is significant support.

A crucial change for the better since 1991 is that the notion of a pilot has been accepted as being a sensible way forward when there is no way of distinguishing between the merits of different policies or no way of identifying what policies to try. The Primary Care Act 1997 encapsulated piloting and was itself based on a systematic and genuine attempt to listen to what people in the Service thought ought to be done. Furthermore, through the general stimulus they gave to experiment, the 1991 reforms led to a range of innovations such as multi-funds and commissioning groups and total purchasing pilots which were not envisaged at the time the 1990 Act was passed.

The *New NHS* backtracked to some degree on that way of working by introducing a blanket policy for purchasing by general practice – primary care groups – and a number of other changes on the same basis. But it has the merit of allowing for different rates of progress and for slightly different forms of organisation within primary care. Furthermore, the Labour Government has continued with the Primary Care Act pilots which the 1997 Act provided for and decided to introduce Health Action Zones on a selective and voluntary basis. All will be evaluated independently.

Although piloting and experiment are valuable in themselves, their use has had an impact outside the areas immediately affected. To a degree, the notion of constant innovation has entered the culture of the NHS. As a result, it is possible to entertain ideas for change in the way that services are designed and delivered which would have been rejected out of hand even at the beginning of the decade. Perhaps the only 'downside' to this development is that the process of learning by which knowledge gained in parts of the NHS is disseminated to others has not always been effective. But there are signs of improvement here too, such as the proposals for an NHS Learning Network.[1]

## Greater budgetary flexibility

The obstacles to change embodied in the boundary between the budgets for general medical services and hospital and community health services were recognised with the provision of the Primary Care Act 1997. The Act allowed for a relaxation of these boundaries on a selective basis, which was subsequently accepted for general application under the new regime of primary care groups. At an administrative level, the unification of health authorities and family health service authorities in 1996 took this a stage further by finally removing organisational boundaries within the local supervisory structure. Provided that the NHS retains and develops contracting expertise and the financial costing skills that, in principle at least, should underpin it, the way towards a greater degree of flexibility across the primary–secondary boundary should be opened up.

But budgetary flexibility is only permissive: the potential benefits can only be enjoyed if other factors are present such as the requisite knowledge, service design and contracting skills. These, earlier chapters have suggested, cannot be taken for granted. Moreover, there are signs that the Centre is moving in the opposite direction by seeking to earmark funds centrally for particular purposes, for example for winter pressures, for the reduction of waiting lists and for primary care 'walk-in' centres. At the moment, the scale of these 'tied' funds is modest relative to the total budget, but they can represent a substantial proportion of the extra money a health district gains over its previous year's budget. Furthermore, the introduction of new rules disallowing virement between financial years and between revenue and capital funds has also reduced financial flexibility. There is a risk, therefore, that the scope of real flexibility at local level will be narrowed.

## More and better external audit

The work of the Audit Commission, the National Audit Office, the Clinical Standards Advisory Group and the Health Service Commissioner, along with the professionally run National Confidential Enquiry into Peri-operative Deaths, have vastly increased awareness of the weaknesses in current performance as well as identified ways of improving it which both managers and policy-makers can respond to. The overall significance of these developments is that they provide assurance that the performance of the Service is subject to assessment by expert bodies which are not themselves part of it. The NHS is possibly now the most scrutinised organisation in the UK.

But despite this achievement, the current system of external audit is not properly structured for the needs of the NHS. It has in fact grown up in a piecemeal way with resultant overlaps and gaps. The way in which the auditors work means that certain issues are not properly addressed.

A prime example emerging from Chapters 6, 7 and 8 is given by the links, or lack of them, between the various elements required for a cost-effective and clinically effective system of service delivery. Monitoring of the impact of policies rather than the process of implementation remains weak: the gap, as noted in Chapter 11, is not yet adequately filled by the NHS R&D programme.

The NHS performance assessment framework provides for greater disclosure of information on performance on a routine basis. The additional 'policing' of performance through the Commission for Health Improvement further strengthens the audit function. But the precise ways in which this role will be carried out and its relationship with the existing auditors still require clarification. Whatever the final arrangements, the weaknesses identified above seem likely to remain. In particular, the challenge posed by the emphasis that the Labour Government has placed on links between organisations has yet to be fully recognised through the development of 'cross-boundary' audit procedures, although the need for them has been recognised by the auditors themselves.[2]

## Evidence-based care

The drive for evidence-based clinical care and better information management, for example through NICE and the new National Electronic Library for Health, is pushing the NHS in the right direction. Although clinical practice cannot rely solely on formally produced evidence, it should not proceed in the absence of it either. The extensive reviews of the available evidence by organisations such as the Cochrane Centre not only provide guidance to day-to-day practice but also identify where understanding is poor and more research is required.

But the main emphasis of most of the effort currently devoted to assessing the existing state of knowledge and to establishing new knowledge of 'what works', continues to be directed to particular clinical interventions rather than the broad organisational context within which the interventions would be carried out. For example, evidence on the most effective way to treat a patient with asthma is far more likely to be available than evidence on how to manage a whole system of care for a population of asthma sufferers.

As pointed out in Chapter 11, there remains a vast range of issues that are fundamental to the Service, which are not being systematically addressed. These include general clinical issues, such as the benefits and costs of greater specialisation among the medical workforce and alternative ways of providing hospital services. Topics such as the demand for and management of elective care – which require both clinical and non-clinical skills – and the control of costs – where the skills required are managerial and analytic – remain largely unrecognised.

There are some signs that these gaps are being recognised in the new subject areas emerging from the NHS R&D programme, such as service delivery and organisation. But the scale of the change required is, if our analysis is correct, enormous, demanding not simply a switch of resources, but also changes in the way that the search for evidence and understanding is carried out and the dissemination of the results organised.

## Engagement by clinicians in management

We have argued that one of the key weaknesses in the NHS over the years has been the separation of clinical from other forms of decision-making. This weakness is slowly being reduced. In both secondary and primary care, clinicians' involvement in decision-making on a wider range of issues has been growing: GP fundholding; the total purchasing pilots, primary care groups; and medical and clinical directorships for hospital clinicians are all pushing further in this direction.

But these developments are not yet sufficiently supported by continuing medical education, by undergraduate and postgraduate training in management or by systematic development work to support further clinical engagement at a service level, for example in drawing up long-term service agreements or developing health improvement plans.

More fundamentally, our analysis suggests that the nature of the clinical role has historically been too narrowly defined. In the short term the issue may be whether or not it makes sense to use the limited clinical resources available to the NHS in management tasks – there may well be scope for re-deploying consultants at later stages in their careers when they may be keen to reduce their clinical commitments. In the longer term, the issue is how the role of clinical staff is defined, how clinicians are trained, how their field of knowledge is defined and what kind of careers are available to them at different stages of their professional lives. In short, the very notion of what it means to be a doctor needs to be renegotiated – as some of the leaders of the profession have recognised. As Sir Cyril Chantler[3] has put it:

> The time has come to make a fundamental examination of the role of physicians in our society and in the health care we provide for our people (p.1181).

## Workforce flexibility

The professions still remain entrenched in their respective colleges and similar organisations. But in a number of areas the significance of the barriers between them is beginning to diminish. Nurses can now prescribe although progress has been painfully slow; nurse practitioners are taking over work from general medical practitioners; the contribution of specialist nurses – along with other skills – to clinical teams within hospitals is now widely recognised. The Primary Care Act 1997 opened up new structures for primary care provision potentially involving a wide range of professions. In a few pilots, nurses are taking the lead in providing and managing primary care, and even employing general practitioners. All this is good news.

But the potential agenda remains massive. The range of issues identified in *The Future Healthcare Workforce* is still to be systematically tackled and, despite the improvement in the way training is commissioned, described in Chapter 8, the structure still presents significant obstacles to thinking and acting across the workforce as a whole.

## Primary care

At times, the rhetoric of a 'primary care-led' NHS seems rather strained, as hospitals continue to expand their activity. Furthermore, many aspects of primary care remain much as they were at the beginning of the 1990s. To date the impact of the 'primary care-led' slogan may have been slight, in part because of the financial, professional and cultural obstacles described in earlier chapters.

Nevertheless, significant changes are afoot. As regards provision, the proportion of single-handed practices is declining, and group practices with multidisciplinary teams are becoming the norm. The isolation of the individual practice has already been broken down in favour of more collective forms of provision, for example, out-of-hours co-operatives. As more practices become computerised, and with the introduction of GP*Net*, practices will become more connected with each other as well as with the rest of the NHS. Tele-medicine and other new technologies will accentuate this trend.

Fundholding and its subsequent variants unleashed the beginnings of a huge culture change, one that will accelerate with the formation of the new primary care groups. Giving practices significant purchasing power (primary care groups have an average budget of £60 million in 1999) will have enormous knock-on effects. It will underline the need for GPs and other primary care staff to take responsibility for the local health care system, its management and necessary strategic decision-making. To respond, key staff will have to develop management skills and a broader perspective, as well as to function effectively, particularly when dealing with powerful providers. Managing a budget will be an important incentive to audit and peer review activity (in particular of utilisation) within the primary care group and also in local providers, and to take into account clinical effectiveness and cost-effectiveness in decision-making. It will also give greater responsibility to clinicians for setting priorities for care. Many of these are steps taken in other OECD countries to reform the health sector, and, as we have argued in the preceding chapters, all move the NHS significantly in the right direction.

This is a long-term agenda. Primary care groups will not become effective functioning organisations overnight, even in two to three years. Significant leadership and careful management will be required, particularly from health authorities, to support this process. Primary care groups will also need a great deal of support to develop the managerial skills of key players within them. In turn this depends more on the recognition by the professionals within them that such managerial skills are required.

## User orientation

The *Patient's Charter*, limited though it was, was significant for what it reflected – the need to make the Service more responsive to users – as much as for what it has achieved. The *Patient Partnership Initiative*, also begun by the Conservatives, has been pushing the NHS in the right direction but it still remains tentative and low key.

As we have noted, the Labour Government has taken a number of initiatives which greatly extend the Service's commitment to the user: at national level, the People's Panel, the National Patient Survey; NHS *Direct* currently on a local pilot basis, but soon to be national; and the notion of expert patients put forward in *Saving Lives* and the development of NHS *Direct Online*. All these policies push the NHS in the right direction.

There are risks involved in going down the track of adapting the services to users; more information and engagement may fuel more demand. But equally there are obvious risks in not doing this. More information will become available via the Internet, come what may. The NHS cannot control or even influence this but it can be more proactive than it has been so far in providing information to users.

Outside the Service itself, the advice issued by the medical profession to its members in *Duties of a Doctor*[4] reflects a significant change in professional attitudes, at least by the General Medical Council, towards the role of the patient.

## Information technology

The NHS has had some spectacular failures and embarrassments over the introduction of information technology, but it has been successful on a small scale, and the scope for its greater deployment is immense. It will allow much better internal communications, more flexible forms of service delivery, more effective learning and spread of good practice, and greater user empowerment. The NHS, being a near monopoly purchaser and provider of health care, is in a uniquely advantageous position in the developed world to provide seamless nationwide communications between purchasers and providers within a single national information template. This is an enormous advantage.

Currently, many parts of the NHS remain effectively isolated in terms of knowledge. IT can change that by allowing much greater and much faster interchange between different parts of the Service, including between the local NHS and the Centre. There are now signs with *Information for Health* that the route to improving the scientific basis for the practice of clinical skills is at least opening up. With the development of the electronic patient records and the NHS*Web*, the potential for sharing information should grow rapidly. There have been many false starts in the development of an effective NHS strategy for information, which suggests remaining cautious as to the speed at which the proposals put forward in *Information for Health* will be realised. But there are signs, such as the successful implementation of PRODIGY, as well as many local initiatives, that the potential of information technology is at last being grasped.

## Greater awareness of costs

The NHS is still not efficient at costing particular activities: but a greater degree of cost awareness, including the opportunity costs of choosing particular forms of treatment or service designs, has permeated the Service, in part as a result of specific features of the NHS reforms such as contracting, and budgets for clinicians through, for example, fundholding and in part as a result of a greater realism towards general financial pressures on the Service.

The development of the role of primary care groups should further promote these developments. The National Schedule of Reference Costs also represents a further push in the right direction, potentially allowing comparisons between NHS trusts for most common procedures, as the data become more reliable.

The changes suggested by Sir Kenneth Calman to the Hippocratic Oath, noted in Chapter 10, would, if generally accepted, encourage individual professionals to use such information. The Secretary of State's decision on Viagra[5] may prove to be a turning point.

There remains a long way to go. As we have argued in Chapter 1, the gap between expectations and resources is inevitable, but much of the rhetoric surrounding the NHS continues to deny that, emphasising as it does the need to raise quality and improve access regardless of the cost implications. More mundanely, costing skills remain weak, particularly for whole systems of care running across a range of providers. As a result, there is no sound base for costing the implications of national commitments to 'world-class' service standards or to other broad policy goals.

## Overall

In all the areas briefly set out here, very significant changes can be observed, even if a great deal remains to be done in each of them. But it can, at minimum, be concluded that the Service is:

- encouraging innovation and flexibility in service delivery and organisation
- making a start in tackling areas which for most of its history the NHS has neglected – the evidence underpinning clinical practice and the user view point
- breaking down some of the artificial barriers which have hindered its development in the past and becoming more open-minded at individual and institutional level
- developing the role of clinicians as managers of resources
- better informed than ever about its performance through the development of external audit and greater availability of information.

In these respects, therefore, the NHS is technically much better equipped to 'face the future' than it was some ten years ago. What else needs to be done we consider in the paragraphs below.

## Areas requiring 'technical' improvement: some key problems not faced in *The New NHS*

Despite the progress noted above, there remain a number of areas in which there is scope for technical improvement and where the need has not been fully recognised:

- the wider environment
- service configuration
- demand management
- organisational and contractual frameworks
- relationships within the Service
- developing staff.

### The wider environment

As we have stressed above, the NHS does not have within it a systematic means of identifying and appraising the factors which might impinge upon it, be they in the labour force, the physical environment or among those it delivers care to. It has never attempted to produce a vision of the future within which it will have to operate, nor to speculate in public about the different forms the Service might take in future, nor the possible impact of greater integration with Europe on both professionals and users, or information technology on the balance of power between users and professionals. The National Institute for Clinical Excellence will support a process of horizon-scanning in respect of new clinical technologies but not the broader service environment, still less the economic and social environment discussed in Chapter 2. The need for this intelligence function will grow in future.

### Service configuration

*The New NHS* is typical of the White Papers of the last 20 years in that does not look ahead. It gives no serious consideration to the way in which services might be delivered in ten or 20 years time. Given the rate at which technology and other critical factors develop, that task is inherently difficult. *A Service With Ambitions*, using pen portraits, did attempt to do this in an impressionistic way but it lacked any solid underpinning. There is no systematic programme of work designed to identify the areas where existing knowledge is weak or the implications of technological change. *The New NHS* makes virtually no reference to these issues.

The principal gap is in the hospital system. As noted in Chapter 6, official documents have fought shy of discussing the hospital system as a whole with the result that many key issues have not been addressed: the running has been left to individual parts of the professions. While this contribution is vital, it is only part of what is required.

As this book was going to press, the results of the National Bed Inquiry were about to be published – the first such document to emerge from the Centre for 20 years. But it is only a start: the issues it raises and the gaps it identifies reflect the lack of serious attention paid to hospitals and their role in the health care system by the Centre since the 1960s.

## Demand management

The task of demand and utilisation management has not been acknowledged, but the nettle must be grasped. As noted in Chapter 9, some of the requisite techniques are being developed, in particular the linking of clinical and financial decisions, but many key areas remain to be addressed. In particular, the notion of systematically trying to understand why users seek professional help (and why they do not), what influences these decisions and how through changes in service design or the availability of information they may be influenced, has yet to take hold.

The pilots such as NHS *Direct* are being introduced against a background of minimal information about who uses what services and when. In only one or two parts of the country have attempts been made to map the current pattern of demand and how that divides up between different providers. As a result, the interaction between demand for different forms of service, even though that is an essential feature of any attempt to reduce or modify user pressures on the Service, is not well understood. NHS *Direct* should prompt such analysis in future, as should the introduction of primary care groups, but if it is to be done properly it will require a much greater investment in attempts to describe, monitor and predict user behaviour than has yet become apparent.

## Organisational and contracting frameworks

Very little thinking is apparent about the different forms of organisation and contractual frameworks that might be required within the collaborative framework the Government is intent on introducing. *The New NHS* does not, for example, discuss what the relationship might be between the services designed within the national service framework programme, and the role of NHS trusts or health authorities. As Chapter 7 noted, these developments may require new forms of organisation and a rethinking of the role of NHS trusts and health authorities, together with new lines of accountability. The notion of a primary care trust has emerged without there being, in public at least, any serious study of its merits and of the best way of handling the complex contractual relationships they are likely to require, to deal properly with their different roles – those of purchaser and provider – and what may be the conflicting ambitions of different providers.

*The New NHS* alone contains a vast agenda of technical development at both national and central levels bearing on both organisations and contracting. Despite this, the discussion of the contribution that R&D could make was confined to a single paragraph. It offers no discussion of the scale of the analytic work required to support its own proposals or who should do it. This is symptomatic of the wider failing identified in Chapter 11 to develop the NHS knowledge-base required to provide systems of health care delivery.

### Relationships within the Service

As we noted in Chapter 7, the recognition that it would be desirable to integrate the various parts of the NHS has been accompanied by persistent failure to do so. The word 'partnership' or synonyms for it appears throughout *The New NHS* but – finance apart – it does not tackle directly the obstacles that have hindered integration of services in the past.

Past failures have been in part a reflection of inappropriate policies based on inadequate knowledge of the way that the various elements of particular services fit together and in part due to organisational and professional barriers. *The New NHS* proposals for national service frameworks and unified financial budgets may gradually overcome this weakness, but a proper knowledge base for these remains to be developed. Although there is substantial merit in the service-by-service approach implicit in national service frameworks, it is over-simple to suggest that it solves the question of how the various part of the Service should relate to each other, because, as we argued in Chapter 7, any way of slicing up a health service will benefit some, but will disadvantage others. These trade-offs remain to be properly identified and their implications for the accountability of the Service explored.

## Developing staff

As we noted in Chapters 5 and 8, the weaknesses in national approaches to workforce planning have not properly taken into account the economic and social environment within which the NHS has to work. A further implication of our analysis is that while the development of clinical skills has been – properly – emphasised, others, particularly those required for the effective delivery of services, such as analytic and management skills, have not. The Centre published a Human Resources Strategy in 1999 and *Saving Lives* notes the need for training programmes designed to support its proposals. But neither addresses the tasks identified here. There are signs, for example in the work of the British Association of Medical Managers, that these weaknesses have been recognised, but they have yet to be actively acknowledged within the Royal Colleges responsible for postgraduate education and training.

## Conclusion

The issues identified here are primarily 'technical' ones, to which technical solutions must be found. The lack of adequate technical solutions in recent years has, however, contributed significantly to the perception that the NHS is not able to cope with the demands placed upon it and in that way undermines it.

But while the failings might be described as technical, the reasons they arise stem from the wider context within which the NHS operates and also its internal 'constitution' – that is the definition of clinical and managerial roles. As we have argued in Chapters 11 and 12, lack of clarity about roles and the artificial boundary between clinical and non-clinical knowledge has meant that key issues such as those listed above have been neglected.

While technical improvements of the kinds listed here are clearly important, a key theme of the argument in previous parts of this book is that the wider environment within which the NHS works is equally critical to its survival. The 'signs of hope' listed above overall contribute favourably to that environment, both within the Service and outside it. But in some respects they have the opposite effect. The very attributes that we identify as desirable may appear to many professionals within the Service as threatening their roles within it and to users and the public as threatening the institutions that they hold dear. In the final chapter of this book, therefore, we consider how the wider context may be addressed directly.

## References

1. Langlands A. Learning the steps. *NHS Magazine* 1999; 17: 16–18.
2. Public Audit Forum. *Implications for audit of the modernising government agenda.* London: Public Audit Forum, 1999.
3. Chantler C. The role and education of doctors in the delivery of health care. *Lancet* 1999; 353: 1178–81.
4. General Medical Council. *Good Medical Practice.* London: GMC, 1997.
5. Department of Health. PN 1999/0315.

Chapter 15

# Facing the future

In Chapter 2 and elsewhere in this book we have referred to the environment within which the NHS has to function. Much of it, particularly the external environment, it cannot hope to influence. Instead, the NHS must attempt to anticipate and adapt to the changes in it as best it can. These areas include the kinds of social transformation that are leading to changing attitudes towards clinical careers, demography and the physical environment. Some areas such as the media and public opinion may be influenced though not controlled by the NHS. But within the NHS, the environment is not given but may be altered, albeit slowly and with difficulty. It is this that is our prime concern in this chapter.

Our analysis and the historical material it has drawn on have repeatedly identified a small number of recurring issues running right across the NHS, which have been present and acknowledged in official reports and White Papers since its early days and yet which remain as difficult to resolve as ever. These are:

• the balance between medical and other professional interests on the one hand, and other service requirements on the other
• the balance between central and local control/discretion
• the relations between users and the Service and the wider political process.

These all turn on the perennial triangle of interests at the heart of the NHS professionals, the public and the State.

A theme running through much of our argument has been that the distribution of power within the NHS – between the three main stakeholders, the State, the medical profession and the public – which characterised its early days up to the 1990s is changing and as a result its implicit internal constitution is breaking down. The professions, particularly the medical profession, are no longer simply entrusted to use well the resources made available to them. Instead, the Centre, acting for the taxpayer and the general public, presses increasingly hard for evidence that resources are being well used. Meanwhile users are also seeking a greater voice in how services are organised and provided. These shifts taken together mean that a new constitution will have to emerge which may be less implicit than the first one. Without it, we believe, needed change will be blocked by a resistant, and increasingly isolated, medical profession.

In this final chapter we consider how the internal environment of the NHS, in particular the dynamics between the three main stakeholders, might be managed to ensure that needed change can take in the NHS. We consider in turn:

- the medical profession
- users, citizens and taxpayers
- the political process.

## Changing the environment

### The medical profession

At present, the tide appears to be running against the notion of professionalism and for greater external control over clinical decision-making. The implicit trust in clinicians that has characterised most of the life of the NHS has largely broken down and, as in other areas of social and economic life such as education, the move has been to greater regulation and policing of professional activity by the State on behalf of the public.

Although it was repeatedly argued in *The New NHS* that self-regulation should continue, its proposals actually point to a greater external regulation through the National Institute for Clinical Excellence and the Commission for Health Improvement. The implementation of national service frameworks and the performance assessment framework will also add to the scope of external scrutiny of clinical activities. As Sir Donald Irvine[1] has acknowledged, professional self-regulation is a privilege that has to be earned by being demonstrably effective: otherwise external regulation will take over entirely.

In the light of measures such as these, combined with pressures from users to take greater control over their own care, the professions could retreat into their shells and attempt as best they can to fight a rearguard action in defence of their current position. Our argument points the other way, towards their being more engaged with the wider issues running across the Service as a whole.

Underlying the whole of our analysis is the view that as far as the management of the NHS is concerned, in both the narrow and the broader senses of the term, the distinction between medical and clinical on the one hand and other issues on the other, is unhelpful. Virtually all the critical issues that NHS management must face require a broad view, not that of a specific discipline or profession.

In our view, the reason these issues have not been systematically analysed or tackled, despite the fact that many were identified in the early days of the NHS, stems from the way that effective responsibility for the NHS has been divided between clinical and non-clinical bodies. Despite the nominal integration at NHS Executive level, in fact the Service is run from a number of centres. The introduction of general management has proved insufficient to bridge this gap and indeed has been largely irrelevant to building links at national level.

At several points in this book we have pointed to issues such as service design, or research into the organisation on care delivery, which have suffered precisely because the professions have defined their role too narrowly. A *British Medical Journal* editorial by Donald Berwick[2] addressed to the US health care system rather than the British nevertheless addressed precisely this point.

His central argument is that the medical profession should develop its role away from its old, restrictive guild status to a new role that extends beyond the sectional interest of the profession. This means accepting rather than resisting many of the changes that bear upon it, particularly the pressures on it – and on other clinical professions – to demonstrate that spending on health care delivery is effective. As he puts it:

> *Doctors, like others, tend to regard measurement of performance as a threat. In their role as system leaders, both individual doctors and medical associations will need to embrace the measurement of performance as a step in their own learning* (p.1565).

The central implication of this approach is that doctors, along with other clinicians, will have to accept explicitly what in effect they have implicitly accepted in the past, responsibility for service delivery and the choices that involves. Such a role would have to extend beyond the clinical care of individual patients to planning whole systems of care, having budgetary responsibility for them, and being called to account for the clinical quality of care offered.

The difference between this situation and the current position is that the terms on which the medical and other professions accept this responsibility would be largely defined by others, albeit in co-operation with them. It is only on this basis, we believe, that the professions will earn back the trust the user, taxpayer and citizen once placed in them.

The key element in this new 'contract' would be a combination of better information available to the patient and greater transparency – not only through the development and publication of performance measures but also prospective information on risks and the likely effectiveness of procedures and treatments.

Another key element would be an acceptance of responsibility for the use of resources and all that goes with that. In Sir Cyril Chantler's words:[3]

> I believe that we can serve our patients' best interests and retain the necessary degree of independence to be the patient's advocate by participating more fully in the problems our society faces and in the health care systems that we have developed (p.1181).

If doctors and other professionals do accept this wider role and the conditions attached to it, that will have fundamental implications for the role and definition of the professions, training and subsequent career structures, opportunities and rewards. Being a leader of a 'system' is not a professional role as currently understood: it requires essentially managerial, analytic and rhetorical skills and a wide-ranging view, the qualities required to lead and persuade others of the need for change and for tough choices. It would have to draw on skills and techniques that are not currently part of professional development either at undergraduate or postgraduate level. It would lead to the complete blurring of boundaries between what are now seen as different activities and different professions.

Perhaps the most difficult part of the transformation we are suggesting here is a change in attitude and range of knowledge of clinicians, from a focus solely on the clinical, the scientific and the hierarchy of status that the professional has embodied in the past, towards an acknowledgement that a number of other dimensions of thinking and behaving are also important for the health and health care of the population. Most significant in this respect is a change in the relationship between clinician and user – an acknowledgement that the user has something important to say with respect to the decisions affecting him or her and that an open relationship of partnership must be fostered.

The change could go further: the professions could take seriously what the rhetoric of serving the patient's interests suggests and accept that research into the market they serve is as important as research into the interventions they carry out. If our conclusion in Chapter 2 is correct – that regardless of the absolute level of mismatch between supply and demand, the *perceptions* of such a mismatch are just as, if not more, important for the long-term survival of the NHS – then the market served by the NHS will be critically important to understand.

One tough question then to be answered is where should the burden of managing scarcity lie? Can that role be reconciled with the role of patient adviser? Individual clinicians currently play the dual role and can find it hard: it will get harder unless the Centre and fellow professionals support them in it. The Centre can offer support through new institutions such as the National Institute for Clinical Excellence and the Commission for Health Improvement, by ensuring that the work of these institutions has broad acceptance by the major clinical stakeholders and does not result in conflict. Fellow professionals can offer support by taking a wider and more long-term view and accepting at 'collegiate' level their role in achieving a cost-effective Service, by infusing this philosophy into the training of all professionals and by implementing technical developments such as clinical guidelines and care pathways that help to manage demand down where appropriate.

## Users, citizens and taxpayers

All health systems, not just the NHS, face difficult choices about what to provide and on what terms. In the past, these hard choices have been hidden, within implicit rationing and in the confusion that continues over local and central responsibilities. The essence of our argument in Chapter 10 is that in future the issues must be tackled openly.

This is a risky course which politicians will be understandably reluctant to adopt. But we believe that the alternative is riskier – that the NHS will continue to appear to be 'crumbling' when in fact it is making sensible decisions about the allocation of its resources and making sensible attempts, through local experiment and innovation, to develop new services and new ways of delivering them in an uncertain and changing environment.

To move in this direction, the NHS has to be proactive, aiming to promote among the media and the public an understanding of the way the Service is changing and the nature of the choices it has to make. Some of this should be quite straightforward. For example, the NHS could provide (or ensure the provision of) objective briefings in current topics which would be designed to provide the essential context within which particular developments or events could be assessed. Non-political spokespeople could be used in the media to explain the context of particular decisions in a non-partisan way – too often the Service is at the mercy of an array of independent (often ill-informed) commentators or lobby groups in the national media, which leads to confusion, half-truth and conflict.

This proactive role would comprise areas in which scarcity of resources must be explicitly faced, not in terms of individual decisions whether or not to provide care, but rather in broad areas such as hospital reconfiguration or ambulance standards or the terms on which new drugs are licensed or new surgical procedures brought into use. It might extend, drawing on developments such as citizens' juries and deliberative polling, to determination of priorities at local or even national level.

It would also have to tackle some of the tensions described in earlier chapters between innovation and equity. As noted already, there are strong arguments for accepting the diversity that comes from encouraging innovation, but this will only be acceptable if the underlying reasons are understood. Achieving such an understanding is essentially a task of the political Centre.

A related requirement, also stemming from the arguments set out in Chapter 10, would be a commitment to justify explicitly changes to the scope of the NHS. This would involve a commitment to justify planned withdrawals of service (or of subsidy), such as those that have occurred in long-term care, dentistry and podiatry, where types of service or need may be judged to be outside the range of the NHS.

As we noted in Chapter 10, experience in other countries has shown that exclusions are difficult to achieve for whole classes of treatment; for example while some forms of cosmetic surgery may be judged purely cosmetic – and hence thought to be outside the bundle – others may be judged to have therapeutic value, such as the treatment of gross deformities. A debate needs to be held on what criteria justify removing services from the NHS package and how far they should be dropped in whole or in part, according to some threshold, based perhaps on the degree of severity of disease or the individual's ability to benefit.

Defining thresholds for treatment has not been a focus of activity in the NHS at national level. However, national policies are likely to have had significant knock-on effects on the thresholds actually applied. For example, over the last two years acute hospitals have rebalanced the pattern of their activities towards emergency and away from elective and then back again during 1998 as they have striven to reach the waiting list targets set in the 1997 election. It is not known what implications these switches in policy at national level will have for thresholds at the local level.

Equally, the implicit trade-off between the extent of the bundle and the threshold at which care is received for services within the bundle needs to be debated. What if, for example, the nursing element of long-term care was re-classified as falling within the NHS bundle, as the Royal Commission's report *With Respect to Age* suggested? Would this mean that less elective care could be carried out and hence the threshold for access to it raised?

At present, the clinical threshold (level of disease) at which patients receive care for different services is not measured in any objective way. As noted in Chapter 9, there are some examples up and down the country where clinicians and others have tried to develop 'clinical scoring systems'. This work should be extended, through the National Institute for Clinical Excellence as well as audit and peer review and the results made available for public debate.

Similarly, explanations of how new services or treatments should enter the bundle also need to be made and the criteria for entry debated. The previous Government made significant progress in this direction through the introduction of health technology assessment, but much more could be done in respect of both drugs and new surgical procedures.

So far the UK is a long way from grasping this nettle even in the most obvious circumstances. A good example arose under the previous Government in relation to ambulance services. The notion of a category of call which would not attract an ambulance response was rejected, no doubt because Conservative Ministers wished to avoid the charge that they were cutting back services and also the risk that they would be blamed if a patient in urgent need did not receive a rapid response. But such non-essential calls, which amount to some 15 per cent of the total, are often trivial; as has now become accepted, some form of gate keeping is required, based ultimately on the judgement that certain forms of need can and should be met outside the NHS.

The impact of greater debate and the development of nationally agreed and understood rules should help to make certain types of change and forms of policy easier to introduce. It could also help to support professionals and patients in their decisions about clinical care, by helping to sanction some of the limits to the NHS. In this way the political process can support the day-to-day professional roles as well as the management of change.

If this takes place, then the limits of the NHS will be made more explicit and that might in turn encourage more use of private sector services. If so, then the Government may have to consider further what its responsibility is towards those who do so. That might lead to a more active regulation of both private insurers and privately provided care than the Government proposals set out in the Care Standards Bill currently allow for. Such a role seems entirely appropriate for the Government to exercise, but it could only be squared with the overall objectives of the NHS if the precise scope of the NHS, and the reasons for setting limits to it, were widely accepted.

## The political process

We have argued that the Service has become too politicised, in part as a response to, and in part because of, a growing load on the Centre. That, however, reflects the nature of the British political system, as much as the current state of the NHS, so it is clear that ways of deflecting attention from the Centre will be hard to find. The present time should be more propitious. First, the phrase used in *The New NHS* 'what counts is what works' implies that it is the outcomes that policy achieves rather than the ideological correctness of the policies themselves which should count in future. If so, that should allow issues to be debated not only in a less heated and partisan way than in the first part of the 1990s but also less at central and more at local level.

Second, although there is a current emphasis, typified by the waiting list initiative, on a centrally directed approach to managing performance in the NHS, this is also combined with an encouragement to the NHS to build 'horizontal networks' with other organisations to promote partnership within the local NHS through, for example, the duty of partnership placed on the NHS in developing local health improvement plans. If partnership is allowed to develop – that is if it is not crowded out by too much central direction – then this would lead to more local freedoms and flexibilities and greater scope for local initiative.

Third, there is an obvious impatience within the Government to itself solve problems faced by the public and users of public services, rather than simply design 'top-down' solutions for local implementation. Hence the exhortation for more of a 'joined-up' approach to problem solving, evidenced by the work, for example, of the Social Exclusion Unit. Some commentators[4] of current influence have even suggested that the Government should be organised around problems, not traditional Departments. This represents a potentially exciting new approach to policy-making, but again is difficult to reconcile with the tendency for the Government to increase central influence control and direction.

Another development is the emergence of devolution at country level, and the growing possibility of change at local, *i.e.* city level. This might create a political environment in which it was possible to envisage new forms of local accountability such as elected health authorities. But at present, developments below national level are not strong enough to rely on for support for changes of this kind. As education and social services policy indicates, the Centre clearly intends to keep a tight grip on local service provision with regard both to its content and the manner of its provision.

The alternative is reform at the Centre. In principle, the Agency approach widely adopted under the previous Government with the express aim of isolating the management role from political interference, would relieve central government ministers from the day-to-day pressures and allow those actually responsible for service delivery to defend their record in public. It would mean, for example, that officials such as the NHS Chief Executive would 'front' the NHS rather than the Secretary of State when matters such as hospital closures were being publicly debated.

The central difficulty with this approach, at least at the present time, was well illustrated in the case of prisons where the then newly appointed Director General was required to resign by a Home Secretary unable to make the distinction between policy and execution. As we noted in Chapter 12 that line would be even harder to draw in the health field but in the field of economic policy the Chancellor surprised nearly everyone by handing over control of monetary policy to an expert committee chaired by an official, the Governor of the Bank of England, and, more recently, the Secretary of State for Trade and Industry, Stephen Byers, has indicated his intention to de-politicise mergers policy by handing over his role to the Office of Fair Trading and the Competition Commission.

Another possible direction is to attempt to limit the range of issues with which the Centre is actively involved through more effective delegation. The way forward here is extremely difficult to make out. If the potential for muddle and frustration is to be avoided then a clearer definition of the roles of the Centre, including the professionals' own 'centre', and the locality, including the 'professional locality', has to be reached. This is of course a very old dilemma but the terms in which it might be solved might be slowly changing in such a way as to allow new solutions to emerge.

For example, improved central intelligence allied to the development of information technologies could allow genuinely effective centrally-determined of some services. Improvements in IT combined with centralised service frameworks, agreed thresholds for elective care and much greater analytic capacity could be the basis for the centralised management of the hospital system as a whole, particularly elective care.

In the present context, the advantages of such a system would be that it would allow a much clearer identification of responsibility than currently exists and also the pooling of analytic resources and relevant clinical and organisational intelligence about hospital performance. It would allow managerial experiment in hospital organisation, by for example using new ways of dividing work between clinicians to be carried out as part of a systematic programme of improvement. It would open the way for a more rigorous approach to capital planning in a limited number of areas where central direction was feasible.

A second example is that outcome indicators and improved external audit on the lines suggested in Chapter 14, could allow a genuinely *local* NHS to emerge. The basic terms of any major delegation or relaxation of central rules must be that in return for greater local flexibility, accountability is more rigorous. Essentially the nature of the 'deal' would be the same as that with professional interests as a whole: trust would have to be earned by greater transparency, severer sanctions in the event of failure, and clear central rules in those areas considered a part of a *national* health service.

The cause of transparency is now more hopeful than it once was. Whatever the merits of the particular sets of performance indicators proposed in *The New NHS*, the context in which they have been put forward marks them as being a much more significant development than the initiatives taken by the Conservatives in the 1980s which were never developed or applied in a systematic way. The issue of sanctions has also been addressed in *The New*

*NHS* through the proposals relating to the Commission for Health Improvement.

A third example is increased emphasis on the public, their views on the quality of services and their involvement in decision-making at all levels of the NHS. Of course it could be that this emphasis will make central decision-making more likely – everyone will want what others appear to be getting – but it could work the other way, particularly if the public proves to be more concerned with influencing the way their local services are provided than with the national picture.

It will be readily apparent that there are severe obstacles in the way of effective delegation. As we have remarked at several points, the rhetoric of the Centre has been consistently in favour of local discretion but its behaviour has been otherwise. Although *The New NHS* indicates there will be a stronger role in some areas and more effective local delegation, what is missing, as we have pointed out elsewhere, is any serious discussion of what range of decisions can properly be made locally and which not. In particular *The New NHS* does not address those areas surrounding the scope of the NHS and thresholds of access to it.

The failure to tackle these issues reflects in turn the pressures on the Centre to demonstrate obvious results in the short time horizon of a political term in office, and the desire of national politicians to impose their priorities on the Service. Because of 'short-termism', process is favoured over outcome and particularly over the steps needed to secure an environment most favourable to the longer-term survival of the Service.

## New forms of policy-making

As noted in Chapter 14, recent developments have been encouraging. The 'listening exercise' conducted by the previous Government within primary care did lead to proposals which genuinely addressed the concerns of those in the field, and they were nonetheless radical for that. Another has been the widespread use of pilots. The present Government stated in *The New NHS* that 'what matters is what works'. If they really believed that, the way would be open for a less politicised and more evidence-based form of policy-making.

The technical suggestions made in Chapter 14 will also help: more learning from past experience within the Service; more international comparisons; more reliance on sound intelligence. The aim should be to avoid abrupt changes of policy based purely on political hunch or expediency and move towards evidence or consensus-based policy.

## More objective reporting

What exactly the 'State of the NHS' is remains hard even for insiders to know. The National Survey of Patients and Users is a step in the right direction. But it should be accompanied by publicly available, regular, authoritative and independent monitoring of trends within the Service such as changes in resources, levels of activity, trust finance and so on. This need not be done within the Service itself provided that the agency responsible had unrestricted access to the information it required and the standing to be taken seriously.

In effect this represents a unification of the roles of the existing auditors – the Health Service Commissioner, the Audit Commission and the National Audit Office. As we noted in Chapter 11, their roles to some degree overlap but by virtue of their different powers and reporting arrangements, they do not present a coherent picture of the Service and many areas such as the health of the workforce are omitted from regular review. Furthermore they make no attempt, either individually (with the exception of the Health Service Commissioner) or collectively, to come to an overall view of the Service or to draw out the general lessons from their specific findings.

The central purpose of such an exercise would be to reassure the public, in their capacity as taxpayers, citizens and users, that resources are being effectively and efficiently used. There is no direct way in which taxpayers can make their views known but even if there were, any views they might express would be almost worthless for lack of any useful information about what any additions to the NHS budget might be spent on, still less what they might achieve. This deficiency has only been tenable because of the general public goodwill towards spending on the NHS.

There can be no quick solutions to the problem of finding a way to measure what the NHS achieves by way of health outcomes. But it would be feasible to devise a much better system of reporting how NHS resources have been used in the past, and what the intention is as to the future. Some such debate must take place between Department and Treasury but it is shrouded in the usual secrecy. It should be opened up and a much better attempt made to show why the NHS deserves more, how well or badly its staff are paid, and which services or groups of the population are benefiting from extra resources.

One simple step might be to publish an annual report on 'The State of the NHS'. This would go far beyond the present style of annual departmental report by providing a much more comprehensive and objective account of progress in the NHS as a whole, reporting performance, significant changes, impact of policy and public perceptions. It could draw on the large amount of data being presented in the performance assessment framework, the National Schedule of Reference Costs as well as audit findings. Such a report, which could be available on the Internet as well as the bookshop, could even include reflections by independent observers of the NHS (from the UK and abroad) and a summary of relevant trends in other countries.

## Conclusion

The starting point of this book was the initial settlement made when the NHS was established between the State and the medical profession. The central thread running through the subsequent chapters is that this settlement is changing and must change further.

We have not attempted in this book to put forward precise solutions or particular proposals except in broad terms. But our analysis suggests some key requirements for the future:

- the NHS will have to continue to change and adapt, in the light of new circumstances and new knowledge. That change should be rooted either in consciously designed experiments or in evidence of 'what works' particularly in the area of management and service delivery or in a greater consensus about the limits to the Service, especially among the public
- its basic orientation must shift from a preoccupation with the professions and the requirements of the Government to those of its users and ultimate financiers. This is not just a matter of designing services that are more responsive to individuals: it also involves being more open about the limits to the Service
- within the NHS the role of clinicians should be extended to comprise responsibility for the management of resources and of services: clinical training should be overhauled to reflect this. The Government should actively encourage this and seek support from the national medical institutions
- communication between the Service and the public should not primarily run through the political process. The NHS itself needs a clearer non-partisan voice

- in policy-making, there should be less emphasis on process and more emphasis on longer-term impact. Impact assessments should be regularly reviewed by policymakers possibly in the annual review of the 'State of the NHS'.

What these very general proposals imply is a change in the political role. It may seem quixotic to propose that, but if the Government really means what it says about public services in general – 'what counts is what works' and, that providers should listen to users – then that would be the consequence.

Progress in the each of the areas discussed above can be made in isolation and indeed there are signs of change in what our argument suggests is the right direction in most of them. But the most important changes needed essentially involve mutual adjustment of roles, which must start with the political role.

Such a process is not once and for all nor can it be rapid. Rather, it must take place over a long period of time and through an informal rather than a formal process. While the Government would clearly have a key role, there is no reason why other interested parties could not make their own contribution.

If the Government does not play its part, then the challenge might, perhaps, be taken up by a leading figure in the professions who might begin to lead both them and the NHS into the 21st century. The critical point is to accept that the old relationships must change and that a sustained dialogue and development process involving all the interested parties is required. Our hope is that we have contributed in some measure to this process.

## References

1. Irvine D. The performance of doctors: the new professionalism. *Lancet* 1999; 353: 1174–77.
2. Berwick D. Medical Associations: guilds or leaders? *BMJ* 1997; 314: 1564–65.
3. Chantler C. The role and education of doctors in the delivery of health care. *Lancet* 1999; 353: 1178–81.
4. Leadbetter C. *Living on Thin Air: the new economy.* London: Viking, 1999.

# Appendix 1

# Important events

**1948** National Health Service established.

**1950** Ceiling on NHS expenditure first imposed.

**1951** Authorisation of charges for dental and optical appliances.

**1956** Guillebaud Committee established to examine expenditure in the NHS.

**1962** Publication of Hospital Plan for England and Wales.

**1965** Charter for GPs introduced.

**1966** New GP contract introduced.

**1968** Department of Health and Social Security (DHSS) formed.

**1969** Ely Hospital report published. Hospital (later Health) Advisory Board established.

**1972** NHS Reorganisation White Paper published.

**1973** NHS Reorganisation Act passed. Health Service Commissioner first appointed.

**1974** NHS Reorganisation Act implemented. English regional health boards (RHBs) reconstituted with minor boundary changes as 14 regional health authorities (RHAs). These became responsible for strategy, building programmes, staffing matters and the allocation of resources to 90 area health authorities (AHAs), which replaced local authority health departments. District health authorities were created and were further sub-divided into sectors. Executive Councils were abolished and replaced by 90 family practitioner committees (FPCs) administering general practices.

**1976** Report of the Resource Allocation Working Party (RAWP) published, proposing ways of allocating resources to regional health authorities in relation to health care need.

Royal Commission on NHS established.

**1979** *Patients First*, a consultative paper on the structure and management of the NHS, published.

Royal Commission reports.

**1982** NHS restructured – the area tier was abolished.

**1983** Griffiths Management Review published, identifying the need for a general management function in the NHS.

**1984** Griffiths management reforms introduced.

**1985** Family practitioner committees (FPCs) achieved independent status.

**1986** NHS Management Board established.

**1988** DHSS split, to become the Department of Health (DoH) and the Department of Social Security (DSS).

**1989** *Working for Patients* published, setting out the Conservatives' proposals for reform of the NHS.

NHS Management Executive created.

**1990** NHS and Community Care Act – purchasing and provision were separated. District health authorities became purchasers and were given allocation of funds directly. Hospital and community services could apply for self-governing status as trusts. GP practices could apply to manage their own budget for staff costs, prescribing, out-patient care and some hospital services. Successful practices were called GP fundholders. The responsibility for the funding of residential and nursing homes transferred from the Department of Social Security to local authority social services departments.

New national contract introduced for GPs.

**1991** Implementation of 1990 reforms began on 1 April.

Clinical Standards Advisory Group established.

*Patient's Charter* introduced.

NHS R&D Initiative launched.

**1992** Tomlinson Inquiry into London's health services was published. The report emphasised the need to improve the provision of primary care and bring it up to national standards.

**1994**  The 14 regional health authorities were reduced to eight.

NHS Management Executive becomes NHS Executive.

**1995**  Health Authorities Act provided for the abolition of regional health authorities and their transformation into Regional Offices of the NHS Executive. The Act also facilitated the creation of 100 health authorities by merging the remaining 105 district health authorities and 90 family health services authorities in 1996.

**1996**  Primary Care White Papers published.

**1997**  NHS (Primary Care) Act provided opportunities for developing new ways of delivering primary care.

NHS (Private Finance) Act eased the way for the use of private finance in capital investment projects.

**1998**  *The New NHS* published, setting out Labour's new proposals for reform of the NHS.

**1999**  National Institute for Clinical Excellence and the Commission for Health Improvement set up.

Primary care groups came into operation.

Health Act passed.

Appendix 2

# Glossary

**Area Health Authorities** – created in 1974 and then removed in the 1982 restructuring. They were in charge of district management teams (responsible for hospital and community health services) and family practitioner committees (responsible for primary care).

**Audit Commission** – oversees the expenditure audit of local authorities and the NHS in England and Wales. It reviews the financial value of the service provided and undertakes studies and audits of selected topics.

**Citizen's Charter** – introduced in 1991. Organisations and institutions in both the public and private sector were encouraged to set standards of service to which they aimed and then to measure their performance.

**Clinical Standards Advisory Group (CSAG)** – established in 1991 and wound up in 1999. It reported on clinical standards on the basis of site visits and analysis of data from those sites.

**Commission for Health Improvement (CHI)** – established during 1999. It will act as a monitor of clinical governance within the NHS at local level.

**Comprehensive Spending Review (CSR)** – first carried out in 1998, sets out public spending programmes for the next three years.

**Department of Health (DoH)** – formed in 1988 when the Department of Health and Social Security was split into the Department of Health and the Department of Social Security.

**Family Health Services (FHS)** – services provided in the community by GPs, dentists, pharmacists and opticians. These professionals are independent contractors.

**Family Health Services Authorities (FHSAs)** – managed family health services from 1991 until their abolition in 1996.

**Family Practitioner Committees (FPCs)** – administered family health services from 1977 until the establishment of FHSAs. Their line of accountability to health authorities was dropped in 1984 and they were abolished in 1991.

**General Medical Services (GMS)** – services provided by general practitioners.

**GP Fundholders** – practices that chose to accept a budget for all or part of their practice and to manage the budget for hospital and community health services themselves. Introduced by the NHS and Community Care Act 1990, they were effectively abolished in 1997, but this was not made official until 1999.

**Griffiths' Reforms** – introduced as a result of the 1983 review into NHS management. The review's main recommendation was the establishment of a small, strong general management board for the NHS as a whole and that all hospitals should be run by general managers.

**Health Action Zones (HAZs)** – introduced by Labour, they bring together organisations within the NHS and others, such as local authorities, to promote health improvement in specially designated areas.

**Health Authorities (HAs)** – now serve a population of around 500,000. Originally smaller, they were the purchasing half of the purchaser–provider split. They retain some purchasing functions as well as strategic leadership at a local level.

**Health Improvement Programme (HImP)** – a local plan of action to improve health and modernise local health services.

**Health Service Commissioner** – investigates complaints from individuals about failures in service and administration within the NHS.

**Healthy Living Centres (HLCs)** – funded from national lottery monies, these are intended to promote health, particularly in areas of deprivation.

**Hospital and Community Health Services (HCHS)** – consist of hospital and community health care services such as district/home nursing.

**House of Commons Health Select Committee** – has a roving remit reviewing policy for health and social services.

**Long Term Service Agreements** – in 1999 these replaced the annual contracting procedures introduced by the 1990 Act; they are intended to run for three years or more.

**Medical Practices Committee (MPC)** – established in 1948, it aims to ensure that all parts of the country are adequately provided with GPs.

**Medical Research Council (MRC)** – established in 1918 to replace the Medical Research Committee. This publicly funded body oversees medical research aimed at improving public health, health services, pharmaceutical and other health-related industries.

**Modernisation Fund** – created following the Comprehensive Spending Review. It is used to finance specific projects that the Government wishes to see implemented, such as NHS *Direct*, or to meet particular targets such as waiting list reductions.

**National Audit Office (NAO)** – verifies the accounts of all Government departments and many public sector bodies and conducts value for money studies within the NHS and other spending programmes.

**National Electronic Library for Health** – currently under development, this is intended to provide NHS professionals with 24-hour-a-day access to health care information.

**National Health Service Executive (NHSE)** – comprises eight regional offices, each with a regional director and a head office within the Department of Health, led by the chief executive Sir Alan Langlands. It is responsible for policy development and implementation and it monitors the performance of NHS trusts and health authorities.

**National Institute for Clinical Excellence (NICE)** – a special health authority, which offers specialised advice to the Secretary of State and NHS clinicians and managers on the cost-effectiveness of new technologies, including medicines, tests and surgical procedures, and how they can add value to existing treatments.

**National Service Frameworks (NSFs)** – intended to define how major services, such as mental health or coronary heart disease are best provided.

**National Schedule for Reference Costs** – shows the variations in the recorded costs of clinical care within NHS trusts.

**National Specialist Commissioning Advisory Group (NSCAG)** – makes recommendations on the provision of specialist services such as liver transplantation.

**NHS *Direct*** – nurse-led telephone line providing 24-hour medical advice, introduced in 1998 in parts of the country but rapidly becoming available nationwide.

**NHS R&D Initiative** – begun in 1991, it led to the creation of a series of R&D programmes focused largely on NHS service requirements.

**NHS Supplies Authority** – works to enable the NHS to obtain the maximum benefit from the money it spends on procuring supplies.

**NHS Trusts** – providers of hospital services, community health services, mental health services and ambulance services.

**Patient Partnership Initiative** – launched in 1996 to promote individual involvement in one's own care and to make services more responsive to the needs and preferences of users.

**Patient's Charter** – the NHS section of the Citizen's Charter. Most of the indicators concentrate on the process of health care received by NHS patients, such as waiting times. In 1997 further standards were added relating to clinical performance.

**Performance Assessment Framework (PAF)** – consists of a wide range of indicators for each health authority and NHS trust, covering efficiency, equity, access, clinical quality and the user experience.

**Personal Social Services (PSS)** – social care provided at a local level for the vulnerable in society, for example residential care for the elderly.

**Pharmaceutical Price Regulation Scheme (PPRS)** – a voluntary agreement between the Government and pharmaceutical industry on acceptable profit levels.

**Policy Research Programme** – an R&D programme for the Department of Health, the programme aims to provide a knowledge base for health service, social service and central health related policy.

**Primary Care Act Pilots (PCAPs)** – introduced by the NHS (Primary Care) Act 1997. They allow for relaxation of the rules governing general medical services and hence allow new forms of service to be developed.

**Primary Care Groups (PCGs)** – consist of groups of general practices serving on average about 100,000 people. Formed in 1999 to replace GP fundholding, they are beginning to assume responsibility for commissioning health services.

**Primary Care Trusts (PCTs)** – provision for these was made in the 1999 Health Act. They are expected to come into effect in 2000 in some areas. They offer trust status to organisations providing general medical and related services.

**Private Finance Initiative (PFI)** – introduced by the Conservatives and continued under Labour, it seeks to use private capital to finance public sector capital projects such as hospitals.

**Regional Health Authorities (RHAs)** – emerged after the reorganisation of the NHS in 1974. They were responsible for strategy, the building programme, staffing matters and allocation of resources to area health authorities. They were abolished in 1995.

**Regional Hospital Boards** – acted at regional level in the NHS between 1948 and 1974. They acted mainly as the Minister's agents but had discretion to plan among other things medical staffing and manage financial allocations.

**Resource Allocation Working Party (RAWP)** – set up in 1975 to devise a method for resources to health authorities on the basis of health care need.

**Social Exclusion Unit** – located within the Cabinet Office. It tackles issues that run across departments such as urban decay, teenage pregnancies and school truancy.

**Special Health Authorities** – provide health services for the whole of the population, not specific geographical areas, for example the National Blood Authority.

# Bibliography

All the references cited in the text are listed below. However, because of the wide-ranging nature of this book, we have drawn on, been influenced by, or otherwise found useful a much wider range of literature which we have not explicitly cited. These sources are also included below.

Adam S and Platt D. *Ex parte Coughlan: follow up action*. Leeds: Department of Health, 1999.

Aiken LH, Sloane DM and Sochalski J. Hospital organisation and outcomes. *Quality in Health Care* 1998; 7: 222–26.

Allen I. *Committed but critical: an examination of young doctors' views of their core values*. London: British Medical Association, 1997.

Association of Community Health Councils for England and Wales. *Medical records: restricted access, limited use*. London: ACHCEW, 1998.

Audit Commission. *Improving the Supplies Service in the NHS*. London: Audit Commission, 1991.

Audit Commission. *NHS Estate Management and Property Maintenance*. London: HMSO, 1991.

Audit Commission. *A prescription for improvement: towards more rational prescribing in general practice*. London: HMSO, 1994.

Audit Commission. *United they stand: co-ordinating care for elderly patients with hip fracture*. London: HMSO, 1995.

Audit Commission. *Goods for Your Health: Improving Supplies Management in NHS Trusts*. London: Audit Commission, 1996.

Audit Commission. *What the doctor ordered: a study of GP fundholders in England and Wales*. London: HMSO, 1996.

Audit Commission. *Finders, Keepers: The management of staff turnover in NHS Trusts*. London: Audit Commission, 1997.

Audit Commission. *Coming of Age: improving care services for older people 1997*. London: Audit Commission, 1997.

Audit Commission. *Higher Purchase: commissioning specialised services in the NHS.* London: Audit Commission, 1997.

Baker M and Kirk S, editors. *Research and Development for the NHS: evidence, evaluation and effectiveness.* 2nd edition. Abingdon: Radcliffe Press, 1998.

Batchelor I and Williams A. *Issues of Manpower Planning and Management in the NHS.* London: King's Fund Centre, 1980.

Beech R *et al.* Spatial Equity in the NHS: the death and rebirth of RAWP. In: Harrison A, editor. *Health Care UK 1990.* Hermitage: Policy Journals, 1990.

Blendon RJ *et al.* Who Has the Best Health Care System? A Second Look. Data Watch. *Health Affairs* 1995; 14: 220–30.

Bone M *et al. Health expectancy and its uses.* London: HMSO, 1995.

Bonneux L *et al.* Preventing fatal diseases increases health care costs: cause elimination life table approach. *BMJ* 1998; 316: 26–29.

British Medical Association – Health Policy Research Unit. *Core Values for the Medical Profession in the 21st Century: survey report.* London: BMA, 1995.

British Medical Association – Central Consultants and Specialists Committee. *Towards Tomorrow: The future role of the consultant.* London: BMA, 1996.

British Medical Association – Health Policy and Economic Research Unit. *Leaner and fitter: What future model of delivery for acute hospital services?* London: BMA, 1997.

British Medical Association – Health Policy and Economic Research Unit. *BMA Cohort Study of 1995 Medical Graduates: Second Report: February 1997: the pre-registration year.* London: BMA, 1997.

British Medical Association – Health Policy and Economic Research Unit. *BMA Cohort Study of Medical Graduates 1995: Third Report: June 1998: career intentions of 1st year senior house officers.* London: BMA, 1998.

British Medical Association – Health Policy Research Unit. *The Workforce Dynamics of Recent Medical Graduates: a report from the BMA cohort study of 1995 medical graduates.* London: BMA, 1998.

British Medical Association. *The waiting list problem.* London: BMA, 1998.

British Medical Association, Royal College of Physicians of London, Royal College of Surgeons of England. *Provision of Acute General Hospital Services: a consultation document.* London: Royal College of Surgeons, 1998.

Broadbent J, Dietrich M and Roberts J. *The End of the Professions? The restructuring of professional work.* London: Routledge, 1997.

Cabinet Office Advisory Council for Applied Research and Development. *Medical Equipment.* London: HMSO, 1986.

Cabinet Office Advisory Council on Science and Technology. *A Report on Medical Research and Health.* London: HMSO, 1993.

Cabinet Office. *NHS Procurement Review.* London: Cabinet Office, 1998.

Calabresi G and Bobbitt P. *Tragic Choices: The Conflicts Society Confronts in the Allocation of Tragically Scarce Resources.* New York: WW Norton, 1978.

Calman K and Hine D. *Breast cancer services in Exeter and quality assurance for breast screening: report to the Secretary of State.* Leeds: Department of Health NHS Executive, 1997.

Cave M and Towse A. *Regulating the Prices Paid for NHS Medicines: Lessons from utility regulation.* OHE Briefing 34. London: Office of Health Economics, 1997.

Chalkley M and Robinson R. *Theory and evidence on cost sharing in healthcare: an economic perspective.* London: Office of Health Economics, 1997.

Chantler C. The role and education of doctors in the delivery of health care. *Lancet* 1999; 353: 1178–81.

Clinical Standards Advisory Group. *District elective surgery: access to and availability of services.* London: Stationery Office, 1996.

Clinical Standards Advisory Group. *Cleft Lip and/or Palate: Report of a CSAG Committee.* London: Stationery Office, 1998.

Clinical Standards Advisory Group. *Community health care for elderly people: report of a CSAG committee.* London: Stationery Office, 1998.

Commission on Social Justice. *Social Justice: strategies for national renewal: the report of the Commission on Social Justice.* London: IPPR; Vintage, 1994.

Coulter A, Entwhistle V and Gilbert D. *Informing Patients: an assessment of the quality of patient information materials.* London: King's Fund, 1998.

Culyer A (chair). *Supporting research and development in the NHS: a report to the Minister of Health.* London: HMSO, 1994.

Davis P. *Managing Medicines: public policy and therapeutic drugs.* Buckingham: Open University Press, 1997.

Department of the Environment, Transport and the Regions. *Modernising local government: local democracy and community leadership.* London: DETR, 1998.

Department of Health. *Practice Budgets for General Medical Practitioners – Working Paper 3.* London: HMSO, 1989.

Department of Health. *Self-governing Hospitals – NHS Review Working Paper 1.* London: HMSO, 1989.

Department of Health. *Research for health: a research and development strategy for the NHS.* London: Department of Health R&D Division, 1991.

Department of Health. *Planning the Medical Workforce – Medical Manpower Standing Advisory Committee: First Report.* London: HMSO, 1992.

Department of Health. *Local Voices.* London: NHS Management Executive, 1992.

Department of Health. *Priority Setting in the NHS: the NHS drugs budget: Government Response to the Second Report from the Health Committee sessions 1993/94.* Cm. 2683. London: HMSO, 1994.

Department of Health. *Improving NHS Dentistry.* Cm. 2625. London: HMSO, 1994.

Department of Health. *Managing the New NHS: functions and responsibilities in the new NHS.* Leeds: NHS Executive, 1994.

Department of Health. *Medical Research and the NHS Reforms.* Cm. 2894. London: HMSO, 1994.

Department of Health. *Centrally Commissioned Research Programme.* London: Department of Health, 1995.

Department of Health. *Planning the Medical Workforce – Medical Manpower Standing Advisory Committee: Second Report.* London: HMSO, 1995.

Department of Health. *Primary care: the future.* Cm. 3390. London: HMSO, 1996.

Department of Health. *Pharmaceutical Price Regulation Scheme: Report to Parliament.* London: HMSO, 1996.

Department of Health. *The National Health Service: A service with ambitions.* Cm. 3425. London: HMSO, 1996.

Department of Health. *In the Patient's Interest: multi-professional working across organisational boundaries – Report by the Standing Medical and Nursing & Midwifery Advisory Committees.* London: HMSO, 1996.

Department of Health. *Pharmaceutical Price Regulation Scheme: Second Report to Parliament.* London: HMSO, 1997.

Department of Health – Standard Medical Advisory Committee. *Future patterns of medical care: a paper by the Standard Medical Advisory Committee.* London: SMAC, 1997.

Department of Health – Medical Workforce Standing Advisory Committee. *Planning the Medical Workforce – Third Report.* London: HMSO, 1997.

Department of Health – Policy Research Programme. *Providing a Knowledge Base for Health, Public Health and Social Care.* London: HMSO, 1997.

Department of Health. *A first class service: quality in the new NHS.* London: Department of Health, 1998.

Department of Health – Emergency Services Action Team. *Emergency Services Action Team 1998 report.* London: Department of Health, 1998.

Department of Health. *Health in partnership: patient, carer and public involvement in health care decision making.* London: Department of Health, 1998.

Department of Health. *Modernising Health and Social Services: National Priorities Guidance 1999/00–2001/02.* London: Department of Health, 1998.

Department of Health. *Nurse prescribing: implementing the scheme across England.* London: Department of Health, 1998.

Department of Health. *Emergency services action team 1998 report.* London: Department of Health, 1998.

Department of Health. *Working Together: Securing a quality workforce for the NHS.* London: Department of Health, 1998.

Department of Health. *Primary care: delivering the future*. London: Department of Health, 1998.

Department of Health. *Modernising Social Services: Promoting independence, improving protection, raising standards*. Cm. 4169. London: HMSO, 1998.

Department of Health. *Capital Investment Strategy for the Department of Health*. Leeds: Department of Health, 1999.

Department of Health. *Future Staffing Requirements: The Government's Response to the Health Committee's Report on Future Staffing Requirements*. London: Stationery Office, 1999.

Department of Health. *The Government's Expenditure Plans 1999–2000*. London: Stationery Office, 1999.

Department of Health. *Modernising Health and Social Services: Developing the Workforce*. London: Department of Health, 1999.

Department of Health. *Agenda for Change: Modernising the NHS pay system*. London: Department of Health, 1999.

Department of Health, National Audit Office. *Cost Over-runs, Funding Problems and Delays on Guy's Hospital Phase III Development: report by the Comptroller and Auditor General*. London: Stationery Office, 1998.

Department of Health, NHS Executive. *Managing the New NHS, Functions and Responsibilities in the New NHS*. Leeds: NHS Executive, 1994.

Department of Health, NHS Executive. *Seeing the wood, sparing the trees: efficiency scrutiny into the burdens of paperwork in NHS trusts and health authorities*. Leeds: NHS Executive, 1996.

Department of Health, NHS Executive. *The new NHS 1998 reference costs: National schedule of reference costs*. Leeds: NHS Executive, 1998.

Department of Health, NHS Executive. *Quality and performance in the NHS: high level performance indicators*. London: Department of Health, 1999.

Department of Health, Welsh Office, Scottish Office. *Choice and Opportunity: primary care: the future*. Cm. 3390. London: HMSO, 1996.

Department of Health and Social Security. *The National Health Service: the future structure of the National Health Service*. London: HMSO, 1970.

Department of Health and Social Security. *Management Arrangements for the Reorganised National Health Service*. London: HMSO, 1972.

Department of Health and Social Security. *Priorities for Health and Personal Social Services in England, A Consultative Document*. London: HMSO, 1976.

Department of Health and Social Security. *The Way Forward*. London: HMSO, 1977.

Department of Health and Social Security. *Medical Manpower – the next twenty years*. London: HMSO, 1978.

Department of Health and Social Security. *Review of Health Capital: a discussion document on the role of capital in the provision of health services*. London: HMSO, 1979.

Department of Health and Social Security. *Patients First*. London: HMSO, 1979.

Department of Health and Social Security. *Medical Manpower Steering Group Report*. London: HMSO, 1980.

Department of Health and Social Security. *Hospital Services: the future pattern of hospital provision in England: a consultation paper*. London: HMSO, 1980.

Department of Health and Social Security. *Care in Action*. London: HMSO, 1981.

Department of Health and Social Security, Operational Research Service. *Nurse Manpower Planning: approaches and techniques*. London: HMSO, 1983.

Department of Health and Social Security. *Health care and its costs: the development of the National Health Service in England*. London: HMSO, 1983.

Department of Health and Social Security. *Report of the Advisory Committee for Medical Manpower Planning*. London: HMSO, 1985.

Department of Health and Social Security. *Neighbourhood Nursing – A Focus for Care, Report of the Community Nursing Review*. London: HMSO, 1986.

Department of Health and Social Security, The Welsh Office. *Report of the Committee on Hospital Complaints Procedure*. London: HMSO, 1973.

Department of Trade and Industry – Office of Science and Technology. *Science, Engineering and Technology Statistics 1998*. Cm. 4006. London: HMSO, 1998.

Dixon J, Inglis S and Klein R. Is the English NHS underfunded? *BMJ* 1999; 318: 522–26.

Dixon J, Harrison A and New B. Is the NHS underfunded? *BMJ* 1997; 314: 58–61.

Dixon P, Gatherer R and Pollock A. *Hospital Services for the 21st Century: a report to Oxford Regional Health Authority.* Reading: West Berkshire Health Authority, 1992.

Dopson S. *Managing Ambiguity and Change: the case of the NHS.* London: Macmillan Business, 1997.

Drummond MF and Maynard A, editors. *Purchasing and Providing Cost-Effective Health Care.* Edinburgh: Churchill Livingston, 1993.

Dunnell K. Are we healthier? *Population Trends* 1995; 85: 12–18.

Dunning AJ (chair). *Choices in Health Care.* Report by the Government Committee on Choices in Health Care. Zoetermeer: Government Committee on Choices in Health Care, 1992.

Ebrahim S and Redfern J. *Stroke Care – A Matter of Chance: A National Survey of Stroke Services.* London: The Stroke Association, 1999.

Edwards N and Harrison A. Hospitals: a research and policy programme. *BMJ* 1999, forthcoming.

Eve R and Hodgkin P. Professionalism and Medicine. In: Broadbent J, Dietrich M and Roberts J. *The End of the Professions? The restructuring of professional work.* London: Routledge, 1997.

Ferguson B, Sheldon T and Posnett J, editors. *Concentration and Choice in Health Care.* London: Financial Times Healthcare, 1997.

Financial Secretary to the Treasury. *Treasury Minutes on the Sixty-eighth and Sixty-ninth Reports from the Committee of Public Accounts 1997–98.* Cm. 4279. London: Stationery Office, 1999.

Foot M. *Aneurin Bevan* Vol. 2. St Albans: Paladin, 1975.

Francis B and Humphries J. Commissioning Nurse Education. *Nursing Standard* 1998; 12: 45–47.

Fulop NJ, Hood S and Parsons S. Does the national health service want hospital-at-home? *Journal of the Royal Society of Medicine* 1997; 90: 212–15.

Gaffney D, Pollock AM, Price D *et al.* NHS capital expenditure and the private finance initiative – expansion or contraction? *BMJ* 1999; 319: 48–51.

Gaffney D, Pollock AM, Price D *et al.* PFI in the NHS – is there an economic case? *BMJ* 1999; 319: 116–19.

Geljins AC and Rosenberg N. Making choice about medical technology. In: *Conference on fundamental questions about the future of health care.* Amsterdam: Scientific Council for Government Policy, 18–19 April, 1996.

General Medical Council. *Duties of a Doctor.* London: GMC, 1997.

General Medical Council. *Good medical practice: guidance from the General Medical Council.* London: General Medical Council, 1998.

Goddard M and Smith P. *Equity of Access to Health Care.* York: University of York, 1998.

Gray A and Buchan J. Pay in the British NHS: a local solution for a national service? *Journal of Health Services Research and Policy* 1998; 3: 113–20.

Griffiths R. *NHS management inquiry* ('The Griffiths Report'). London: DHSS, 1983.

Guillebaud CW (chair). *Report of the Committee of Enquiry into the Cost of the National Health Service.* London: HMSO, 1956.

Harrison A. Cost Containment in the NHS 1979–1990. In: Harrison A, editor. *Health Care UK 1990.* London: King's Fund Institute, 1990.

Harrison A. *London's Health Care System.* London: King's Fund, 1997.

Harrison A. National Service Frameworks. In: Klein R. *Implementing the White Paper: Pitfalls & opportunities.* London: King's Fund, 1998.

Harrison A and Prentice S. *Acute Futures.* London: King's Fund, 1996.

Harrison A, Dixon J, New B and Judge K. Is the NHS sustainable? *BMJ* 1997; 314: 296–98.

Harrison A, Dixon J, New B and Judge K. Can the NHS cope in future? *BMJ* 1997; 314: 139–42.

Hazell R and Jervis P. Devolution and health: dynamics of change in the post-devolution health services. In: Harrison A, editor. *Health Care UK 1997/98.* London: King's Fund, 1998.

Heald D and Scott DA. NHS capital charging after five years. In: Harrison A, editor. *Health Care UK 1995/96.* London: King's Fund, 1996.

Healthcare 2000. *UK Health and Healthcare Services: challenges and policy options: a report*. London: Healthcare 2000, 1995.

Health Service Circular. *Commissioning in the new NHS – Commissioning Services 1999–2000*. HSC 1998/198. London: Department of Health, 1998.

Health Service Circular. *Nurse prescribing: implementing the scheme across England*. HSC 1998/232. London: Department of Health, 1998.

Health Service Circular. *Agenda for change – modernising the NHS pay system*. HSC 1999/035. London: Department of Health, 1999.

Health Service Commissioner. *Failure to provide long-term NHS care for a brain-damaged patient (Leeds case) – Second Report for Session 1993–94*. London: HMSO, 1994.

Health Service Commissioner. *Health Service Commissioner for England, Scotland and Wales Annual Report 1997–98*. London: HMSO, 1998.

Health Service Commissioner. *Health Service Commissioner: fourth report for session 1997–98: investigations completed October 1997 to March 1998*. London: Stationery Office, 1998.

Health Service Commissioner. *Health Service Commissioner for England, Scotland and Wales Annual Report 1998–99*. London: Stationery Office, 1999.

Health Service Management Unit. *The Future Healthcare Workforce*. Manchester: University of Manchester, 1996.

Hinchcliffe D (chair). *The long-term care of the elderly: 4th report together with the proceedings of the Committee and minutes of evidence*. House of Commons Health Committee – Session 1998–99 – Paper No. 318. London: Stationery Office, 1999.

HM Treasury. *Competing for quality: buying better public services: presented to Parliament by the Chancellor of the Exchequer, November 1991*. Cm. 1730. London: HMSO, 1991.

HM Treasury. *Public services for the future: modernisation, reform, accountability: comprehensive spending review: public service agreements 1999–2002*. London: Stationery Office, 1998.

HM Treasury. *Modern Public Services for Britain: Investing in Reform. Comprehensive Spending Review: New Public Spending Plans 1999–2002*. Cm. 4011. London: HMSO, 1998.

HM Treasury. *Budget 1999 Leaflet*. London: HMSO, 1998.

House of Commons. *Open government: code of practice on access to Government information*. 2nd edition. London: HMSO, 1997.

House of Commons. *Treasury minute on the first to fourth reports from the Committee of Public Accounts 1997–98: first report: NHS supplies in England; second report: Health and Safety in NHS acute hospital trusts in England; third report: South and West Regional Health Authority: disposal of Swift; fourth report: Ministry of Defence: management of utilities*. London: Stationery Office, 1998.

House of Commons Committee of Public Accounts. *Financial Control and Accountability in the National Health Service*. London: HMSO, 1981.

House of Commons Committee of Public Accounts. *NHS Supplies and the Pharmaceutical Price Regulation Scheme*. London: HMSO, 1985.

House of Commons Committee of Public Accounts. *Control of Nursing Manpower*. London: HMSO, 1986.

House of Commons Committee of Public Accounts. *National Health Service Supplies in England – Forty-second Report*. London: HMSO, 1991.

House of Commons Committee of Public Accounts. *West Midlands Regional Health Authority: Regionally Managed Services Organisation*. London: HMSO, 1993.

House of Commons Committee on the Parliamentary Commissioner for Administration. *Independent Review of Hospital Complaints in the National Health Service*. London: HMSO, 1977.

House of Commons Committee on the Parliamentary Commissioner for Administration. *Independent Review of Hospital Complaints in the National Health Service*. London: HMSO, 1977.

House of Commons Health Committee. *Priority Setting in the NHS: the NHS drugs budget. Volume 1: Report, together with an Appendix and the Proceedings of the Committee*. 2nd report. London: HMSO, 1994.

House of Commons Health Committee. *Public Expenditure on Health and Personal Social Services*. London: HMSO, 1997.

House of Commons Health Committee. *Long-term Care: NHS Responsibilities for Meeting Continuing Health Care Needs Volume I. Report, together with Annexes and the Proceedings of the Committee*. London: HMSO, 1995.

House of Commons Health Committee. *Priority setting in the NHS: purchasing: first report [of the] Health Committee. Volume 1: Report, together with annexes and the proceedings of the Committee.* London: HMSO, 1995.

House of Commons Health Committee. *Future NHS Staffing Requirements – Volume 1: Report and Proceedings of the Committee.* London: Stationery Office, 1999.

House of Commons Health Committee. *Future NHS Staffing Requirements – Volume 2: Minutes of Evidence and Appendices.* London: Stationery Office, 1999.

House of Commons Health Committee. *Long-term Care of the Elderly.* London: Stationery Office, 1999.

House of Commons Public Accounts Committee. *Wessex Regional Health Authority: management of the regional information systems plan.* London: HMSO, 1993.

House of Commons Public Accounts Committee. *NHS Supplies in England – First Report.* London: HMSO, 1997.

House of Commons Public Accounts Committee. *The former Yorkshire Regional Health Authority: the inquiry commissioned by the NHS Chief Executive together with the proceedings of the Committee relating to the report and the minutes of evidence, and appendices.* London: HMSO, 1997.

House of Commons Social Services Committee. *Medical Education, with special reference to the number of doctors and the career structure in hospitals, Volume I – Fourth Report.* London: HMSO, 1981.

House of Commons Social Services Committee. *Medical Education Report: follow-up.* London: HMSO, 1985.

House of Commons Social Services Committee. *Resourcing the National Health Service: Whitley Councils. Volume 1 Together with the Proceedings of the Committee.* London: HMSO, 1989.

House of Commons Social Services Committee. *Resourcing the National Health Service: Whitley Councils – Third Report, Volume I.* London: HMSO, 1989.

House of Lords Select Committee on Science and Technology. *Priorities in Medical Research.* London: HMSO, 1988.

House of Lords Select Committee on Science and Technology. *Medical Research and the NHS Reforms.* London: HMSO, 1995.

Hunter DJ. Accountability and local democracy. *British Journal of Health Care Management* 1995; 1: 78–81.

Hunter DJ. The Changing Roles of Health Care Personnel in Health and Health Care Management. *Social Science and Medicine* 1996; 43: 799–808.

Impicciatore P, Pandolfini C, Casella N *et al.* Reliability of health information for the public on the world-wide web: systematic survey of advice on managing fever in children at home. *BMJ* 1997; 314: 1875.

Irvine D. The performance of doctors: the new professionalism. *Lancet* 1999; 353: 1174–77.

Jarman B, Gault S, Alves B *et al.* Explaining differences in English hospital death rates using routinely collected data. *BMJ* 1999; 318: 1515–20.

Jones A and Duncan A. *Hypothecated Health Taxes: an evaluation of recent proposals.* London: Office of Health Economics, 1995.

Kasper JK *et al.* Developing shared decision making programmes to improve the quality of care. *Journal of Quality Improvement, Quality Review Bulletin* 1992; 18: 183–86.

Kelliher C. Competitive Tendering in NHS Catering: a suitable policy? *Health Manpower Management.* 1997; 23: 170–80.

Kerr D. The Future of General Medicine. *Journal of the Royal College of Physicians of London* 1998; 32: 97.

Key T. Contracting out ancillary services. In Maxwell RJ, editor. *Reshaping the National Health Service.* Hermitage: Policy Journals, 1988.

King's Fund. Managing demand in general practice. *BMJ* 1998; 316: 1895–98.

Kirkness B, editor. *Putting Patients First: the emerging role of patients in the provision of healthcare.* London: The Association of the British Pharmaceutical Industry, 1996.

Klein R. *The New Politics of the NHS.* London: Longman, 1995.

Klein R, editor. *Implementing the White Paper: Pitfalls and opportunities.* London: King's Fund, 1998.

Klein R. Regulating the medical profession: doctors and the public interest. In: Harrison A, editor. *Health Care UK 1997/98.* London: King's Fund, 1998.

Klein R and New B. *Two cheers?: reflections on the health of NHS democracy.* London: King's Fund, 1998.

Kneeshaw J. Does the public mind having to wait? In: Harrison A, editor. *Health Care UK 1997/98*. London: King's Fund, 1998.

Laing & Buisson. *Laing's Review of Private Health Care 1998/99*. London: Laing & Buisson, 1999.

Langlands A. *Improving quality and performance in the new NHS: Clinical Indicators and High Level Performance Indicators*. Leeds: Department of Health, 1999.

Langlands A. Learning the steps. *NHS Magazine* 1999; 17: 16–18.

Lattimer M and Holly K. *Charity and NHS reform: a report into charitable funds in the NHS*. London: Directory of Social Change, 1992.

Leadbetter C. *Living on Thin Air: the new economy*. London: Viking, 1999.

Legoretta AP, Silber JH, Constantino GN, Kobylinski RW and Zatz SL. Increased cholecystectomy rate after the introduction of laparoscopic cholecystectomy. *JAMA* 1993; 270: 1429–32.

Le Grand J, Mays N and Mulligan J, editors. *Learning from the NHS Internal Market: a review of the evidence*. London: King's Fund, 1998.

London Implementation Group. *Reports of an independent review of specialist services in London: cancer, neurosciences, plastics & burns, cardiac, renal and children*. London: Department of Health, 1993.

Long AF and Mercer G, editors. *Manpower Planning and the National Health Service*. London: Gower, 1981.

Loux A, Kerrison S and Pollock AM. Long term nursing: social care or health care? *BMJ* 2000; 320: 5–6.

Mackenzie WJM. *Power and responsibility in health care: The National Health Service as a political institution*. Oxford: Oxford University Press for the Nuffield Provincial Hospitals Trust, 1979.

McGlone F and Cronin N. *A Crisis in Care?: the future of family and state care for older people in the European Union*. London: Family Policy Studies Centre, 1994.

McLachlan G, editor. *Positions, Movements and Directions in Health Services Research: the papers and proceedings of a meeting held at Hertford College, Oxford, 1974*. London: Oxford University Press for Nuffield Provincial Hospitals Trust, 1974.

McLachlan G, editor. *Five Years After: a review of health care research management after Rothschild*. Oxford: Oxford University Press, 1978.

McLachlan G, editor. *A fresh look at policies for health service research and its relevance to management*. Nuffield Provincial Hospitals Trust Occasional Paper 3. London: Nuffield Provincial Hospitals Trust, 1985.

McLachlan G. *What Price Quality? The NHS in Review*. London: The Nuffield Provincial Hospitals Trust, 1990.

McMichael AJ and Haines A. Global climate change: the potential effects on health. *BMJ* 1997; 315: 805–9.

Maxwell RJ, editor. *Reshaping the National Health Service*. Hermitage: Policy Journals, 1988.

Maynard A and Bloor K. Regulating the Pharmaceutical Industry. *BMJ* 1997; 315: 200–1.

Maynard A and Walker A. *Planning the Medical Workforce: Struggling Out of the Time Warp – Discussion Paper 105*. York: University of York Centre for Health Economics, Health Economics Consortium, 1993.

Maynard A and Walker A. Managing the medical workforce: time for improvements? *Health Policy* 1995; 31: 1–16.

Maynard A and Walker A. *The Physician Workforce in the United Kingdom: Issues, Prospects and Policies*. London: The Nuffield Trust, 1997.

Mays N and Dixon J. *Purchaser Plurality in UK Health Care: is consensus emerging and is it the right one?* London: King's Fund, 1996.

Mays N et al. *What Were the Achievements of Total Purchasing in Their First Year and How Can They be Explained?* London: King's Fund, 1998.

Mays N, Keen J and Willman J. Patient charges: the way to crack the funding conundrum? *British Journal of Health Care Management* 1998; 4: 433–37.

Mays N, Morley V, Boyle S et al. *Evaluating Primary Care Development: A review of evaluation in the London Initiative Zone primary care development programme*. London: King's Fund, 1997.

Medical Manpower Steering Group. *Report*. London: HMSO, 1980.

Merrison, Sir Alex (chair). *Report of the Royal Commission on the National Health Service.* Cmnd. 7615. London: HMSO, 1979.

Merrison, Sir Alex (chair). *Report of the Committee of Inquiry into the Regulation of the Medical profession.* Cmnd. 6018. London: HMSO, 1975.

Minister of Health and Secretary of State for Scotland. *Report of the Committee of Enquiry into the Cost of the National Health Service.* London: HMSO, 1956.

Ministry of Health. *The Dawson report on the future provision of medical and allied services 1920: an interim report to the Minister of Health.* Consultative Council on Medical and Allied Services. London: King Edward's Hospital Fund for London, 1950.

Ministry of Health. *Final Report of the Committee on Hospital Supplies.* Central Health Services Council. London: HMSO, 1958.

Ministry of Health. *National Health Service: A hospital plan for England and Wales.* Cmnd. 1604. London: HMSO, 1962.

Ministry of Health. *National Health Service: the administrative structure of the medical and related services in England and Wales.* London: HMSO, 1968.

Ministry of Health. *The Future Structure of the National Health Service.* London: HMSO, 1970.

Ministry of Health. *National Health Service Reorganisation.* Cmnd. 5055. London: HMSO, 1972.

Ministry of Health Central Health Services Council. *Final Report of the Committee on Hospital Supplies.* London: HMSO, 1958.

Ministry of Health and Department of Health for Scotland. *A National Health Service.* London: HMSO, 1944.

Munro J et al. *Evaluation of NHS Direct first wave sites: first interim report to the Department of Health.* Sheffield: University of Sheffield, School of Health and Related Research – Medical Care Research Unit, 1998.

National Audit Office. *National Health Service: control over professional and technical manpower, Report by the Comptroller and Auditor General.* London: HMSO, 1986.

National Audit Office. *National Health Service Supplies in England: report by the Comptroller and Auditor General.* London: HMSO, 1991.

National Audit Office. *Income Generation in the NHS.* London: HMSO, 1993.

National Audit Office. *National Health Service Supplies in England: report by the Comptroller and Auditor General.* London: HMSO, 1996.

National Audit Office. *NHS Residential Health Care for Elderly People.* London: HMSO, 1996.

National Audit Office. *NHS Residential Health Care for Elderly People: Appendices.* London: HMSO, 1996.

National Audit Office. *Cataract Surgery in Scotland.* London: HMSO, 1997.

National Audit Office. *The PFI Contract for the new Dartford and Gravesham Hospital.* London: Stationery Office, 1999.

New B. The new NHS: accountability and control in the NHS. In: Harrison A, editor. *Health Care UK 1992/93.* London: King's Fund Institute, 1993.

New B. The NHS: what business is it in? In: Harrison A, editor. *Health Care UK 1997/98.* London: King's Fund, 1998.

New B. *A good-enough service: values, trade-offs and the NHS.* London: Institute for Public Policy Research and King's Fund, 1999.

New B and Klein R. *Rationing: talk and action in health care.* London: BMA & King's Fund, 1997.

New B and Le Grand J. *Rationing in the NHS: Principles & pragmatism.* London: King's Fund, 1996.

Newhouse J. *Free for all: lessons from the RAND health insurance experiment.* Cambridge, Mass: Harvard UP, 1993.

New Zealand Ministry of Health. *Core Services for 1995/96 – Third report of the National Advisory Committee on Core Health and Disability Support Services.* Wellington: NZ Ministry of Health, 1994.

NHS Centre for Reviews and Dissemination. *Relationship between volume and quality of health care: a review of the literature 1995.* York: University of York NHS CRD, 1995.

NHS Executive. *Patient Partnership: building a collaborative strategy.* London: NHS Executive, 1996.

NHS Executive. *Specialist Workforce Advisory Group (SWAG): Annual Report for 1995/96.* London: Department of Health, 1996.

NHS Executive. *Education and Training Planning Guidance.* Executive Letter EL (96) 46. Leeds: NHSE, 1996.

NHS Executive. *A Working Draft to Develop a Quality Framework for HCHS Medical and Dental Staffing.* Executive Letter EL (97) 25. Leeds: NHSE, 1997.

NHS Executive. *Workforce Planning for General Medical Services.* Executive Letter EL (96) 69. Leeds: NHSE, 1996.

NHS Executive. *Priorities and Planning Guidance for the NHS: 1998/99.* London: Department of Health, 1997.

NHS Executive. *Workforce Planning for General Medical Services.* HSG (97) 9. London: NHS Executive, 1997.

NHS Executive. *The Annual Report of the NHS Health Technology Assessment Programme 1997.* London: NHS Executive, 1997.

NHS Executive. *The NHS Home Healthcare Guide.* Leeds: NHSE, 1998.

NHS Executive Anglia and Oxford Region. *Opportunities in emergency health care: summary report from the Anglia and Oxford emergency health care project.* London: Arena Communications and Design, 1995.

NHS Executive Anglia and Oxford Region. *Opportunities in intermediate care: summary report from the Anglia and Oxford intermediate care project.* Milton Keynes: NHS Executive Anglia & Oxford, 1997.

NHS Executive, Institute of Health Services Management, NHS Confederation. *In the Public Interest: Developing a Strategy for Public Participation in the NHS.* London: Department of Health, 1998.

NHS Executive North Thames. *The Right Team for the Job.* London: NHS Executive, 1997.

NHS Executive North Thames. *The Workforce Project: a report of two behavioural simulations exploring the interaction between health care and education and training pressures on the clinical workforce.* London: NHS Executive North Thames and Office for Public Management, 1997.

NHS Executive South Thames. *Review of Cervical Screening Services at Kent and Canterbury Hospitals NHS Trust.* London: NHS Executive South Thames, 1997.

NHS Management Executive. *Integrating Primary and Secondary Health Care.* London: Department of Health, 1991.

NHS Management Executive. *Managing Resource Management Projects: Practical Experience.* London: Department of Health, 1991.

NHS Wales. *Involving the Public*. Cardiff: Welsh Office, 1998.

Office of National Statistics. *General Household Survey 1995*. London: HMSO, 1996.

Office of National Statistics. *General Household Survey 1996*. London: HMSO, 1997.

Office for Public Management. *The workforce project: a report of two behavioural simulations exploring the interaction between health care and education and training pressures on the clinical workforce*. Leeds: Department of Health, 1997.

Owen D (MP), editor. *A Unified Health Service*. London: Pergamon Press, 1968.

Parliament of Great Britain. *Your right to know: freedom of information*. London: HMSO, 1997.

Parliamentary Office of Science and Technology. *Factors Affecting Pressure on Healthcare Resources*. London: POST, 1994.

Peckham M and Smith R, editors. *Scientific Basis of Health Service*. London: British Medical Journal Publishing, 1996.

Pencheon D. Matching demand and supply fairly and efficiently. *BMJ* 1998; 316: 1665–67.

Pollock AM, Dunnigan MG, Gaffney D *et al*. Planning the 'new' NHS: downsizing for the 21st century. *BMJ* 1999; 319: 179–84.

Powell JE. *Medicine and Politics: 1975 and after*. London: Pitman, 1976.

Public Audit Forum. *Implications for audit of the modernising government agenda*. London: Public Audit Forum, 1999.

Report of the Resource Allocation Working Party. *Sharing Resources for Health*. London: HMSO, 1976.

Review Body on Doctors' and Dentists' Remuneration. *Nineteenth Report 1989*. Cm. 580. London: HMSO, 1989.

Review Body on Doctors' and Dentists' Remuneration. *Twenty-Eighth Report 1999*. Cm. 4243. London: Stationery Office, 1999.

Review Body for Nursing Staff, Midwives, Health Visitors and Professions Allied to Medicine. *First Report on Professions Allied to Medicine 1984*. Cmnd. 9257. London: HMSO, 1984.

Review Body for Nursing Staff, Midwives, Health Visitors and Professions Allied to Medicine. *Sixth Report on Professions Allied to Medicine 1989.* Cm. 78. London: HMSO, 1989.

Review Body for Nursing Staff, Midwives, Health Visitors and Professions Allied to Medicine. *Fourteenth Report on Nursing Staff, Midwives and Health Visitors 1997.* Cm. 3538. London: Stationery Office, 1997.

Richardson G and Maynard A. *Fewer Doctors? More Nurses? A Review of the Knowledge Base of Doctor-Nurse Substitution – Discussion Paper 135.* York: University of York Centre for Health Economics, Health Economics Consortium, NHS Centre for Reviews & Dissemination, 1995.

Rivett G. *From Cradle to Grave: fifty years of the NHS.* London: King's Fund, 1998.

Robine JM, Blanchet M and Dowd J. *Health expectancy: first workshop of the international healthy life expectancy network.* London: HMSO, 1992.

Robinson R, Evans D and Exworthy M. *Health & The Economy.* Birmingham: NAHAT, 1994.

Robinson R and Steiner A. *Managed health care: US evidence and lessons for the National Health Service.* Buckingham: Open University Press, 1998.

Rogers A, Entwistle V and Pencheon D. A patient-led NHS: managing demand at the interface between lay and primary care. *BMJ* 1998; 316: 1816–19.

Rogers A, Hassell K and Nicolaas G. *Demanding Patients? Analysing the Use of Primary Care.* Buckingham/Philadelphia: Open University Press, 1999.

Rosen R and Mays N. The impact of the UK NHS purchaser/provider split on the 'rational' introduction of new technologies. *Health Policy* 1998; 43: 103–23.

Royal College of Physicians of England. *The Consultant Physician: responding to change.* London: Royal College of Physicians, 1996.

Royal College of Physicians of England. *Future patterns of care by general and specialist physicians: meeting the needs of adult patients in the UK.* London: Royal College of Physicians, 1996.

Royal College of Surgeons. *Report of the Working Party on Head Injuries.* London: Royal College of Surgeons, 1986.

Royal College of Surgeons of England. *The Provision of Emergency Surgical Services: an organisational framework.* London: Royal College of Surgeons, 1997.

Royal Commission on the National Health Service, Brunel University Department of Government. *The working of the National Health Service: a study for the Royal Commission on the National Health Service by a team from the Department of Government, Brunel University – Research Paper 1.* London: HMSO, 1978.

Royal Commission on the National Health Service. *Doctor Manpower 1975–2000: alternative forecasts and their resource implications – Research Paper 4.* London: HMSO, 1978.

Royal Commission on the National Health Service. *Report.* Cmnd. 7615. London: HMSO, 1979.

Salter B. *The Politics of Changes in the Health Service.* London: Macmillan, 1998.

Saltman RB. Medical Savings Accounts: a notably uninteresting policy idea. *European Journal of Public Health* 1998; 8: 276–78.

Scheffler R and Yu W. Medical Saving Accounts: A worthy experience. *European Journal of Public Health* 1998; 8: 274–76.

Scottish Office. *Designed to care: renewing the National Health Service in Scotland.* Edinburgh: Stationery Office, 1997.

Scottish Office. *Acute services review report.* Edinburgh: Stationery Office, 1998.

Secretaries of State for Health. *Working for Patients.* Cm. 555. London: HMSO, 1989.

Secretaries of State for Social Services. Wales, Northern Ireland and Scotland. *Primary Health Care: An Agenda for Discussion.* Cm. 9771. London: HMSO, 1986.

Secretary of State for Health. *The new NHS: modern, dependable.* Cm. 3807. London: Stationery Office, 1997.

Sheldon R (chair). *West Midlands Regional Health Authority: regionally managed services organisation: fifty-seventh report [of the] Committee of Public Accounts. House of Commons paper – Session 1992–93 No. 485.* London: HMSO, 1993.

Sheldon R (chair). *Wessex Regional Health Authority regional information systems plan: sixty-third report – session 1992–93. House of Commons paper, Session 1992–93, No. 658.* London: HMSO, 1993.

Sheldon R (chair). *The former Yorkshire Regional Health Authority: the inquiry commissioned by the NHS Chief Executive together with the proceedings of the Committee relating to the report and the minutes of evidence, and appendices – House of Commons Committee of Public Accounts – Session 1996–97.* London: Stationery Office, 1997.

Shocket G et al. *Efficiency in the NHS: a study of cost improvement programmes*. London: King's Fund Institute, 1989.

Simpson J and Smith R. Why Healthcare Systems Need Medical Managers. *BMJ* 1997; 314: 1636–37.

South-East Thames Regional Health Authority. *Shaping the Future: a review of acute services*. Bexhill-on-sea: SETRHA, 1991.

Specialist Workforce Advisory Group. *Annual report 1995/96*. Leeds: Department of Health, 1996.

Stowe, Sir Kenneth. *On Caring for The National Health*. London: The Rock Carling Fellowship, 1988; and Nuffield Provincial Hospitals Trust, 1989.

Sutherland S (chair). *With respect to Old Age: a report by the Royal Commission on Long-term Care*. Cm. 4192-1. London: Stationery Office, 1999.

The Health Service. *Practice Budgets for General Medical Practitioners – Working Paper 3*. London: HMSO, 1989.

*The Times*, 3 February 1998.

Tomlinson, Sir Bernard (chair). *Report of the Inquiry into London's Health Service, Medical Education and Research*. London: HMSO, 1992.

Total Purchasing National Evaluation Team (TP-NET). *Total purchasing: A Step Towards Primary Care Groups – National evaluation of total purchasing pilot projects working paper*. London: King's Fund, 1998.

Total Purchasing National Evaluation Team (TP-NET). *What Were the Achievements of Total Purchasing Pilots in their First Year and how can they be explained? – National evaluation of total purchasing pilot projects working paper*. London: King's Fund, 1998.

Total Purchasing National Evaluation Team (TP-NET). *Developing Primary Care in the New NHS: Lessons from total purchasing – National evaluation of total purchasing pilot projects working paper*. London: King's Fund, 1999.

Towse A, editor. *Financing health care in the UK: a discussion of NERA's prototype model to replace the NHS*. London: Office of Health Economics, 1995.
Tudor Edwards R. Points for Pain: waiting list priority systems. *BMJ* 1999; 318: 412–14.

Turnberg L (chair). *Health services in London: strategic review* ('The Turnberg Report'). London: Department of Health, 1998.

Vaughan B and Lathlean J. *Intermediate care: models in practice*. London: King's Fund, 1999.

Warlow D. *Review of the Conditions of Employment of Staff Employed in the National Health Service (England, Wales and Scotland)*. London: Department of Health, 1989.

Warner M, Longley M, Gould E *et al*. *Healthcare Futures 2010*. Pontypridd: Welsh Institute for Health and Social Care, 1998.

Webster C. *The health services since the war*. London: HMSO, 1996.

Webster C. *The National Health Service: a political history*. Oxford: OUP, 1998.

Weed LJ. New Connections Between Medical Knowledge and Patient Care. *BMJ* 1997; 315: 231–35.

Wells W (chair). *Review of cervical screening services at Kent and Canterbury Hospitals NHS Trust*. London: South Thames NHS Executive, 1997.

Welsh Office. *NHS Wales: Putting Patients First*. London: HMSO, 1998.

West P. *Future Hospital Services in the NHS: one size fits all? – Nuffield Occasional Papers, Health Economics Series: Paper No 6*. London: The Nuffield Trust, 1998.

Whelan J. *Equal access to cardiac rehabilitation: age-discrimination in the NHS: cardiac rehabilitation services*. London: Age Concern England, 1998.

Whynes DK and Baines DL. Income-based incentives in UK general practice. *Health Policy* 1998; 43: 15–31.

Williams S *et al*. *Improving the Health of the NHS Workforce*. London: The Nuffield Trust, 1998.

Willman J. *A better state of health: a prescription for the NHS*. London: Profile in association with Social Market Foundation, 1998.

Wilson A (chair). *Being heard: The report of a review committee on NHS complaints procedures*. London: Department of Health, 1994.

Wistow G. *Aspirations and Realities: Community Care at the Crossroads*. Inaugural Lecture delivered at the Nuffield Institute for Health 28 November. Leeds: University of Leeds, 1994.

Woolf HK. *Access to Justice*. London: HMSO, 1996.